Standpoints an

Gender and Psychology
Feminist and Critical Perspectives

Series editor: Sue Wilkinson

This international series provides a forum for research focused on gender issues in – and beyond – psychology, with a particular emphasis on feminist and critical analyses. It encourages contributions which explore psychological topics where gender is central, which critically interrogate psychology as a discipline and as a professional base; and which develop feminist interventions in theory and practice. The series objective is to present innovative research on gender in the context of the broader implications for developing both critical psychology and feminism.

Sue Wilkinson teaches social psychology and women's studies at Loughborough University. She is also Editor of *Feminism & Psychology: An International Journal.*

Also in this series

Subjectivity and Method in Psychology
Wendy Hollway

Feminist Groupwork
Sandra Butler and Claire Wintram

Motherhood: Meanings, Practices and Ideologies
edited by Ann Phoenix, Anne Woollett and Eva Lloyd

Emotion and Gender: Constructing Meaning from Memory
June Crawford, Susan Kippax, Jenny Onyx, Una Gault and Pam Benton

Women and AIDS: Psychological Perspectives
edited by Corinne Squire

Attitudes toward Rape: Feminist and Social Psychological Perspectives
Colleen A. Ward

Talking Difference: On Gender and Language
Mary Crawford

Feminism and Discourse: Psychological Perspectives
edited by Sue Wilkinson and Celia Kitzinger

Resisting Gender
Rhoda Unger

Standpoints and Differences

Essays in the Practice of Feminist Psychology

edited by

Karen Henwood, Christine Griffin and Ann Phoenix

SAGE Publications
London • Thousand Oaks • New Delhi

First published 1998

Chapter 5 reprinted by permission of the publisher from
RAISING THEIR VOICES by Lyn Mikel Brown, Cambridge,
MA: Harvard University Press, copyright © 1998 by the
President and Fellows of Harvard College.

 SAGE Publications Ltd
6 Bonhill Street
London EC2A 4PU

SAGE Publications Inc.
2455 Teller Road
Thousand Oaks, California 91320

SAGE Publications India Pvt Ltd
32, M-Block Market
Greater Kailash – I
New Delhi 110 048

British Library Cataloguing in Publication data

A catalogue record for this book is available from the British Library

ISBN 0 7619 5443 0
ISBN 0 7619 5444 9 (pbk)

Library of Congress catalog card number 98–060685

Typeset by Mayhew Typesetting, Rhayader, Powys
Printed in Great Britain by Biddles Ltd, Guildford, Surrey

Contents

Notes on Contributors

Karen Henwood lectures at the School of Psychology, University of Wales, Bangor. She has done research in the areas of psychology, 'race' and racism, women's relationships (especially between mothers and their adult daughters), and qualitative research methods. She has published articles in journals such as *Feminism and Psychology, Theory and Psychology, British Journal of Psychology*, and *Journal of Ageing Studies*. She is currently Chair Elect of the Psychology of Women Section of the British Psychological Society.

Christine Griffin teaches social psychology at the University of Birmingham, UK. Her research interests include the representations and experiences of young people, especially young women; the use of qualitative research methods in social psychology; and feminist perspectives on teaching and research. She is one of the founding editors of the journal *Feminism and Psychology*, and is the author of *Typical Girls: Young Women from School to the Job Market* (1985) and *Representations of Youth: The Study of Youth and Adolescence in Britain and America* (1993).

Ann Phoenix works in the Department of Psychology, Birkbeck College, University of London. Her research interests include motherhood and the social identities of young people, particularly those associated with gender, 'race', social class and adoption. Her publications include *Young Mothers?* (1991), *Motherhood: Meanings, Practices and Ideologies* (edited with Anne Woollett and Eva Lloyd, 1991), *Black, White or Mixed Race? Race and racism in the lives of young people of mixed parentage* (with B. Tizard, 1993) and *Shifting Identities Shifting Racisms*, (edited with Kum-Kum Bhavnani, 1994).

Rosalind Gill is a lecturer in gender theory and gender studies at the Gender Institute, LSE. She is editor of *The Gender-Technology Relation* (with Keith Grint, 1995) and author of *Gender and the Media: Representations, Audiences and Cultural Politics* (1998). Politically active since her teenage years she is currently working on issues about the nature of critique and resistance in these 'post' times/places.

Stevi Jackson is Professor of Women's Studies and Director of the Centre for Women's Studies at the University of York. Her writings include *Childhood and Sexuality* (1982) and *Christine Delphy* ('Women of Ideas' Series, 1996). She has co-edited *Women's Studies: A Reader* (1993), *Feminism and Sexuality* (1996), and *Contemporary Feminist Theories* (1998). She has also published a number of articles on romance, sexuality and family relationships and is currently working with Sue Scott, Kathryn Milburn and Jennifer Harden researching the impact of risk and adult risk anxiety on the everyday world of children.

Corinne Squire is at the University of East London. She is the author of *Significant Differences: Feminism in Psychology* (1989), and with Ellen Friedman of *Morality USA* (1998). She also edited *Women and AIDS: Psychological Perspectives* (1993). She is currently working on a book about HIV, narrative genre and citizenship.

Lyn Mikel Brown is Associate Professor and Co-chair of the Education and Human Development Program at Colby College, Waterville, Maine. She is author (with Carol Gilligan) of *Meeting at the Crossroads: Women's Psychology and Girls' Development* (1992) and *Raising Their Voices: The Politics of Girls' Anger* (1998). She has written numerous articles on girls' and women's psychological development, girls' education, and feminist research methods.

Harriette Marshall is a Reader in the Psychology division at Staffordshire University. Her main research interests include identity, issues around gender, ethnicity and the role of psychology in relation to inequalities.

Anne Woollett is a Professor in the Psychology Department at the University of East London. Her research interests are in families, children's development and women's experiences of childbirth and parenting.

Neelam Dosanjh is a Clinical Psychologist at Newham Psychology and Counselling Service, and Head of Primary Care Psychology (Newham Community NHS Trust) in East London. Her interests include using the psychoanalytic framework in clinical and organisational settings, research on mental health of young Asian women, and the teaching of 'race' and culture in clinical psychology courses.

Irene Bruna Seu lectures in social psychology at the Department of Human Sciences, Brunel University. She is also a psychoanalytic psychotherapist in private practice. Her research interests are in gender, oppression, psychoanalysis and qualitative methodologies. She has conducted research on women's experiences of shame and is currently researching 'Bystanders and Human Rights Abuses'. She is the co-editor (with Colleen Heenan) of *Feminism and Psychotherapy: Reflections on Contemporary Theories and Practices* (1998).

Margaret Wetherell is a senior lecturer in the Faculty of Social Sciences, Open University. Her research interests include work on discourse and identity, particularly in relation to gender and 'race' issues. She is author of *Discourse and Social Psychology* (1987) and *Mapping the Language of Racism* (1992) (both with Jonathan Potter) and editor of *Identities, Groups and Social Issues* (1996). Her recent work has focused on the formation of masculine subjectivities and she is author of *Men in Perspective: Practice, Power and Identity* (with Nigel Edley, 1995).

Nigel Edley is a lecturer in social psychology at Nottingham Trent University. For some years now he has been interested in looking at the issues of ideology, identity and subjectivity from a social constructionist framework. He is the co-author of *Men in Perspective: Practice, Power and Identity* (with Margaret Wetherell, 1995).

Sara Willott is a Lecturer in gender and social and critical psychology (including psychology and gender) at the School of Health and Social Sciences, Coventry University. She has done research in the area of masculine identity, unemployment and crime, and has published in *Feminism and Psychology*.

Janneke van Mens-Verhulst lectures in clinical and health psychology at the Faculty of Social Sciences of Utrecht University, and she is a member of the Netherlands' Research School of Women's Studies. Much of her work focuses on the principles and theories of Feminist Mental Health Care. The *1996 Simulation and Gaming Yearbook* contains a report of her efforts to model FMHC in a simulation game. One of her main projects has been *Daughtering and Mothering* (1993). She has published in journals such as *American Journal of Psychotherapy*, *Women and Health* and *Social Science & Medicine*. From 1995 until 1997 she was visiting professor at the University for Humanist Studies.

Erica Burman is Professor of Developmental Psychology and Women's Studies at The Manchester Metropolitan University. Alongside trying to encourage a critical, feminist approach to psychological theories, methods and practices, her research interests lie in promoting social theories of subjectivity and change that support political action. Her publications include *Feminists and Psychological Practice* (edited, 1990), *Discourse Analytic Research* (co-edited, 1993), *Deconstructing Developmental Psychology* (1994),

Challenging Women: Psychology's Exclusions, Feminist Possibilities (co-authored, 1996), *Psychology Discourse Practice: From Regulation to Resistance* (co-authored 1996) and *Deconstructing Feminist Psychology* (edited, 1998).

1

Introduction

Karen Henwood, Christine Griffin and Ann Phoenix

A new research student is about to start work on an exciting new research project on the construction of womanhood in daytime TV programmes. As a critical social psychologist, she wants to use a feminist perspective and a discursive analytical framework to conduct interviews with TV producers, presenters and women viewers. She has a fairly clear idea of what a feminist perspective on this issue might look like, and has read a couple of recent books on women and TV. She is far more worried about the discourse analytic side of the research. She spends a considerable amount of time and effort reading Foucault, Derrida, Baudrillard, and lots more besides, becoming increasingly anxious and confused. Gradually, however, she begins to get a sense of their arguments and how they relate to one another and to her project. This doesn't leave much time to read (or think) so deeply about the feminist element of her work, although some of the poststructuralist texts she has read do adopt a feminist perspective. She comes across quite a few critiques of what is called feminism in her reading, although she never gets a chance to read any of these feminist texts before she starts her interviewing. Perhaps she will have time to catch up on these feminist debates when it comes to writing up . . .

The above is a brief story, or perhaps a cautionary tale, about the relationship between feminism(s) and poststructuralism(s) in psychological research. It is both a fiction and a compilation of some women's experiences as feminist researchers in psychology, and it is one of the reasons why we decided to compile this book. This story constructs feminism(s) and poststructuralism(s) as two relatively distinct entities or perspectives with minimal overlap, and also suggests that one way in which feminists in psychology are differentiated is in relation to their orientation towards feminist and poststructuralist debates – to the extent that these can be disentangled. Of course, to represent feminism(s) and poststructuralism(s) as two distinct perspectives is a gross, and in some cases, an inaccurate over-simplification. However, we would argue that the tale described above is of relevance to many feminists working in psychology. Partly it may arise as a problem of inaccessibility and (excessive) semantic complexity in many poststructuralist texts, but there is also an issue of political engagement which has different implications in relation to feminism and to poststructuralism. All researchers and practitioners working in psychology operate in relation to an institution that remains profoundly patriarchal as well as being steadfastly positivist in orientation. Thus, for feminists and those who adopt other critical approaches that have a less 'acceptable' status within the academy than poststructuralism, their relationship with psychology must be constantly negotiated. Such negotiations may well be quite different from those operating from a base in sociology, cultural studies or anthropology: in mainstream psychology, the dominance of positivism and the scientific method is still clear in most degree programmes and in the content of most academic journals. For researchers new to the area, these negotiations may prove extremely fraught. This book aims to address the debates over and within feminism(s) and poststructuralism(s) in relation to psychology.

As editors, we have struggled with how to represent the relationship between feminism(s) and poststructuralism(s), because of the difficulty of avoiding the construction of these perspectives as distinct binary opposites. Our aim is to recognize the relevance of the 'two distinct entities' construction, while remaining unhappy with its over-simplistic formulation. This is epitomized by a quote from our proposal to potential contributors and to the eventual publishers of this book which illustrates all too clearly some of the difficulties we have faced in putting this text together:

> This book is concerned with the debate in feminist scholarship around its interface with poststructuralist theories, and in particular with the implications of this for research practice within feminist psychology.

This construction of binary opposites is common to other texts in this area – albeit often along with some expressed reservations about reproducing such a dichotomy. However, the contributors to this book have either taken issue with the polarization of feminism(s) and poststructuralism(s), or found various ways of circumventing it. This they have done by: (a) highlighting those aspects of poststructuralism that reinforce and contribute to feminist analyses (Wetherell and Edley); (b) carefully refining contested theoretical positions and concepts (Brown); (c) demonstrating ways in which feminist standpoint theory has long addressed issues considered important in poststructuralist theory, although it is often set up as a 'straw woman' and demonized (Jackson); (d) problematizing aspects of both theories (Burman; van Mens-Verhulst; Squire); and (e) using the strengths of one to remedy deficiencies in the other (Gill; Marshall, Woollett and Dosanjh; Seu; Willott).

It would be remarkable, of course, if no difficult issues were raised by this general approach. The women who declined to write for the book raised several of these as they commented on the possible danger of forcing an unwanted and perhaps unnecessary engagement between perspectives. They considered that postmodernism[1] produces 'alienated knowledge' which can be understood and used only by a few academics. For this reason they decried what they see as an increasing separation between feminist political struggles and feminist academic work since this runs counter to feminist attempts to bridge the gap between political struggle and intellectual theorization. A similar point is made by bell hooks when she argues that it is 'sadly ironic that the contemporary discourse which talks most about heterogeneity, the decentred subject and recognition of Otherness, still directs its critical voice primarily to a specialized audience that shares a common language rooted in the very master narratives it claims to challenge' (1991: 25). Furthermore, the women who were not attracted to contributing to the collection argued that postmodernism has incorporated feminist ideas without acknowledging that, for example, feminisms have always been committed to deconstruction (e.g. of gender categories – see Jackson 1992 and this volume). These points are important ones and the contributors to this book produce further critiques of postmodernism (as well as critiques of feminisms, especially a particular variant known as feminist standpoint theory). In doing so, however, they are concerned to use both feminist and postmodernist theories in ways which further feminist politics. This book has, hopefully, not reproduced the problems anticipated by those who did not wish to be part of a project engaging with postmodernism.

Although the title of the book might appear, at first sight, to set up a binary opposition between 'standpoints' and 'differences', one of our aims is to dissolve that dualism. This involves refusing to narrow discussions of feminisms to approaches that either depend upon the notion of having or taking a standpoint or, rebounding from this, privilege notions of difference. (More extensive discussion of why we have chosen to use these two terms as motifs for the book appears later in this introduction.) We know that focusing upon a dichotomy (even if just to criticize it) can have the effect of reinforcing it as the main frame of reference and, thereby, displace other possible ways of discussing the issues it raises (see, for example, Davis, 1992). Within feminism and psychology, the debate about whether 'masculine' moral development is expressed through a voice of justice, while 'women's' moral development is expressed through the ethic of care, provides one example of how such polarizations can be unhelpful. Nevertheless, the contributors to the book have applied themselves enthusiastically to the difficult task of deconstructing the binary opposition between feminism(s) and post-structuralism(s), as well as to examining the notion that feminists should take up either 'pro' or 'anti' positions in relation to something called poststructuralism. While we certainly would not wish to deny the importance of feminist critiques of poststructuralist approaches, nor the potential value of some elements of poststructuralist perspectives for feminists, we have a particular hope for the book. This is that it succeeds in raising critiques of both feminism(s) and poststructuralism(s), and in bringing out creative formulations of the relationship, without having to do so from a position that locates feminisms (especially what is sometimes stereotyped as feminism by those who do not consider themselves feminist) as Other, to be pitied or disdained, and without being vituperative about postructuralism.

The conditions of possibility for this book

Since one of the book's aims is to present a range of examples of recent work by feminists who are engaging with poststructuralism within psychology, it is important to acknowledge that the publication of *Changing the Subject* (Henriques et al., 1984, new edition 1998) over ten years ago provided a highly influential introduction to poststructuralism among researchers (at least in Britain). Written by (as defined at the time) a group of white women and black men involved in the radical and sexual politics of the late 1960s, and who had different involvements in psychology, the book drew on psychoanalytic theory as well as poststructuralism to present a profound critique of the notion of the unitary individual subject which was (and still is) so central to mainstream academic psychology, and to the far broader psychological discourse of the individual that extends into the far reaches of contemporary Western cultures. Some members of the group, notably Valerie Walkerdine, Wendy Hollway and Cathy Urwin, continued to work on and from feminist perspectives on poststructuralism, and have made further important contributions to debates in psychology, cultural studies and feminism (e.g. Hollway, 1989; Walkerdine, 1996, 1997). Yet, both feminism and poststructuralism have struggled to have any impact on the dominance of positivist psychology.

The publication of *Changing the Subject* put a number of issues on the psychological agenda and took forward a number of key themes raised by poststructuralism. These include the disruption of essentialism; the importance of reflexivity in the academic process; the examination of the political power of psychology as a discursively constituted academic discipline; and the use of psycho-analytic theories and poststructuralism as resources to promote an understanding of the fracturing and multiplicity of subjectivities, and the way these are constituted within discursively organized power relations (e.g. of gender, 'race' and social class).

Since that time all these issues have been addressed in different ways, within and outside psychology, and this book is a further contribution to debates which focus on the ways in which feminism, psychology and poststructuralism can make innovative contributions to theory and practice. We recognize that feminisms and poststructuralisms do not reflect the only forms that critical perspectives in psychology have taken in recent years (see for example, Burman and Parker, 1993; Edwards, 1997; Edwards and Potter, 1992; Potter and Wetherell, 1987; Shotter and Gergen, 1989; Wilkinson, 1986; Wilkinson and Kitzinger, 1995). At the same time it is clear that debates are continuing, partly because of resistances within psychology, but also because a critical perspective necessitates the adoption by researchers of continually questioning and reflexive ways of approaching their work. In the words of Patti Lather a requirement of such research is that it 'reflects back at its readers the problems of inquiry at the same time an inquiry is conducted' (1997: 286). Thus, some chapters in the book oppose unitary or essentialist modes of theorizing and of addressing issues, such as women's violence, which are often omitted from psychological work (e.g. Squire). Other chapters argue that many people are able to exert some control in their lives through the 'agentic power' they obtain from claims to 'authentic' identities (e.g. Brown). Yet others demonstrate some of the ways in which psychoanalytic 'origin stories' can help to maintain the *status quo* because of a lack of reflexivity in their theorizing (Jackson).

To offset worries that the conceptualization of 'discursively constructed subjectivities' lacks concrete, experiential and material grounding, some chapters demonstrate the importance of such groundings in researchers' analyses. One way in which this can be done is by studying narratives of socially and historically situated experiences (Jackson; Squire). Another, innovative, way is to provide a sustained focus on various possible modifications to theories of 'the practical' in social life, as a prelude to studying psychological identifications as 'articulations' of gender practices (e.g. in masculinity – Wetherell and Edley). From the point of view of conducting specific analyses, it then remains to find ways of adjudicating between multiple readings of the implications of subject positionings according to whether they are both epistemically supportable and politically informed (Seu).

Another set of concerns raised by the chapters relates to the point that non-foundationalist theorizations of subjectivity are not innocent and may not be definitively split off from Enlightenment models (Burman; Gill). In the case of the 'fictive self', this can be viewed as a 'patriarchal narrative with a postmodern signature' (van Mens-Verhulst). Similarly, the notion of a chaotic, playful, spontaneous, child-like subject may contain the modernist residue of free-spirited explorer, and the metaphor of the cyborg may, despite its transgression of many historical associations (e.g. the association of women with nature), resurrect others (such as the equation of science and technology with progress and an acceptance of the role of the military-industrial complex in this). Hence there is no guarantee against new limitations emerging from novel metaphorical associations that may then act against progressive outcomes (Burman).

Standpoints and differences

We might call the exercise undertaken by the book a feminist and deconstructive analysis of some feminist and postmodernist questions (of both a theoretical/conceptual and practical/methodological nature) within contemporary feminist psychology. This is precisely the kind of activity that we wish to capture by using the hybridized term 'standpoints and differences'. Our purpose in conjoining these two terms in the book's title (as well as in the minds of our authors at the time they were asked to write their chapters) is (and was) to invoke the many and ambiguous ways in which these terms can signify in relation to feminism and poststructuralism. In particular, we wanted to bring to the fore an awareness that these are simultaneously overlapping and contradictory domains of theorizing.

In recent years, theoretical work from a critical perspective (feminist and other) has engaged with ways in which to recognize difference, theorize it productively, while not reproducing pathologizing constructions of the Other (see Brah, 1996). In such work, the term difference(s) is likely to be most immediately recognizable: as connoting known entities (e.g. gender differences and racialized identities); implying criticism of the assumption of taken-for-granted a priori standards where these create pathological difference (namely, deviance from such norms); undermining white, male, middle-class hegemony by introducing diverse sociopolitical positions and identities into the knowledge process; and suggesting a conceptual shift to a more fragmented, shifting and indeterminate view of subjectivities, meanings and differences.

As well as indicating the 'taking of an explicitly political agenda' (Willott), the term 'standpoint' can be a synonym for concrete, materially grounded, or shared experiences, socially defined group identities, or collectively articulated political viewpoints. Some of these associations obviously run a strong risk of implicating a unifying, static and essentializing reading. Nevertheless, non-essentializing theorizations are also possible, in the form of references to ontological fracturing of 'identity' and 'position' (Stanley and Wise, 1993); to the plurality (Devault, 1990) partiality, hybridity and motility of social positions (Haraway, 1991); and to the complications forced by recognition of multiple standpoints to any singular notion of the 'experiences' of marginalized groups (Hill Collins, 1990; Marshall, Woollett and Dosanjh, this volume). Of course, feminist analyses also have a longstanding history of problematizing absolute notions of male–female difference and making explicit their ideological consequences. Moreover, it would be consistent with non-dichotomous thinking to suggest that post-structuralist theorizing is itself likely to be dependent for its survival on keeping alive a notion of a unified, singular and fixed perspective, position or standpoint (since it depends for its existence on opposition to the 'Enlightenment subject').

By pivoting around the notion of 'standpoints and differences' this collection of essays avoids creating the appearance that epistemological and methodological debate is solely the province of the axis between feminism and poststructuralism. This is important since, as will be apparent to many, there are numerous feminist epistemologies (Alcoff and Potter, 1993; Lennon and Whitford, 1994). There is a longstanding and broad range of writings by feminists articulating the social and psychological specificities of gendered and other social relations and their impact on knowledge and science (see for example, Bleier, 1979, 1986; Fox-Keller, 1985; Haraway, 1991; Harding and Hintikka, 1983). A formalized version of 'standpoint theory' is one attempt to legitimize the idea of classed, gendered/sexed, racialized subjects as knowers at the same time as debunking claims to neutrality and objectivity in science (Harding, 1991; Hartsock, 1983, 1990). Yet, as much as we can find by way of commonalities between feminist standpoint epistemology and poststructuralism, there does seem to be, at least at a meta-theoretical level, a prima-facie case for viewing the two approaches as irreconcilably different (see the chapters by Gill and by Squire). Standpoint theory's argument that researchers can foster more egalitarian (or at least less oppressive) social relationships and meanings by being concerned with women's concrete, materially grounded experiences (see for example, Smith, 1992) or by starting from a politically informed and theorized position regarding the perspectives or standpoints of women (Harding, 1986, 1991) stands in stark contrast to poststructuralism's rejection of the idea that foundations of any kind can form the basis for knowledge generation and political practice (Flax, 1987; see also, for example, Derrida, 1976; Foucault, 1984; Lyotard, 1984). According to the poststructuralist account, research and emancipatory politics should flow from the relentless pursuit of personal and political fragments, inconsistencies and differences (Butler, 1990; Squire, 1989, 1994).

While there are many sources of discontent with feminist 'standpoint theory' (see especially Gill; Squire; and Marshall, Woollett and Dosanjh), silence on these debates would merely amount to opting out of the ongoing lines of research and deliberation of which it is a part. For instance, paying attention to women's experiences, and the particular, before proceeding to generalizations has been used to propose proportional representation in health care and bioethics (Mahowald, 1996). The project of asking people to write for this book has itself generated the insight that, having avoided any suggestion that classed and gendered experiences and locations offer a 'correct' view, it may be possible to illuminate how processes of personal, political and intellectual struggle can move 'experiences' and social positioning towards a theorized, political standpoint (Gill). In general terms, many of the chapters in this volume would seem to provide valuable examples of ways of 'minding the gaps' as one moves analytically between experience, social/material location and political action (Brown; Jackson; Marshall, Woollett and Dosanjh; Willott).

In addition, psychology has generally not paid attention to the structuralist-materialist link that first moved us from asocial conceptions of knowing to socially constructed (albeit sometimes standpoint) ones. To ignore this moment in the chain of debates within feminism and about epistemology would not adequately reflect the variety of scholarship within feminist psychology. One of the distinctive aspects of psychological research and practice in relation to feminism and poststructuralism has been its particular history of lack of engagement with these specific debates. In disciplines such as sociology, the dominant approach of liberal humanism had already been subject to structuralist critique, especially by those influenced by Marxist ideas, before feminism 'hit' academia in the late 1960s. In psychology, structuralism has had even less of a foothold, such that positivism and a liberal humanist perspective have retained much of their dominance (Hollway, 1989). In addition, psychology has retained its central role outside the academy in reinforcing the discourse of individual agency and the unitary rational subject. Some (though not all) of those critical psychologists who took up (a form of) poststructuralism, postmodernism and/or feminist ideas with such alacrity in the mid-1980s, did so without having any great sense of engagement with structuralism – or with structuralist critiques of liberal humanist positions. This has helped to configure the 'take-up' of feminism and poststructuralism within critical psychology in fundamental ways.

Engaging with standpoints *and* differences

The proposal for the collection of essays in the book was not prescriptive about the kind of accounts that should be given of the feminist–poststructuralist axis. Our stated aim was to put together a varied set of essays written by feminists engaged in work on psychological issues (whatever their disciplinary perspectives). Their brief was to: (a) take up the issues at stake in the feminism–poststructuralism controversy within their own substantive area(s) of study; (b) identify the position(s) their own work occupies within the wider theoretical debate; and (c) reflect upon the influence of this positioning on their research and/or other areas of feminist and psychological practice. What we have been rewarded with is a rich and challenging set of chapters on a wide variety of issues. Several themes addressed in the volume have already been discussed (above) and several others emerge from a reading of the text. Three of these are discussed below.

(i) Diverse ways of engaging in feminist politics

The chapters illustrate various ways of taking forward a commitment to feminist politics that reproduces neither foundationalism nor relativism. Hence, they do not reproduce essentialist assumptions about the experiences or social positions of women. Nor do they relativize accounts and arguments as merely one possible version of plural possibilities, each having equal weight. As a general approach this is most explicit in the first two chapters that set out and deconstruct the dualism (Gill; Jackson), but there are a number of more specific illustrations in relation to particular psychological studies. Marshall, Woollett and Dosanjh focus strategically on their findings of commonalities or differences among groups of ethnically 'Asian' and white women, as part of a wider project whose stipulated (feminist) goals are to challenge universalizing, marginalizing and pathologizing understandings of motherhood, childbirth and childcare. In addition, they address the possible consequences of the researchers' silence about difference(s) for blocking the development of further understanding power relations. Brown discusses 'adolescent' girls' compromises and resistances with dominant and constraining constructions of femininity as sites of struggle against normalizing discourses which are fissured by what she calls the 'accents' of class. Seu discusses an issue rarely addressed within feminist psychological literature – shame. She uses psychoanalytic theory to interrogate 'shameful' subject positions as 'practical ideologies', and argues against any dilution of concern for the iniquitous and health-implicating effects of relations of power and domination.

Other chapters reinforce a relational approach to the construction, contestations and consequences of gender. Wetherell and Edley do this by comparing differences and similarities between men. Squire's approach is to hold the category 'woman' continually in question and to attribute as much interpretive importance to gender similarities as to differences. This, she argues, does not depoliticize feminism through being endlessly relativist. Instead, relativism is avoided through strategies 'like a strategic, even metaphorical essentialism about the category "women"'; by paying attention to the possible limitations produced by conditions of consumption and by studying language itself. The concern of van Mens-Verhulst's chapter is with the shifting agenda of feminist mental health care (involving both mainstream and alternative systems) in the Netherlands, and this brings on to the agenda feminist 'grass roots' politics and the process of change in organizing for women. Her argument is that 'women's liberation is an endless process' and that poststructuralism has provided some useful insights. However, in contrast, for example, to Squire's chapter, she concludes that it cannot guide feminist mental health care since it refuses to take any standpoints. Erica Burman's chapter subjects developmental psychology to a deconstructive critique. In doing so, it focuses on the multiple and contradictory effects of power relations and gendered subject positions among women in the classroom and in the international women's and children's rights arenas. She argues that 'no metaphor can guarantee a positive outcome: rather, what matters is what we do with it'. It is this political sensitivity that allows Burman's chapter to provide another example of the productive possibilities of reconciling feminist standpoint and a 'commitment to a postmodern-style multiplicity and diversity'.

(ii) Textuality of experience, dialogics of voice: questions of engagement/mutuality, accountability and authority in knowing and science
One of the severest challenges for researchers whose affinity is with feminism and psychology is to be able to move forward, rather than be paralysed by the questioning of notions of 'representing

experience' or 'giving voice'. This type of questioning was initially directed at positivistic notions of distanced, impartial objectivity, but it has been extended into ideas that were at one time thought to be disruptive of the subject–object binary. The assumption that accounts of experience speak for themselves or that ethnographies allow the pure representation of people's lives, uncontaminated by researchers' interpretations and selections, has long been deconstructed (Gillespie, 1995; hooks, 1991). While metaphors of speaking and listening are clearly different from the more usual specular one of knowing by observing or looking, they do not necessarily break completely with modernist representational practices if speech is treated as a more direct indicator of thought than writing and if listening is treated as an acoustic mirror. In that formulation, metaphors of speaking and listening remain bound into an ocular epistemology, or spectator approach to knowing and science (Denzin, 1997). Seeking to represent or to speak for another then runs the risk of creating an object of researchers' gaze and pathologizing the Other (Wilkinson and Kitzinger, 1996).

In her chapter, Gill focuses on the specialized fields that apply poststructuralist ideas to research (such as social studies of science in the tradition which has come to be known as the Sociology of Scientific Knowledge – SSK). She argues that, while these have provided many useful insights, they do not provide the solution to the problems raised by consideration of a spectator approach to knowledge. She suggests that many reservations can be expressed about the practical means such researchers use to build reflexivity into their research and writing. Certain uses of reflexive practices can reinforce, as much as challenge, textual authority. Multiple voices may only apparently be invoked when they are in fact those the authors want to present to us (and, usually their own). There can be a problem of lack of accountability if any and all statements can be passed off as irony. New literary forms may themselves become 'guarantees' of reflexiveness; and focusing upon writing alone as the site of reflexive practice may obviate the need for interrogations of the whole research process on issues such as mutuality and involvement. This results in a non-productive 'engagement' with the ethical and political concerns that have been paramount within feminism. Seen in this light, the Sociology of Scientific Knowledge would seem to fall short of its promise of promoting reflexive practice within social science research although it raises several crucial issues (see also Gill, 1995).

This argument opens up the possibility of a recuperative strategy – and all the chapters point towards (different) ways in which possible problems of postmodern approaches can be addressed through feminist engagement. Gill suggests that in their 'rejection of the idea of value freedom, of objectifying research relationships, and of the omnipotent and distant researcher', feminist researchers have already made some of the most significant contributions to 'new ways of writing engendered by new ways of thinking about and doing research'. Jackson's chapter attempts to reclaim a space for feminist theorizing and research that insists on the specific and important uses of investigating everyday experiences, accounts and reflections upon them, as part of a more contingent, contextually specific, perspective on the operation of power and knowing. Within this space the potential of researching 'experiences and lives' can be reclaimed as a research strategy with the potential to stimulate insights on material 'realities' (namely, 'subjugated knowledges') that counter claims to reflect a so-called universal, neutral view – or a position-less, objective standpoint (see also Willott, this volume), while accepting that such an epistemic outcome cannot be guaranteed. Such an approach accommodates a research strategy that is designed to help develop a language for encoding what might otherwise be ignored because it is associated with socially dis-advantaged or marginalized peoples (including women – see Brown, this volume). At the very least, it makes a case for assigning value to the mundane and the everyday, just as other approaches to research place value on, for example, numbers or media images/texts (Squire).

At the same time, Jackson recognizes some of the problems that need to be addressed in feminist research. Indeed, her chapter acknowledges some of the continuing strains in feminist work that can be brought out more clearly by forging an alliance with poststructuralism. For example, if (as Jackson argues) treatments of the concept of 'experience' are not necessarily reductionist, it is still important to explain those moments when they are. One of Jackson's main concerns here is that a considerable pull may still be exerted by conventions of social science practice towards accepting researchers – even the qualitative, feminist social scientist – as 'knowers' and 'experts'. In this way feminist research can fail in its promise to avoid the more hierarchical relationship between researcher and researched demanded by both feminist writers' and deconstructionism's destabilization of the observer–observed dichotomy. To counter this tendency in her own work, Jackson strives to exemplify the kind of personally and politically self-reflexive social science practices referred to by Gill. For example, her study of autobiographical narratives includes studying, not just other people's, but her own autobiography in an attempt to take forward ways of understanding how 'the personal is political'. The more impersonal or structural types of explanations to be found within academic theorizing are considered as socially/culturally available stories, and she reflects upon the wider epistemic ramifications of the different ways in which researchers tell their stories. Her argument also takes her to one of the epistemological 'turning points' which led Gill to reflect upon her own preference for presenting a transparently argued – and hence authoritative and accountable – position within academic debate or discourse.

(iii) Generating new research strategies
The presentation within the chapters in this book of a wide variety of research strategies also makes a significant contribution to contemporary debates about methodology within feminism and psychology. In particular, they find ways to disrupt the binary between theory and research, and are thus part of attempts to undermine the hegemony of empirical science. Many of the new approaches and concepts used in the chapters function to disrupt the 'Othering' which is common to work which 'represents the Other' (Wilkinson and Kitzinger, 1996) as well as the assumption of commonality when women study women (Squire). Marshall, Woollett and Dosanjh's research includes Asian women – a group which is frequently omitted from studies of 'normal' motherhood – and also refuses to treat this group as an homogeneous one. Van Mens-Verhulst explores a feminist initiative which is currently not well-researched – feminist mental health care. Brown examines commonalities and differences in relation to social class among young women. Authors variously refer to their work as a 'politics of articulation' (Marshall, Woollett and Dosanjh; Wetherell and Edley); a specifically 'dialogic' treatment of the concepts of 'ventriloquation' and 'voice' (Brown); and developing a 'critical reflexivity that is politically accountable' (Willott). The latter involves combining action-oriented approaches with a caution about representation in order to reflect upon the dilemmas for a feminist researcher of adopting the position of 'outsider within'. Willott's account of her contradictory positioning, and that of her research participants, both takes forward understandings of the non-exclusivity of (dis)empowerment and complicates understandings of what it means to be a feminist doing research with men.

For several authors a central feature of their research strategies is the construction and discussion of various forms of 'readings'. For example, Erica Burman reflects on her positioning as a feminist teacher of developmental psychology by providing a reading of her experiences using the intersections of poststructuralist theory and feminisms. Ros Gill is concerned that, while writing is crucial to academic disciplines, 'the forms we use, the genres we employ, the narratives we construct – has been given little sustained critical attention'. Therefore she begins the (difficult) process of subjecting academic writing to critical 'readings'. Jackson lays biographical narratives open to critical (and reflexive) reading. Seu presents multiple readings of the same accounts which pay attention to the political consequences of different readings. Having built into her research a process of mutual interrogation between psychoanalysis, poststructuralism and feminist accounts of the psychology of women and oppression, she is able also to discuss the different and contradictory implications of subject positions for women's well-being and sense of self (an aim she shares with van Mens-Verhulst). Squire presents readings from a standpoint perspective and demon-strates why she finds a genre perspective, informed by psycho-analysis, more satisfactory for reading subject positions and for understanding 'violence'. Wetherell and Edley present a careful discursive analysis in order to examine the utility of different theoretical readings for understanding young men's accounts of masculinity.

Conclusion

One of our reasons for editing this book is that it has become difficult to ignore the disputatious air in contemporary feminist scholarship. This affects our understanding of both the categories, concepts and codes that are the building blocks of feminist analyses and the forms of questioning that give a distinctive framing to feminist work. While critical self-reflection is, of course, part and parcel of the deliberation and debate that is endogenous to feminism(s) (hooks, 1982; Lorde, 1984; Essed, personal commu-nication), it has been given a specifically 'deconstructive' edge by an emergent interface with poststructuralist theorizing (Diamond and Quinby, 1988; Hekman, 1990; McNay, 1992; Weedon, 1987). A central aim of this book is to contribute to the development of an appreciation of the productive tensions and disputes associated with the feminist–poststructuralist interface (see also Nicholson, 1990; Ramazanoglu, 1993; Soper, 1993), as they play out in the investi-gations and practices of feminist psychology.

The ten chapters that we have brought together deal with the challenges posed by the relationship of feminisms and poststructur-alism, and its implications for psychological and feminist practice. Each chapter is so thoroughly embroiled in debating the relation-ship, and in considering the issues at stake once the relationship has been represented, that they do not fit readily into any previously occasioned classification – such as that which has framed the implications of discourse analysis for feminist psychology as either 'optimistic', 'questioning' or 'equivocal' (Wilkinson and Kitzinger, 1996). We have sub-divided our chapters into three parts: (i) Modes of arguing/theoretical positionings; (ii) Diverse positionings; and (iii) Reflections on theory and practice. These sections are, however, less concerned with delineating overall positions on the feminism–poststructuralism controversy, than with mapping out the different ways in which the authors approach the issues they address. The sections and the content of the chapters also overlap to some extent.

Given the complexity of the subject matter they address, the contributors to this volume have presented their arguments admirably clearly. Through focusing on a consideration of 'standpoints and differences', they address some of the key academic and political issues of our time. These include: understandings of subjectivities; the intersection of feminist politics, practices and research; processes of historical change in contexts where power relations of, for example, gender, 'race', social class and sexuality continue to be central; the place of language in theoretical understandings. Each chapter problematizes (to different extents) the binary between 'standpoints' and 'differences', demonstrating, in some cases, that feminist standpoint theories are deconstructive and, in others, that poststructuralism is reconcilable with analyses of the complexities of everyday 'lived experiences' and language. There is no easy, formulaic agreement between the contributors on how best to move forward these debates. However, each chapter refuses a 'standpoints' *or* 'differences' impasse embedded either in a foundationalist essentialism or in relativism. None demonize either 'standpoints' or 'differences'. The contributors' rich and varied methodologies and arguments will, hopefully, contribute to moving forward theoretical and methodological debates within, and beyond, feminisms and psychology.

Note

1 Although we mainly use the term poststructuralism in this book, it has a close relationship with postmodernism and so at times they are used interchangeably. Strictly speaking, one important differentiation is that poststructuralism (see e.g. Henriques et al., 1984) refers specifically to a movement in linguistics and literary studies that has sought to extend further structuralist critiques of a referential theory of meaning. Poststructuralism has also been developed in the service of social science critique, and in this form promotes a radical scepticism about the possibilities for knowledge in the social and human sciences, on the grounds that social and psychological life can best be construed as webs of multiple, shifting, contradictory meanings that are formulated within discourse-power relations or

texts. Postmodernism (Lyotard, 1984) is in some ways a more encompassing term which brings into focus analyses of a greater fracturing and fluidity of social organization (including of knowledge and subjectivity) in the post-industrial, post-Enlightenment Age.

References

Alcoff, L. and Potter, L. (1993) *Feminist Epistemologies*. London: Routledge.
Bleier, R. (1979) 'Social and political bias in science', in Ruth Hubbard and Marian Lowe (eds), *Genes and Gender II*. New York: Gordian Press.
Bleier, R. (ed.) (1986) *Feminist Approaches to Science*. New York: Pergamon.
Brah, A. (1996) *Cartographies of Diaspora*. London: Routledge.
Burman, E. and Parker, I. (eds) (1993) *Discourse Analytic Research: Repertoires and Readings of Text in Action*. London: Routledge.
Butler, J. (1990) *Gender Trouble: Feminism and the Subversion of Identity*. London: Routledge.
Collins, P.H. (1990) *Black Feminist Thought*. Boston, MA: Unwin Hyman.
Davis, K. (1992) 'Towards a feminist rhetoric: the Gilligan debate revisited', *Women's Studies International Forum* 15 (2): 219–31.
Denzin, N. (1997) *Interpretive Ethnography*. Thousand Oaks, CA: Sage.
Derrida, J. (1976) *Of Grammatology*. Baltimore, MD: Johns Hopkins University Press.
Devault, M.L. (1990) 'Talking and listening from women's standpoint: feminist strategies for interviewing and analysis', *Social Problems* 37 (1): 96–114.
Diamond, I. and Quinby, L. (eds) (1988) *Feminism and Foucault: Reflections on Resistance*. Boston: Northeastern University Press.
Edwards, D. (1997) *Discourse and Cognition*. London: Sage.
Edwards, D. and Potter, J. (1992) *Discursive Psychology*. London: Sage.
Flax, J. (1987) 'Postmodernism and gender relations in feminist theory', *Signs* 12 (4): 621–43.
Foucault, M. (1984) *The Foucault Reader* (P. Rabinow, ed.). Harmondsworth: Penguin.
Fox-Keller, Evelyn (1985) *Reflections on Gender and Science*. New Haven, CT: Yale University Press.
Gill, R. (1995) 'Relativism, reflexivity and politics: interrogating discourse analysis from a feminist perspective', in S. Wilkinson and C. Kitzinger (eds), *Feminism and Discourse: Psychological Perspectives*. London: Sage.
Gillespie, M. (1995) *Television, Ethnicity and Cultural Change*. London: Routledge.
Haraway, D. (1991) *Simians, Cyborgs and Women: The Reinvention of Nature*. New York: Routledge.
Harding, S. (1986) *The Science Question in Feminism*. Milton Keynes: Open University Press.
Harding, S. (1991) *Whose Science? Whose Knowledge? Thinking from Women's Lives*. Milton Keynes: Open University Press.
Harding, S. and Hintikka, M.B. (eds) (1983) *Discovering Reality*. Dordrecht: D. Reidel.
Hartsock, N.C.M. (1983) 'The feminist standpoint: developing the ground for a specifically feminist historical materialism', in S. Harding and M.B. Hintikka (eds), *Discovering Reality*. Dordrecht: D. Reidel.

Hartsock, N.C.M. (1990) 'Foucault on power: a theory for women?', in L.J. Nicholson (ed.), *Feminism/Postmodernism*. London: Routledge.

Hekman, S. (1990) *Gender and Knowledge: Elements of a Postmodern Feminism*. Cambridge: Polity Press.

Henriques, J., Hollway, W., Urwin, C., Venn, C. and Walkerdine, V. (1984) *Changing the Subject: Psychology, Social Regulation and Subjectivity*. London: Methuen.

Hollway, W. (1989) *Subjectivity and Method in Psychology*. London: Sage.

hooks, b. (1982) *Ain't I a Woman? Black Women and Feminism*. London: Pluto Press.

hooks, b. (1991) *Yearning: Race, Gender and Cultural Politics*. London: Turnaround.

Jackson, S. (1992) 'The amazing deconstructing woman', *Trouble and Strife* 25 (Winter): 25–31.

Lather, P. (1997) 'Drawing the line at angels: working the ruins of feminist ethnography', *Qualitative Studies in Education* 10 (3): 285–304.

Lennon, K. and Whitford, M. (eds) (1994) *Knowing the Difference: Feminist Perspectives in Epistemology*. London: Routledge.

Lorde, A. (1984) *Sister Outsider*. New York: Crossing Press.

Lyotard, J.-F. (1984) *The Postmodern Condition: A Report on Knowledge*. Manchester: Manchester University Press.

McNay, L. (1992) *Foucault and Feminism*. Cambridge: Polity Press.

Mahowald, M. (1996) 'On treatment of myopia: feminist standpoint theory and bioethics', in Susan M. Wolf (ed.), *Feminism and Bioethics: Beyond Reproduction*. New York and Oxford: Oxford University Press.

Nicholson, L.J. (ed.) (1990) *Feminism/Postmodernism*. London: Routledge.

Potter, J. and Wetherell, M. (1987) *Discourse and Social Psychology*. London: Sage.

Ramazanoglu, C. (ed.) (1993) *Up Against Foucault: Exploration of Some Tensions Between Foucault and Feminism*. London: Routledge.

Shotter, J. and Gergen, K. (eds) (1989) *Texts of Identity*. London: Sage.

Smith, D. (1992) 'Sociology from women's experience: a reaffirmation', *Sociological Theory* 10 (1): 88–98.

Soper, K. (1993) 'Productive contradictions', in C. Ramazanoglu (ed.), *Up Against Foucault: Exploration of Some Tensions Between Foucault and Feminism*. London: Routledge.

Squire, C. (1989) *Significant Differences: Feminism in Psychology*. London: Routledge.

Squire, C. (1994) 'Empowering women: the Oprah Winfrey Show', *Feminism and Psychology* 4 (1): 63–80.

Stanley, L. and Wise, S. (eds) (1993) *Breaking Out Again: Feminist Ontology and Epistemology*. London: Routledge.

Walkerdine, V. (1996) *Schoolgirl Fictions*. London: Verso.

Walkerdine, V. (1997) *Daddy's Girl: Young Girls and Popular Culture*. London: Macmillan.

Weedon, C. (1987) *Feminist Practice and Poststructuralist Theory*. Oxford: Blackwell.

Wilkinson, S. (ed.) (1986) *Feminist Social Psychology*. Milton Keynes: Open University Press.

Wilkinson, S. and Kitzinger, C. (eds) (1995) *Feminism and Discourse: Psychological Perspectives*. London: Sage.

Wilkinson, S. and Kitzinger, C. (1996) *Representing the Other: A Feminism and Psychology Reader*. London: Sage.

Part 1

MODES OF ARGUING/THEORETICAL POSITIONINGS

2

Dialogues and Differences: Writing, Reflexivity and the Crisis of Representation

Rosalind Gill

The social scientist is not some autonomous being standing outside society. No one is outside society, the question is where he (sic) stands within it. (C. Wright Mills, 1959: 204)

[E]xtreme self-consciousness certainly has its dangers – of irony, of elitism, of solipsism, of putting the whole world in quotation marks. But I trust that readers who signal these dangers will do so *after* they have confronted the changing history, rhetoric and politics of established representational forms. (James Clifford, 1986: 25)

May you live in sceptical times. (Ancient postmodern proverb)

For social science researchers in the West at the end of the millennium, crisis has become the norm. Individual disciplines are said to be in crisis, the academy as a whole – and the role of intellectuals within it – is in crisis, and, indeed, the very epistemological foundations upon which knowledges have been built have been fatally destabilized and plunged into crisis. Talk about 'endings' and 'deaths' – the end of history, the end of representation, the death of the subject, and so on – has become part of the routine currency of academic exchange. In all the discussions about these multiple crises, however, one issue has been relatively neglected: the relationship of the 'postmodern predicament' to writing and reflexivity. Paradoxically, it seems that the lack of attention given to writing in traditional texts has been mirrored in much of the crisis literature, and writing remains, for the most part, invisible, naturalized, and treated as if it were simply the neutral disinterested recording of research.[1] Indeed, it is one of the ironies of academic life that writing, which is so highly prized, is rarely discussed outside the confines of 'how to' pieces designed to socialize PhD students and others into normative disciplinary practices (Madigan et al., 1995) or to convey advice about the process of writing (Robson, 1993). Despite (or perhaps because of) the fact that an important part of 'becoming disciplined' involves learning how to write in a particular way, the *way* that social scientists write – the forms we use, the genres we employ, the narratives we construct – has been given little sustained critical attention.

The aim of this chapter is to begin to redress this and to open up questions about writing, reflexivity and epistemology. More specifically, it hopes to explore the impact of the 'crisis of representation' upon the practice of reflexivity. The bulk of the chapter is devoted to discussion of two different perspectives: standpoint feminism, as exemplified by the work of Sandra Harding, Donna Haraway and Patricia Hill Collins (Harding, 1987, 1991, 1993; Haraway, 1988, 1991; Hill Collins, 1991), and the radical constitutive reflexivity proposed by Sociologists of Scientific Knowledge such as Steve Woolgar and Malcolm Ashmore (Ashmore, 1989; Woolgar, 1988a, 1996a). Criticisms of both perspectives are made, and I argue for a position in which the response to epistemological crisis is to centre politics and the importance of accountability.

The crisis of representation and the 'reflexive paradox'

The nature of the crises afflicting the academy at present can be constructed in radically different ways for a variety of occasioned practices. What I am interested in here is what is variously called the 'end of representation', the 'crisis of objectivism', and the 'death of the metanarratives' (Lynch, 1994; Lyotard, 1984; Nicholson, 1990; Rorty, 1989): broadly, the uncertainty and instability brought about by the interrogation of the epistemologies that have operated as 'foundations' for the production of (scientific) knowledge in the West for the last 300 years. This is not the place to offer a detailed account of this epistemological crisis, but (briefly) I see it as having been precipitated – indeed overdetermined – by a combination of political, intellectual, technological and economic factors. Perhaps most significant has been the emergence of voices (and political movements) of oppressed groups – women, black people, lesbians and gay men, (post)colonial subjects – which challenged both the subject of knowledge and its production. Alongside these challenges, radical intellectual currents of thought – such as psychoanalysis, structuralism and poststructuralism – raised questions about enduring assumptions in Western philosophy – the existence of the rational unified subject, the prevalence of binary oppositions. Meanwhile rapid technological changes have led to an explosion of information and communication technologies, which have accelerated economic and cultural globalization, given rise to new 'modes of information', and offered privileged Northern elites experiences of time–space compression and virtual realities (see Baumann, 1992; Crook et al., 1992; Jameson, 1991; Nicholson, 1990; Poster, 1990; Ross, 1988.)

Taken together, these various factors have produced a situation in which philosophy can no longer claim to offer incontestable foundations for knowledge, and our 'ways of knowing' have been radically problematized. The notion of representation – the idea that our concepts straightforwardly represent real objects in the world – has been shaken to its core. For discourse analysts, constructivists and others who, like myself, take seriously the implications of postmodernist ideas, language is viewed as *constructing* rather than reflecting reality, and there is no transcendent standpoint from which the 'real' can be apprehended. As Hilary Lawson has argued: 'The postmodern predicament is indeed one of crisis, a crisis of our truths, our values, our most cherished beliefs. A crisis that owes to reflexivity its origin, its necessity and its force' (1985: 8). This chapter seeks to explore the implications of this crisis for our own practice as social scientists. How are we to deal with what Lawson (1985) calls the 'reflexive paradoxes' generated by the recognition of the *textuality of social life* – the fact that when we recognize the importance of language we do so within language, that when we talk about constructions of the world we are ourselves constructing versions. If there are no transcendental guarantees, no final source of knowledge which can be invoked as a trump card (e.g. observation or experience), then what kinds of claim can be made for knowledge production? How should we, as researchers, deal with the fact that our own claims are themselves constructions – our own discourse is not somehow exempt, and is no less constructive, contingent and action-oriented than any other discourse? In short, how should we represent our research in writing in ways that acknowledge its essentially reflexive character?

The remainder of the chapter is divided into three parts. In the first I offer a general sense of some of the themes of the newly emergent interest in social science writing. Work on rhetoric, on the blurring of fact and fiction, and postmodern anthropology is discussed. The second part of the chapter examines feminist discussions of writing, reflexivity and epistemology, focusing in particular on standpoint theory. The notions of epistemic privilege and strong objectivity are critically discussed, the mapping of experience on to standpoint is interrogated, and concerns are raised about a slide into 'identity politics'. The third section explores a contrasting tradition of work, which is not well-known among psychologists, but which has been notable for its serious engagement with questions about writing and reflexivity – the Sociology of Scientific Knowledge (SSK). The advocacy by SSK of 'new literary forms' is interrogated, raising questions about authority, ethics and accountability. Finally, in the conclusion, I argue that, despite their differences, standpoint feminism and SSK share a desire to *escape* from the reflexive paradox. I suggest that rather than trying to find some way out, it would be more productive to acknowledge the crisis and produce knowledge on new terms – with only contingent guarantees and politics at the heart – rather than simply 'smuggled in' by default.

Reflexivity and the rhetoric of social science texts

In literature, drama, film and the visual arts reflexivity has been addressed seriously for several decades. Devices such as including the artist or director in a painting or film, moving in and out of character in plays and films, and disrupting the smooth flow of a narrative have long been used to highlight the fact that the text is a construction, and to jolt audiences out of comfortable, habitual ways of seeing the world. It is only in the last few years, however, that social scientists have started to look at, and problematize, their own textual productions. Interest has come from several directions, invigorated by the general interest in discourse and rhetoric, by the collapse of a belief in representation, and by ethical and political concerns about researching and representing Others.

One of the achievements of these diverse strands of work has been to stress that social science texts, far from being simple, neutral or transparent reflections of the research process, are in fact, complex rhetorical accomplishments (Nelson et al., 1987; Stringer, 1990). They depend for their success upon the strategic deployment of particular generic forms, metaphors and other types of rhetoric. Corinne Squire (1990) has analysed research reports written by psychologists and has argued that they are reliant upon a number of genres or styles that are usually associated with fiction. There is the detective narrative in which the researcher presents him or herself as an investigator, who will work 'under cover' if necessary to discover the truth; the autobiographical narrative, which makes use of subjective and confessional qualities to bolster the story being told; and the science fiction narrative in which the researcher portrays him or herself as voyaging into new, uncharted (research) territories – boldly going where no person has gone before. Squire's analysis draws our attention to the fact that the distinction between factual and fictional discourse cannot be sustained; when we write or talk we are involved in producing versions of events, phenomena, feelings and, moreover, that even the 'hardest' scientific texts are dependent upon literary devices for their effect. A similar point has been made by Potter, Wetherell and Chitty (1991) who show, in a discussion of a documentary about cancer research, that even the use of statistics can be viewed as a kind of rhetoric (see also Hacking, 1990, for a more Foucauldian approach).

This insight about the significance of textual constructions has also been central to the work of what is sometimes called 'postmodern anthropology'. Profoundly influenced by postcolonial critiques of anthropology which highlighted the central role played by anthropology in telling colonial stories and providing voyeuristic accounts of encounters with exotic 'others', this work has been concerned to examine how the anthropologist's authority as cultural expert is textually constructed. James Clifford (1986) argues that writing is a *constitutive* part of what researchers (anthropologists) do 'in the field'. It has been seen as peripheral only because of the prevalence of the ideology which asserts the transparency of representation and the immediacy of experience. Clifford argues that anthropological reports are 'cultural fictions' based on systematic and contestable exclusions. These may involve 'silencing incongruent voices or deploying a consistent manner of quoting, "speaking for" or translating the reality of the other' (1986: 6).

Detailed studies of ethnographic rhetoric have fleshed out this claim (e.g. Atkinson, 1990; Van Maanen, 1988). Van Maanen's analyses of realist 'tales from the field' argues that they involve an appeal to the experiential authority of the ethnographer, who is deemed to have a kind of 'immaculate perception', and is presented as an impersonal conduit through which observations are brought to the reader. This is reflected in a 'studied neutrality' of tone, and the complete invisibility of the ethnographer from the account. They also feature a variety of attempts to establish the credibility of the ethnographer as cultural guide, for example the presentation of precise details about some cultural phenomenon, or the use of strategic quotes from members.

Postmodernist or constructivist anthropologists argue that monologic, realist ethnographies should be abandoned. Clifford (1983) has argued that anthropologists should renounce all distancing techniques, break down the distinction between subject and object and become involved in a more 'dialogic' process of inquiry.

> Dialogic and constructivist paradigms tend to disperse or share out ethnographic authority, while narratives of initiation confirm the researcher's special competence. Paradigms of experience and interpretation are yielding to paradigms of discourse, of dialogue and of polyphony. (Clifford, 1983: 133)

Rhetoricians in a variety of disciplines have also become interested in writing in different ways. Michael Billig (1994), for example, has drawn attention to the way in which psychology texts are 'depopulated', by constructing a fictional account of an experiment, written from the point of view of a young undergraduate student who has been recruited as a subject. What this highlights are the manifold exclusions on which the usual psychology report narrative depends. Indeed, if I could be permitted to lapse into a problematic realist mode myself, for a moment, I would argue that Billig's 'fiction' comes far closer to the truth about what took place than the kind of anodyne statement one might find written up in a journal: for example, 'thirty pairs of matched subjects completed word recognition tests . . .'

But of course Billig is not interested in constructing one true or definitive account, but rather in the political *effects* of traditional ways of reporting research. In the remainder of this chapter I turn to the two broad perspectives which have given these questions most attention: feminisms and SSK.

Feminisms, writing and epistemology

There is no single feminist position relating to writing and epistemology, just as there is no single feminist position about anything else, but rather many diverse perspectives. From the array of feminist discussions of writing it would be impossible to distil a single 'line'. Nevertheless, there are some common themes which, with the caveat that none applies to all feminisms, I am going to sketch out here, before considering standpoint feminism in more detail.

Most feminisms share a critique of traditional social science research. Indeed, it was partly feminist attacks on it which heralded the crisis of representation – as feminists highlighted the partiality of the research which passed as universal knowledge. The notion of objectivity came under sustained attack – an early women's movement slogan being 'objectivity is male subjectivity' (Spender, 1980). Feminist writers raised the suspicion that transcendental claims to truth often reflected little more than the experiences of white Western males and, more recently, white middle-class, first-world feminists (Hill Collins, 1991; hooks, 1982; Ramazanoglu, 1989; Segal, 1987; Spelman, 1988).

Feminisms also challenged the notion that the producer of knowledge is irrelevant, that it does not matter whether the researcher is male or female, black or white, middle-class or working-class, and so on. Moreover, they pointed out the contradiction between this 'scientific' view, and the notion that feminist researchers would somehow 'contaminate' the research process – as if only white, middle-class males would get 'authentic' results (Bhavnani, 1993). Patricia Hill Collins recounts how her academic training sought to eliminate all those aspects of her everyday life, which could, looked at differently, be seen as a valuable resource: 'Much of my formal academic training has been designed to show me that I must alienate myself from my communities, my family, and even my own self in order to produce credible academic work' (1991: xiii). In *Breaking Out Again*, Liz Stanley and Sue Wise ask: 'How many other professions, we wonder, make such a fetish of *ignorance*, and elevate it into the only possible claim to professional competence?' (1993: 169).

In recent years some feminists (and others) have become interested in the way that the *rhetoric* of social science writing serves to conceal the fact that research is an active process, engaged in by embodied subjects, with emotions and theoretical and political commitments. Current interest in 'intellectual biography and autobiography' (e.g. Aldridge, 1993; Cotteril and Letherby, 1993; Ribbens, 1993; Stanley, 1992; Stacey, 1997) has paid particular attention to the conventions by which academic writing *textually disembodies* research. The producer of knowledge and the means by which it is produced are systematically effaced in traditional writing. As Ken Plummer has put it: 'Until recently, research reports have often been written as if they were executed by machines: not a hint of the ethical, political and personal problems which routinely confront the human researcher and the research subject can be found' (1983: 136).

Moreover, to the extent that the process of research is discussed at all, it is subjected to *temporal re-ordering*: the shifting of time, in such a way as to make it appear that the research followed a standard invariant sequence – literature review, hypothesis development, selection of method, and so on. In this way, the (often) messy, contingent practice of research is smoothed over and made 'hygienic': '[M]ost social science researchers start off by believing that what is presented in these descriptions is a reasonable representation of the reality of research. Most of us get a nasty shock when we come to do research ourselves' (Stanley and Wise, 1993: 152–3).

Judith Aldridge (1993) shows how the literature review as a piece of rhetoric plays a crucial role not simply in reviewing the field but in constructing others' research and accomplishing the self (the present writer) as having a wider and more sophisticated vision, a greater knowledge of the field. So integral is this form of writing to the establishment of academic credibility, that she even found herself doing it when writing an autobiographical account. She constructed her former self (herself in the past) as a 'straw target', someone with very narrow vision, in such a way as to display her current expertise and sophistication.

Traditional 'quick and dirty research' is accused by some feminists of drawing on 'a rape model' in which the researchers 'take, hit and run. They intrude into their research subjects' privacy, disrupt their perceptions, utilise false pretences, manipulate the relationship and give little or nothing in return. When the needs of the researchers are satisfied they break off contact with the subject' (Reinharz, 1983: 95). In addition to offering critiques of this model, feminists have advocated new approaches with ethical concerns at their heart. For example, many feminists have argued in favour of models which place the researcher and the researched on the same plane (Harding, 1993; Stanley and Wise, 1993). Vertical or hierarchical relationships are challenged and some feminists see research as a co-production not *on* women but *for* women. Maria Mies (1983), for example, follows Paolo Freire in seeing research as inseparable from political struggle, and views its practice as a forum for change and consciousness-raising (for all participants *including the researcher*). The (apparently) disinterested view from above is replaced by the view from below. Many other feminist researchers have argued that *experience* can constitute a key resource for knowledge production, although the precise nature of this is highly contested (e.g. Currie and Kazi, 1987; Reinharz, 1983; Roberts, 1981; Scott, 1992; Stanley and Wise, 1993). Similarly, the self is regarded by some feminists as a valuable starting point. Dorothy Smith (1987) argues that a woman's perspective makes available a radical critique of sociology, which has attempted a kind of 'conceptual imperialism' – the translation of women's experience into theoretical terms.

Feminist concerns about writing have been inextricably linked to these new ways of doing research. Rejection of the idea of value freedom, of objectifying and exploitative research relationships, and of the omnipotent and distant researcher have produced new ways of writing about research. Recent concerns have focused on the very notion of representation, and particularly on questions of how – and indeed whether – we should represent Others. Should white women research black women? Should women without children research mothers? Should able-bodied women do research on disabled women? And so on. These discussions have highlighted the multiplicity of meanings associated with the term representation – the sense that it refers not simply to textual production, but also to speaking for, or on behalf of, and the fact that power is intimately bound up with representation (see Wilkinson and Kitzinger, 1996). Most of this work has been concerned with questions about social structural location and identity, but others have raised questions about how feminists should go about representing (and indeed practising) research with women with different political views, for example women who reject feminism and who espouse openly racist views. In this vein, Cathleen Armistead (1995) has explored dilemmas raised by her lack of empathy with her female respondents, and raises concerns about how she should present her research to the male academic community without reinforcing racism and class prejudices. She asks: 'Would my attempt to describe and analyse working class women's experiences and interpretations, especially their use of racial categories and their rejection of feminism, be merely another objectification of working class women by academia? (Armistead, 1995: 627). There is no straightforward answer to this question; these are complex issues. The point I wish to stress about it, however, is that feminist interest in writing and representation emerges directly from a variety of *ethical* and *political* commitments. New ways of writing are engendered by new ways of thinking about and doing research. Indeed, (as you may have noticed) I am finding it very difficult to stick to the topic of writing – so bound up is it with other issues about the conduct of research.

Finally, one concern that is common to much (though not all) feminist writing is that it should be clear, accessible and empowering. Writing is part of political struggle, and should reach beyond academia to women more generally. bell hooks (1991), who claims to write as much for other black women in her community as for an academic audience, regrets that so much postmodern writing is so opaque and abstract:

> It is sadly ironic that the contemporary discourse which talks the most about heterogeneity, the decentred subject, declaring breakthroughs that allow recognition of Otherness, still directs its critical voice primarily to a specialised audience that shares a common language rooted in the very master narratives it claims to challenge. (hooks, 1991: 25)

Similarly, Alison Light argues: 'If the day ever comes that any woman feels that she cannot put pen to paper without being conversant with Lacan's mirror phase . . . then we may as well stop the bus and get off' (1989: 27–8).

Standpoint feminisms

Most feminist discourse about writing, then, is a response to ethical concerns about the conduct of research and political concerns about democracy and social transformation. Perhaps the perspective which has addressed most directly the *epistemological* issues raised by the crisis of objectivism is standpoint feminism. A number of different standpoint positions have been elaborated by feminists, among them the work of Donna Haraway (1988, 1991), Nancy Hartsock (1983), Patricia Hill Collins (1991) and Alison Jaggar (1983). It would be impossible to do justice to these diverse strands of thought here, so I will rely on Sandra Harding's work as my guide to standpoint epistemologies, and will draw on others' work when it seems appropriate to do so.

Harding's basic thesis is that all knowledge bears the imprint of the communities that produced it. There is no 'news from nowhere', no 'God trick' (Haraway, 1988); there are only situated knowledges. Harding criticizes traditional conceptions of objectivity, not because they are 'too rigorous or objectifying', but because they 'are not rigorous or objectifying enough' (1993: 50–1). She argues:

> In societies where scientific rationality and objectivity are claimed to be highly valued by dominant groups, marginalised peoples and those who listen attentively to them, will point out that, from the perspective of marginal lives, the dominant accounts are less than maximally objective. Knowledge claims are always socially situated, and the failure by dominant groups critically and systematically to interrogate their advantaged social situation and the effect of such advantages on their beliefs leaves their social situation a scientifically and epistemologically disadvantaged one for generating knowledge. (Harding, 1993: 54)

According to Harding, some social locations are better than others for producing knowledge. More specifically, drawing on Hegel and Marx, she argues that the oppressed have the capacity to see more clearly. They may be socially disadvantaged, but they are *epistemologically privileged*; they are better placed to produce 'maximally objective' knowledge. In relation to a feminist standpoint she writes:

> The distinctive features of women's situation in a gender-stratified society are being used as resources in the new feminist research. It is these distinctive resources, which are not used by conventional researchers,

that enable feminisms to produce empirically more accurate descriptions
and theoretically richer explanations than does conventional research.
(Harding, 1991: 119)

Harding argues that research should strive for what she calls 'strong
objectivity'. A necessary condition for this is starting from the lives
of the marginalized or oppressed. One of the problems with this
argument, however, is that no means of identifying who is
oppressed or marginalized – and therefore privileged – is provided.
This may seem to be a minor point; one could, after all, respond
that 'it is obvious' as Harding seems to assume, but I do not believe
that this stands up to scrutiny. In the first place, epistemologically it
introduces a circularity – oppressed groups cannot be identified
independently of epistemology; secondly, history has taught us that
the identification of oppression is *not* obvious: if it were so, why did
it take first-world feminism so long to recognize its own class and
racial biases? Thirdly, at the specific cultural and historical location
in which Harding is writing, the question of who is and who is not
oppressed is profoundly *contested*. As the media herald in an age of
'postfeminism', it is *men* who are, increasingly, claiming the status
of oppressed, backing this up with data about poor educational
attainment and unemployment. The point is not that I give this
argument any credence, but that Harding provides no means by
which we could mount a principled attack on this claim to
entitlement. Class, 'race', gender and sexuality are treated as
unproblematic independent variables, and Harding risks re-
inscribing an essentialism that treats socially constructed categories
as unitary.[2]

Perhaps the issue which has been the source of most contention
for standpoint theorists, though, is what it actually *means* to 'start
from the lives of the oppressed'. In particular, the relationship of a
feminist standpoint to women's experience has been hotly contested.
On the one hand, Harding accords experience a primary position in
her epistemology. She echoes Hartsock's (1983) Marxist position
that just as 'correct vision is only available from one of the two
major class positions in society' so 'women's lives make available a
particular and privileged vantage point which can ground a
powerful critique of the phallocratic institutions and ideology which
constitute the capitalist form of patriarchy' (1983: 284). She asserts
that existing in patriarchal society equips women with a special
'double vision'. She also devotes considerable attention to exploring
precisely what it is that gives women this capacity, considering,
among other possible explanations, the sexual division of labour
and psychodynamic accounts of women's development. From these

perspectives the material nature of women's lives 'really' does give them epistemological privileges compared with men.

Against this, however, Harding explicitly disavows 'experiential foundationalism'. Experience *lies*, she argues (1991: 311), taking on board criticisms from writers like Jane Flax (1990) who accuse her of overlooking ideology and of assuming 'that the oppressed are not in some ways also damaged by their social experience' (1990: 56). This is, of course, a real dilemma – and not just for standpoint theorists. The problem is, in part, how far the deconstruction of experience is to be taken, and to what extent the occupancy of social locations does exert real, material effects on our consciousness. Harding expresses the tension very lucidly:

> On the one hand, we should be able to decide the validity of a knowledge claim apart from who speaks it; this is the desirable legacy from the conventional view. . . . On the other hand, it *does* make a difference who says what and when. (1991: 269)

One way this enduring problem is dealt with is through the distinction which Harding (and Hill Collins) make between mere *claims* on the basis of experience and *standpoints*. For both Harding and Hill Collins experience is a necessary but not sufficient grounds for production of a standpoint.

> For a position to count as a standpoint rather than as a claim . . . we must insist on an objective location – women's lives – as the place from which feminist research should begin. We would not know to value the location so highly if women had not insisted on the importance of their experiences and voices. . . . But it is not the experiences or the speech that provides the grounds for feminist claims; it is rather the subsequently articulated observations of and theory about the rest of nature and social relations – observation and theory that start out from, that look at the world from the perspective of women's lives'. (Harding, 1991: 123–4)

A feminist standpoint, then, does not exist in pure form in the consciousness of women, and likewise, Black feminist standpoint is not lying passively, waiting to be discovered, inside African American[3] women's heads. A standpoint is the outcome of *struggle* (Harding, 1991; Hill Collins, 1991). It is, it seems to me, a *political project*. The development of a standpoint represents the process by which (to use Marxist terms) an oppressed group becomes not merely a group *in* themselves, but a group *for* themselves. The standpoint bears no natural or inevitable relationship to the experience of members of the group; it is constructed and articulated to the experience of the group in question. Is it not perfectly possible, therefore, that entirely different standpoints could be constructed – each with equal claim to speak from 'women's lives' – much in the way that political parties engage in hegemonic struggle to voice the 'authentic' 'will of the people'? What is not clear is why standpoint theorists set so much store by identity and experience when in fact a standpoint is a *political position*. One of the unfortunate outcomes of this is that the relationship between social location and standpoint is treated as unproblematic – indeed self-evident – while *the politics of constructing standpoints becomes invisible.*

A further problem with the notion of starting from the lives of the oppressed concerns how standpoint epistemologies deal with the existence of multiple and contradictory oppressions. Harding's work has been notable for the serious attention it has given to differences between women (as well as between women and men), especially those structured by 'race', class and sexuality. As she puts it:

> [I]t is important to remember that in a certain sense there are no 'women' or 'men' in the world – there is no 'gender' – but only women, men and gender constructed through particular historical struggles over just which races, classes, sexualities, cultures, religious groups and so forth, will have access to resources and power. (Harding, 1991: 151)

Despite the significant engagement with questions about difference and power in her work, Harding does not seem to have addressed adequately the issues that (may) arise from *conflicting* standpoints. How are the claims of knowledge producers from different social locations to be evaluated? How is their epistemic authority to be ranked – if at all? Bat-Ami Bar On suggests:

> The source of the problem is the existence of multiple socially marginalised groups; is any one of these groups more epistemically privileged than the others, and if that is not so – if they are all equally epistemically privileged – does epistemic privilege matter? (1993: 89)

Harding does not specify any criteria or norms which we might use to evaluate different knowledges (Longino, 1993); implicitly, social location (or at least a standpoint based in the experience of oppression) becomes the epistemological guarantee. But this does not help us to distinguish between competing claims from, for example, white, middle-class, lesbian women and black, working-class, heterosexual men. As Bar On (1993) says, it is important to avoid positing a hierarchy of oppression (and therefore privilege), and we should also be wary of approaches which try to create a totalizing, unifying framework that will account for each and every kind of oppression by reference to a single operation of power.

Patricia Hill Collins (1991) provides a useful way of addressing this problem. While being utterly suffused with discussions of power, her work cautions against dividing the world straightforwardly into oppressors and oppressed. In practice, she argues, 'each group identifies the oppression with which it feels most comfortable as being fundamental and classifies all others as being of lesser importance' (Hill Collins, 1991: 229). This happens, according to Hill Collins, because of a failure to recognize that 'a matrix of domination contains few pure victims or oppressors': individuals are frequently members both of multiple dominant groups and multiple subordinate groups (Hill Collins, 1991: 229–30). Hill Collins advocates the use of *dialogue* to deal with assessing competing claims – her notion of dialogue owes much to Afro-centric call and response traditions in which 'everyone has a voice, but everyone must listen and respond to other voices in order to be allowed to remain in the community' (1991: 236–7).

Dialogue is engendered by the fact that each group speaks from its own standpoint and shares its own partial, situated knowledge.

> But because each group perceives its own truth as partial, its knowledge is unfinished. Each group becomes better able to consider other groups' standpoints without relinquishing the uniqueness of its own standpoint or suppressing other groups' partial perspectives. (Hill Collins, 1991: 236; see also Haraway, 1988 and Harding, 1991 for similar formulations)

While this dual notion of dialogue with accountability does not offer a final panacea to the issue of how knowledge claims can be epistemologically 'underwritten' or guaranteed, it does move the debate forward by re-socializing or re-politicizing epistemology. As Nira Yuval-Davies (1994) has noted, conflicting interests and competing claims to truth are *not* always reconcilable, but at least the notion of dialogue shifts the discussion on to a terrain where standpoints can be argued about, rather than treated as givens. From this perspective, standpoint epistemologies can be seen to have much in common with postmodernist feminist calls for coalition politics or transversal politics (e.g. Butler, 1990, 1992, 1993; Elam, 1994; Nicholson and Fraser, 1990; Yuval-Davies, 1994).

The very success of the engagement of feminist standpoint epistemologies (and postmodernist feminists ideas) with class and 'race' and sexuality paradoxically raises a further question: what does it mean to be a feminist – or to take a feminist standpoint and to produce feminist knowledge? Harding argues that 'the subject/ agent of feminist knowledge is multiple and contradictory, not unitary and coherent; the subject/agent of feminist knowledge must also be the subject/agent of every other liberatory knowledge project' (1991: 180). According to this view, feminism is (or should be) inextricably linked to other liberation struggles – a position with which I would agree. The question is, then, what does it mean to produce knowledge from a *feminist* standpoint, since the agent of feminist knowledge 'must also be the subject/agent of every other liberatory knowledge project?' While I do not have a simple answer to this question, I do believe that it would be much more readily addressed if the politics of standpoints were discussed, rather than being cloaked behind the experiences of people in particular social locations.

Standpoint epistemologies remain profoundly ambivalent about the role of experience and identity (as I have discussed above), and in this respect encounter problems which postmodernist feminisms avoid. One example is Harding's advocacy of reflexiveness. She (rightly) criticizes both traditional approaches and radical SSK approaches to reflexivity for failing to identify the cultural values and interests of researchers. But her own approach seems primarily to involve reflecting on social location. Alcoff and Potter (1993) suggest that this may accord the individual as epistemic agent too much significance; it is the community, rather than the individual knower, which is the key unit of knowledge production – a point with which I am sure Harding would agree. More worryingly, it can easily descend into identity politics – a perspective in which fixed, essential differences between groups are assumed a priori, differences within groups are homogenized, and political action is often collapsed into lifestyle choices (see Brah, 1992; Burman, 1994; Donald and Rattansi, 1992; Hall, 1996; Mohanty, 1992; Rutherford, 1990, for critical discussions). Too often – and I have been guilty of this – papers start with what seems to be little more than a ritual incantation of the identities occupied by the author – with little or no attempt to reflect on the significance of those positions for the research. It is as if by simply stating them one has somehow been reflexive, and eradicated their effects. As Kum-Kum Bhavnani has argued, this can lead to the *micropolitics* of the research encounter being overlooked. Talking about the processes of 'matching' and noting in psychological research – both of which are attempts to register and control for power differences – Bhavnani argues that:

> both matching and noting can take the gaze of the student and reader away from the micropolitics of the research encounter. This is because the processes of matching and noting cannot explicitly take account of the power relationships between the researcher and the researched, and yet both processes imply that unevenness between the two sides in a research study has been dealt with. (Bhavnani, 1993: 101)

To be fair, Harding has herself been scathing about identity politics and about the failure of researchers to address the significance of their social position. However, the lack of clarity about the precise relation of experience and social location to standpoint means that her work is still open to the accusation that identity position acts as the guarantor of the worth of knowledge. There is a tension between this position, and the more fluid one advocated by Donna Haraway which is sceptical of the idea that any subject can pre-exist the encounters which construct it as a subject (Bhavnani and Haraway, 1994).

Finally, I want to raise some questions about Harding's advocacy of 'strong objectivity'. Harding's aim is to appropriate the notion of objectivity and to reconstruct it. She argues that it has a glorious political and intellectual history, and 'one cannot afford to "just say no" to objectivity' (Harding, 1991: 160), but it must be severed from its spurious connection to value-neutrality. She seems to want to argue for the radically contingent, socially situated nature of all knowledge claims, but she also maintains a strong commitment to telling 'more accurate' stories about a 'real' world. It is not clear to me how these desires can be reconciled, without falling into the trap discussed above, namely of policing knowledge claims on the basis of identity position. Some views, it seems, are more 'radically contingent' than others.

Harding argues for an 'outsider within' position. In some ways it is the classic position of the reformist, against – or at least alongside – the revolutionary. It is the position of one who believes that it is worth struggling *within* the existing institutions as well as mounting a full scale attack on them from 'outside'. She contends:

> It is important to work and think outside the dominant modes, as the minority movements have done. But it is also important to bring the insights developed there into the heart of conventional institutions, to disrupt the dominant practices from within by appropriating notions such as objectivity, reason and science in ways that stand a chance of compelling reasoned assent, while simultaneously shifting and displacing the meanings and referents of the discussion in ways that improve it. (Harding, 1991: 160)

In a sense, it seems to me that Harding is adopting a position of 'strategic objectivism', akin to the strategic essentialism espoused by Denise Riley, Gayatri Spivak and others. It is a rhetorical strategy designed to secure speaking rights for people working from the standpoints of the oppressed, in a scientific community still steeped in positivism, as well as to subvert mainstream practice from within. This is not an easy position to occupy, and I admire Harding for taking it on. But there are still questions to be raised. The most important is the one to which all reformist strategies have to answer: namely, is there not a danger that in attempting to reform from within, one finds oneself giving support to positions which ultimately contradict the goals for which one entered the struggle in the first place? It seems to me that just as Harding's emphasis upon the relationship of standpoints to particular social locations serves to efface the *politics* involved in that connection, so too the use of 'strong objectivity' enables her to avoid having to be blunt about the ineluctably political nature of the research enterprise.

Sociology of Scientific Knowledge and new literary forms

Questions about reflexivity have been dealt with in an entirely different way by workers in the sub-domain of the Sociology of Science known as SSK. SSK is characterized by scepticism towards claims about scientific knowledge, and by a thorough-going relativism. SSK studies of a whole range of scientific endeavours have made the point that scientific and technical knowledge is the contingent product of various social, historical and cultural processes. The problem for sociologists of scientific knowledge – or, as some see it, the *opportunity* – is that precisely the same point can be made about SSK. Studying the production of scientific knowledge requires the sociologist to participate in activities that are also the object of that research. She has to produce knowledge claims about the production of knowledge claims, she has to explain how explanation is done, she has to be able to replicate findings about replication, and so on. The question thus becomes what significance should be granted to this self-referential feature of SSK?

Within SSK there are various responses to this question, including outright denial of the tension and advocacy of 'business as usual'. For me, the most interesting response, though, is the injunction to embrace reflexivity as the natural development of relativist or constructivist approaches (e.g. Ashmore, 1989; Ashmore et al., 1995; Mulkay, 1985; Woolgar, 1988b). Reflexivists are critical of researchers who do not subject their own knowledge claims to the same interrogation as those of the scientists they study. As Latour and Woolgar put it:

> It might be reasonable to expect scholars concerned with the production of science to have begun to examine the basis for their own knowledge production. Yet the best of these scholars remain mute on their own methods and conditions of production. (1979: 18)

Writers in the reflexive tradition of SSK argue that an 'in principle' recognition of the reflexive paradox is not sufficient; academic practice must be changed to take on its essentially reflexive character. What is proposed is not simply 'benign introspection', or a loose recommendation to reflect critically on one's own practice, or, indeed, more 'personal' prefaces or addenda to reports. Instead, they are advocating 'radical constitutive reflexivity' (Woolgar, 1988) which strives to prevent closure and reification of categories. Steve Woolgar again:

> It is insufficient to reveal the actual circumstances behind the production of ethnographic texts, as if this revelation was itself a neutral, passive process. In short, we need continually to interrogate and find strange the process of representation as we engage in it. (1988: 28)

It is from this epistemological commitment to reflexivity that SSK's interest in writing derives. Reflexivists have sought to find ways of writing that will disrupt the smoothed-over narratives of objectivism and empiricism. They have attempted to produce texts which do not efface their own production, but draw attention to it, highlighting its artificiality and contingency. In order to do so they have developed 'new literary forms' (NLFs). Thus a 'report' by a SSKer committed to reflexivity might take the form of a play, a limerick, a poem, a letter, a diary, or a piece of 'performance art'. Malcolm Ashmore (1989) wrote a Reflexive (PhD) thesis which included conference transcripts, imaginary meetings between famous scholars, as well as an encyclopaedia of SSK. More recently, he has co-written a 'review' (Ashmore et al., 1995) whose aim was simultaneously to comment on and critique the genre. Most frequently, however, the form chosen is the dialogue – the term is used in a completely different way from Hill Collins (1991). SSK dialogues are 'conversations' between two or more participants. They are usually fictional, although of course this writing is designed to highlight the fact that distinctions between factual and fictional discourse are problematic.

This work is important. It represents a serious attempt to grapple with the 'reflexive paradox' identified by Lawson (1985), and I share its impulse to challenge the authority of writers, and to highlight the fact that (our own) academic texts are constructions. However, there are a number of problems with the way in which reflexivity is practised via NLFs. Elsewhere (Gill, 1995) I have raised two criticisms of the use of NLFs as a 'tool' for reflexivity. The first criticism is that instead of challenging authorial authority, often texts written in NLFs actually reinforce it. They do this by allowing authors to 'script in' critiques of their own position in such a way as to make it seem as if they have been dealt with. By appearing to acknowledge critical points they provide an innoculation for their argument and make it more difficult to rebut. They also sometimes protect authors from criticism through the use of strategic 'leaks' of personal (or other) information, through which authors can offer persuasive 'credentials', rather than needing to work the implications through in the research itself. Secondly, I argued that NLFs sometimes produce a fake pluralism or multivocality. They may seem to take differences seriously, but in fact all the different voices in the text are the author's – what we have (often) is a parody of real debate. Cynically, I suggested a materialist explanation for this, related to the crisis facing contemporary universities.

Here I wish to develop two more critical points, which are also concerned with the political issues raised by this type of practice of reflexivity. The first point concerns the way in which academic texts written in the form of dialogues or plays should be read. In a traditional text like this one, the argument I am making is (I hope) reasonably clear. Anyone wishing to quote me or to disagree with a point can do so with relative ease by singling out a passage verbatim or by producing a summary. Of course, I could reply by saying that I had been quoted out of context or that the critic has misinterpreted my argument, and then the text would become a site of contestation. But the point is that I could (and should) be held responsible or accountable for my argument. This assumption of accountability, however, is made problematic by new literary forms. In an academic article presented as a play, who is responsible for the 'views' of the characters? Although they are all the construction of the author, are they necessarily mouthpieces for him or her? How should the presence of many divergent and even contradictory accounts within the same piece be dealt with? Are the characters meant to represent real positions or are they caricatures? Should they be taken seriously or read ironically?

Ashmore, Myers and Potter (1995) suggest that one of the achievements of reflexivists' work is that they erode all the familiar distinctions between the serious and the non-serious, the important and the trivial. They represent a postmodern move to rework practices of representation in an ironic or self-referential fashion (see also Potter, 1996). The problem with this is that they become very difficult to 'call to account' and to critique, since everything can be passed off as irony. Potential critics can be admonished not simply for having got it wrong, but, more perniciously, for lacking the sophistication to notice that it was ironic. As I have argued in detail elsewhere (Gill, forthcoming), irony is one of the defining features of postmodern popular culture. For example, representations of women in advertising that would once have been targets for feminist campaigns are now 'reworked' and repackaged as 'ironic statements'. That is not an objectified image of a half-naked woman you see in all those bra adverts; it is an ironic comment on 1970s advertising, or, more specifically, a hilarious 'send up' of the 'dumb blonde' stereotype. History repeats itself: first time as sexism, second time as irony. One problem, then, is how 'new texts' should be read, held accountable and criticized.

The second point I wish to discuss concerns the elision of reflexivity and the use of new literary forms. There are actually several issues here. One is the way that new literary forms become a repository for reflexivity – as if writing in a different way somehow guaranteed reflexiveness. Reflexivists do point out that not all unconventional texts are reflexive ones. Nevertheless, for people who have argued so hard that a distinction between form and content cannot be sustained, they seem to set a lot of store by particular *forms* of writing, as if they were inherently disruptive and reflexive. To be fair, some reflexivists have addressed the danger that using NLFs may become a new orthodoxy, and have attended to the criticism that after one or two uses of dialogic form the effect is exhausted (Woolgar and Ashmore, 1988). More recently, there have been a spate of claims that 'reflexivity has moved to the suburbs' (Woolgar, 1996b) – a way of suggesting that new literary forms have become safe and non-threatening.

A further issue which, to my knowledge, has not been addressed concerns why it is that *writing* has become the main vehicle for practising reflexivity. What seems to be missing from discussions of reflexivity within SSK is the sense that it concerns the *entire research process* – not just writing. While the construction of academic accounts is very important, there is surely more to reflexivity than how we write. Feminist concerns about reflexiveness during the conduct of research are conspicuous by their absence. It is as if the (ethnographic) research process can be left unaltered, and all that needs to change are our (*post-hoc*) textual constructions of it. I suggest that it would be far more destabilizing to empiricism and objectivism if the research process as a whole were interrogated. Along these lines, postmodern anthropologist James Clifford (1986) suggests that the dialogue should occur not just in the *textual presentation* of ethnography, but in the practice of the fieldwork too. He points to cases of anthropologists becoming involved in helping people in struggles over land, as one example of this more 'mutual' approach, and also argues that as ethnographers increasingly come to focus on 'insiders' and the familiar, the need for reciprocity and new ways of rendering 'negotiated realities as multi-subjective, power-laden and incongruent' will become apparent (Clifford, 1986: 14).

Finally, the notion of reflexivity proposed by SSK researchers seems to give no space to what Wilkinson (1988) calls 'disciplined self-reflection'. As Paul Rabinow (1986) has argued, despite talk of reflexivity, most academics remain deathly silent about the conditions of their own production. He argues that reflection upon our own social, political, economic and cultural location within the academy is one of the greatest taboos – far greater strictures operate against addressing the significance of 'corridor talk' than operate against the denunciation of objectivism. Until we can bring to the surface and publicly discuss the conditions under which people are hired, given tenure, published, awarded grants and fêted, 'real' reflexivity will remain a dream.

Conclusion

After an initial discussion of a number of different approaches to writing and reflexivity, this chapter has been concerned to examine two distinct positions: feminist standpoint epistemologies and the radical constitutive reflexivity proposed by workers in the Sociology of Scientific Knowledge. These perspectives are, in my opinion, among the most important and challenging responses to the 'crisis of representation' ushered in by postmodernism – or post-positivism more broadly. Both approaches constitute principled positions for dealing with the epistemological dilemma or reflexive paradox identified by Lawson – which concerns the kinds of claim which we can make in an age when there are no 'transcendental guarantees', and the ways in which we should acknowledge the essentially reflexive character of our research. However, I wish to conclude that both positions have responded to the crisis by seeking, in different ways, to *avoid* its full implications.

Standpoint feminism has dealt with the 'problem' that there can be no epistemological guarantees for knowledge claims – no recourse to an unmediated, unconstructed reality – by seeking to ground knowledge in the experiences of marginalized groups. In this way, partial standpoints become the foundation for knowledge, the means of assuring strong objectivity. However, despite recognition that 'science is politics by other means' (Harding, 1991), standpoint positions have failed to acknowledge the *politics* involved in constructing standpoints. Instead they have been made to appear as if they had some natural or self-evident relationship to the lives of the oppressed – as if, for example, a feminist standpoint was somehow naturally connected to women's lives. The effect of this is both to tie experience too unreflexively to standpoint (as if the one implied the other) and to avoid important and difficult questions about social transformation – for example, *how* are standpoints constructed from the lives of marginalized groups, what happens if/when members of the group reject the standpoint, and so on. The correspondence between the marginalized or oppressed group and the standpoint which standpoint epistemologies assume is, for me, the result of politics, the result of a struggle to (re)articulate the meaning of experiences in ways that make sense politically. As yet, though, this remains unexplored.

By contrast, SSK has faced the problem by obsessing about it – like picking at a scab – endlessly reminding their audiences that they are simply telling stories, ceaselessly deconstructing their own discourse, making sure that no knowledge claim can be allowed to stand without being ironized or undermined. As one of the authors of the 'review' (or diary) mentioned earlier (Ashmore et al., 1995) has remarked, inadvertently summing up the whole project: 'The better it worked, the better it unravelled its own basis' (Potter, 1996: 229). The problem with this is that it becomes paralysing; it is impossible to say anything. It is like trying to chase your own shadow. Despite this, it is as if the reflexivists think that they can escape the implications of the reflexive paradox – that if they draw sufficient attention to the contingent status of their own claims, if they disrupt traditional ways of writing, if they script in enough voices, that they will somehow escape.

What both standpoint feminism and reflexive SSK seem, in different ways, to be trying to escape from is the *inevitably political nature of knowledge production*. I want to conclude by arguing that there is no escape. Politics and epistemology are intimately bound up with each other; ethics, values and political commitments suffuse the entire research process. Recognition of this does not lead to paralysis. It simply means that the basis on which we make knowledge claims must change. We should no longer claim to possess what Haraway (1988) calls the 'God's-eye view', to produce 'news from nowhere', but rather we must take on board the contingent and socially situated nature of all knowledge production. Standpoint theory has recognized this, but in attempting to found a new epistemology on social location it has fallen prey to another set of problems. Better that we neither solve the problem by constructing a hierarchy of epistemological privilege, nor attempt to escape it by ceasing to claim anything, but that we face the crisis head on and accept that all knowledge is partial, socially situated and contingent. What we produce are readings or interpretations, warranted to be sure by 'local' evaluative criteria, but not underwritten in any final or definitive way by epistemology. Instead they remain unfinished and open to dialogue. Let us be up-front about this. In this way, politics can take its place next to epistemology – centre stage in the knowledge production process.

Notes

1   Perhaps this is not surprising given the epistemological legacy of positivism which
held sway for so long, in which language is treated as a medium which merely
represents real objects in the world. From this perspective, writing can justifiably
be seen as a process of recording, using the neutral medium of language.
However, since the advent of the diverse crises which have problematized
knowledge production in recent years, it is surprising that discussion of writing
has not gained more prominence, for language is no longer seen as transparent or
reflective, but as active and constructive. The lack of attention to writing is thus
far more troubling in these postmodern times.
2   I am grateful to Ann Phoenix for drawing my attention to this point.
3   My reading of Hill Collins is that she restricts her definition of black feminist
thought to thought produced by *African-American* women.

References

Alcoff, L. and Potter, E. (eds) (1993) *Feminist Epistemologies*. London: Routledge.
Aldridge, J. (1993) 'The textual disembodiment of knowledge in research account
writing', *Sociology* 27 (1): 53–66.
Armistead, C. (1995) 'Writing contradictions: feminist research and feminist writing',
Women's Studies International Forum 18: 627–37.
Ashmore, M. (1989) *The Reflexive Thesis: Wrighting Sociology of Scientific
Knowledge*. Chicago: University of Chicago Press.
Ashmore, M., Myers, G. and Potter, J. (1995) 'Discourse, rhetoric, reflexivity: seven
days in the library', in S. Jasanoff, G. Markle, J. Petersen and T. Pinch (eds),
Handbook of Science and Technology Studies. London: Sage.
Atkinson, P. (1990) *The Ethnographic Imagination*. London: Routledge.
Bar On, Bat-Ami (1993) 'Marginality and epistemic privilege', in L. Alcoff and E.
Potter (eds), *Feminist Epistemologies*. London: Routledge.
Baumann, Z. (1992) *Intimations of Postmodernity*. London: Routledge.
Bhavnani, K.-K. (1993) 'Tracing the contours: feminist research and feminist
objectivity', *Women's Studies International Forum* 16 (2): 95.
Bhavnani, K.-K. and Haraway, D. (1994) 'Shifting the subject: a conversation
between Kum-Kum Bhavnani and Donna Haraway', in K.-K. Bhavnani and A.
Phoenix (eds), *Shifting Identities Shifting Racisms: A Feminism and Psychology
Reader*. London: Sage.
Billig, M. (1994) 'Repopulating the depopulated pages of social psychology', *Theory
and Psychology* 4 (3): 307–35.
Brah, A. (1992) 'Difference, diversity and differentiation', in J. Donald and A.
Rattansi (eds), *'Race', Culture and Difference*. London: Sage.
Burman, E. (1994) 'Experience, identities and alliances: Jewish feminism and feminist
psychology', in K.-K. Bhavnani and A. Phoenix (eds), *Shifting Identities Shifting
Racisms: A Feminism and Psychology Reader*. London: Sage.
Butler, J. (1990) *Gender Trouble: Feminism and the Subversion of Identity*. London:
Routledge.
Butler, J. (1992) 'Contingent foundations: feminism and the question of post-
modernism', in J. Butler and J.W. Scott (eds), *Feminists Theorise the Political*.
London: Routledge.

Butler, J. (1993) Bodies That Matter: On the Discursive Limits of Sex. London: Routledge.

Clifford, J. (1983) 'Power and dialogue in ethnography: Marcel Griaule's initiation', in G.W. Stocking (ed.), *Observers Observed: Essays on Ethnographic Fieldwork*. Madison, WI: University of Wisconsin Press.

Clifford, J. and Marcus, G. (eds) (1986)*Writing Culture: The Poetics and Politics of Ethnography*. Cambridge, MA: Harvard University Press.

Cotteril, P. and Letherby, G. (1993) 'Weaving stories: personal auto/biographies in feminist research, *Sociology*. 27 (1): 67–80.

Crook, S., Pakulski, J. and Waters, M. (eds) (1992) *Postmodernization: Change in Advanced Society*. London: Sage.

Currie, D. and Kazi, H. (1987) 'Academic feminism and the process of de-radicalization: Re-examining the issues', *Feminist Review* 25: 76–96.

Donald, J. and Rattansi, A. (1992) *'Race', Culture and Difference*. London: Sage.

Elam, D. (1994) *Feminism and Deconstruction*. London: Routledge.

Flax, J. (1990) 'Postmodernism and gender relations in feminist theory', in L. Nicholson (ed.) *Feminism/Postmodernism*. London: Routledge.

Flax, J. (1993) *Disputed Subjects: Essays on Psychoanalysis, Politics and Philosophy*. London: Routledge.

Gill, R. (1995) 'Relativism, reflexivity and politics: interrogating discourse analysis from a feminist perspective', in S. Wilkinson and C. Kitzinger (eds), *Feminism and Discourse: Psychological Perspectives*. London: Sage.

Gill, R. (forthcoming) *Gender and the Media: Representations, Audiences and Cultural Politics*. Cambridge: Polity Press.

Hacking, I. (1990) *The Taming of Chance*. Cambridge: Cambridge University Press.

Hall, S. (1996) 'Who needs identity'?, in S. Hall and P. Du Gay (eds), *Questions of Cultural Identity*. London: Sage.

Haraway, D. (1988) 'Situated knowledges: the science question in feminism and the privilege of partial perspective', *Feminist Studies* 14 (3): 581–607.

Haraway, D. (1991) *Simians, Cyborgs and Women: The Reinvention of Nature*. London: Free Association Books.

Harding, S. (1983) 'Why has the sex/gender system become visible only now?', in S. Harding and M. Hintikka (eds), *Discovering Reality: Feminist Perspectives on Epistemology, Metaphysics, Methodology and Philosophy of Science*. Boston, MA: Reidel.

Harding, S. (1987) 'Is there a feminist method?', in S. Harding (ed.), *Feminism and Methodology*. Milton Keynes: Open University Press.

Harding, S. (1991) *Whose Science? Whose Knowledge? Thinking from Women's Lives*. Milton Keynes: Open University Press.

Harding, S. (1993) 'Rethinking standpoint epistemology: what is "strong objectivity?"', in L. Alcoff and E. Potter (eds), *Feminist Epistemologies*. London: Routledge.

Hartsock, N. (1983) 'The feminist standpoint: developing the ground for a specifically feminist historical materialism', in S. Harding and M. Hintikka (eds), *Discovering Reality: Feminist Perspectives on Epistemology, Metaphysics, Methodology and Philosophy of Science*. Boston, MA: Reidel.

Hill Collins, P. (1991) *Black Feminist Thought: Knowledge, Consciousness and the Politics of Empowerment*. New York: Routledge.

hooks, b. (1982) *Ain't I a Woman? Black Women and Feminism*. London: Pluto Press.

hooks, b. (1991) *Yearning: Race, Gender and Cultural Politics*. London: Turnaround.

Jaggar, A. (1983) *Feminist Politics and Human Nature*. Brighton: Harvester.

Jameson, F. (1991) *Postmodernism, or the Cultural Logic of Late Capitalism*. London: Verso.

Latour, B. and Woolgar, S. (1979) *Laboratory Life: The Construction of Scientific Facts*. Princeton, NJ: Princeton University Press.

Lawson, H. (1985) *Reflexivity: The Post-Modern Predicament*. London: Hutchinson.

Light, A. (1989) 'Putting on the style: feminist criticism in the 1990s', in H. Carr (ed.), *From My Guy to Sci-fi: Genre and Women's Writing in the Postmodern World*. London: Pandora.

Longino, H. (1993) 'Subjects, power and knowledge: description and prescription in feminist philosophies of science', in L. Alcoff and E. Potter (eds), *Feminist Epistemologies*. London: Routledge.

Lynch, M. (1994) 'Representation is over-rated: some critical remarks about the use of the concept of representation in science studies', *Configurations* 1: 137–49.

Lyotard, J.-F. (1984) *The Postmodern Condition: A Report on Knowledge*. Manchester: Manchester University Press.

Madigan, R., Johnson, S. and Linton, P. (1995) 'The language of psychology: APA style as epistemology', *American Psychologist* 50 (6): 428–36.

Mies, M. (1983) 'Towards a methodology for feminist research', in G. Bowles and R. Duelli-Klein (eds) *Theories of Women's Studies*. London: Routledge & Kegan Paul.

Mohanty, C. (1992) 'Feminist encounters: locating the politics of experience', in M. Barrett and A. Phillips (eds), *Destabilising Theory: Contemporary Feminist Debates*. Cambridge: Polity Press.

Mulkay, M. (1985) *The Word and the World: Explorations in the Form of Sociological Analysis*. London: Allen and Unwin.

Nelson, J.S., Megill, A. and McCloskey, D.N. (1987) *The Rhetoric of the Human Sciences: Language and Argument in Scholarship and Public Affairs*. Madison: University of Wisconsin Press.

Nicholson, L. (ed.) (1990) *Feminism/Postmodernism*. London: Routledge.

Nicolson, L. and Fraser, N. (1990) 'Social criticism without philosophy: an encounter between feminism and postmodernism', in L.F. Nicolson (ed.), *Feminism/Postmodernism*. London: Routledge.

Plummer, K. (1983) *Documents of Life: An Introduction to the Literature of a Humanistic Method*. London: Allen and Unwin.

Poster, M. (1990) *The Mode of Information*. Cambridge: Polity Press.

Potter, J. (1996) *Representing Reality: Discourse, Rhetoric and Reality Construction*. London: Sage.

Potter, J., Wetherell, M. and Chitty, A. (1991) 'Quantification rhetoric – cancer on television', *Discourse and Society* 2: 333–65.

Rabinow, P. (1986) 'Representations are social facts: modernity and postmodernity in anthropology', in J. Clifford and G. Marcus (eds), *Writing Culture: The Poetics and Politics of Ethnography*. Cambridge, MA: Harvard University Press.

Ramazanoglu, C. (1989) *Feminism and the Contradictions of Oppression*. London: Routledge.

Rattansi, A. (1992) 'Changing the subject? Racism, culture and education', in J. Donald and A. Rattansi (eds), *'Race, Culture, Difference*. London: Sage.

Reinharz, S. (1983) 'Experiential analysis: a contribution to feminist research', in G.

Bowles and R. Duelli Klein (eds), *Theories of Women's Studies*. London: Routledge & Kegan Paul.

Ribbens, J. (1993) 'Facts or fiction? Aspects of the use of autobiographical writing in undergraduate sociology', *Sociology* 27 (1): 81–92.

Roberts, H. (1981) *Doing Feminist Research*. London: Routledge.

Robson, C. (1993) *Real World Research*. Oxford: Blackwell.

Rorty, R. (1989) *Contingency, Irony and Solidarity*. Cambridge: Cambridge University Press.

Ross, A. (1988) *Universal Abandon? The Politics of Postmodernism*. Edinburgh: Edinburgh University Press.

Rutherford, J. (1990) *Identity: Community, Culture and Difference*. London: Lawrence and Wishart.

Scott, J. (1992) 'Experience', in J. Butler and J.W. Scott (eds), *Feminists Theorise the Political*. New York: Routledge.

Segal, L. (1987) *Is the Future Female? Troubled Thoughts on Contemporary Feminism*. London: Virago.

Smith, D. (1987) *The Everyday World as Problematic: A Feminist Sociology*. London: Routledge.

Spelman, E. (1988) *Inessential Woman: Problems of Exclusion in Feminist Thought*. London: The Women's Press.

Spender, D. (1980) *Man Made Language*. London: Routledge & Kegan Paul.

Squire, C. (1990) 'Crisis what crisis? Discourses and narratives of the "social" in social psychology', in I. Parker and J. Shotter (eds), *Deconstructing Social Psychology*. London: Routledge.

Stacey, J. (1997) *Teratologies: A Cultural Study of Cancer*. London: Routledge.

Stanley, L. (1992) *The Auto/Biographical I: The Theory and Practice of Feminist Auto/Biography*. Manchester: Manchester University Press.

Stanley, L. (1993) 'On auto/biography in Sociology', *sociology* 27 (1): 41–52.

Stanley, L. and Wise, S. (1993) *Breaking Out Again: Feminist Ontology and Epistemology*. London: Routledge.

Stringer, P. (1990) 'Prefacing social psychology: a textbook example', in I. Parker and J. Shotter (eds), *Deconstructing Social Psychology*. London: Routledge.

Van Maanen, J. (1988) *Tales of the Field: Writing Ethnography*. Chicago: University of Chicago Press.

Wilkinson, S. (1988) 'The role of reflexivity in feminist psychology', *Women's Studies International Forum* 11 (5): 493–502.

Wilkinson, S. and Kitzinger, C. (1996) *Representing the Other: A Feminism and Psychology Reader*. London: Sage.

Woolgar, S. (ed.) (1988a) *Knowledge and Reflexivity: New Frontiers in the Sociology of Knowledge*. London: Sage.

Woolgar, S. (1988b) 'Reflexivity is the ethnographer of the text', in S. Woolgar (ed.), *Knowledge and Reflexivity: New Frontiers in the Sociology of Knowledge*. London: Sage.

Woolgar, S. (1996a) 'Psychology, qualitative methods and the idea of science', in J.T. Richardson (ed.), *A Handbook of Qualitative Research Methods for Psychology and the Social Sciences*. Leicester: BPS Books.

Woolgar, S. (1996b) 'Is there a future for the Sociology of Scientific Knowledge?' paper presented at conference on The Future of SSK at UEL, 7 September.

Woolgar, S. and Ashmore, M. (1988) 'The next step: an introduction to the reflexive project', in S. Woolgar (ed.) *Knowledge and Reflexivity: New Frontiers in the Sociology of Knowledge*. London: Sage.

Wright Mills, C. (1959) *The Sociological Imagination*. New York: Oxford University Press.

Yuval-Davies, N. (1994) 'Women, ethnicity and empowerment', in K.-K. Bhavnani and A. Phoenix (eds), *Shifting Identities Shifting Racisms: A Feminism and Psychology Reader*. London: Sage.

3

Telling Stories: Memory, Narrative and Experience in Feminist Research and Theory

Stevi Jackson

In this chapter I will consider the possible uses of biographical narratives (our own and other women's) as a basis for feminist research and theorizing, and pose more general questions about the relationship between narrative, experience and subjectivity. My central concern here is with the theoretical and political consequences of treating remembered experience as a narrative construction rather than as a 'true' reflection of past events. This renders the concept of 'experience' problematic and also has implications for theories of subjectivity; it suggests that we construct a sense of self, at least in part, through the stories we tell about ourselves.

The problem of personal experience is often traced back to the feminist slogan: the personal is political. This slogan should not be taken as a straightforward evaluation of pre-given experience. Feminists did not 'discover' that the personal is political; we *made* the personal political by understanding it in new ways.[1] There is a parallel here with C. Wright Mills's idea of the 'sociological imagination' which transforms 'personal troubles' into 'public issues' (Mills, 1970: 14–17). The exercise of a feminist imagination enabled us to see that our personal troubles were often shared and hence social in origin and amenable to political change. Further, it encouraged us to look at ourselves in new ways, to see that our subjectivities were shaped by our social milieu. It enabled us to tell new stories about ourselves and our experience. For the personal to be made political in this way, however, required that feminist narratives had some resonance for us, that they 'made sense' in terms of our everyday knowledges and practices. Feminism must inevitably challenge aspects of commonsense understandings of the world but, if it is to retain its potential for making the personal political, it cannot afford to do so without reference to the lived actualities of women's existence. However, this need not mean treating women as a unitary category or taking experience as given and unproblematic.

Feminists writing from poststructuralist and postmodernist perspectives often imply that it is only they who call experience into question. Other feminists, often unnamed, are said to hold more naive beliefs: for example, 'many feminists assume that women's experience, unmediated by further theory, is the source of true knowledge and the basis for feminist politics' (Weedon, 1987: 8). Similar charges are sometimes made against named feminist standpoint theorists, particularly those who seek to ground their work in women's everyday lived experience. For example, Liz Stanley and Sue Wise (1983) stand accused of being concerned only with 'raw', untheorized experience (Currie and Kazi, 1987; Hollway, 1989). Similarly, Susan Hekman (1997) has recently taken Dorothy Smith's (1987) concern with the 'lived, actual world of everyday experience' as positing 'an absolute dichotomy between abstract concepts . . . and lived experience' (Hekman, 1997: 347). These are gross misrepresentations. The forms of theorizing proposed by Stanley and Wise and by Smith question oppositions between the conceptual and theoretical on the one hand and the experiential on the other. For them 'experience is never "raw"' but is always subject to lay theorizing and hence constructed (Stanley and Wise, 1990: 42, 1993: 10–11); it is never separate from the ways in which it is talked about and conceptualized as part of social relations and, conversely, concepts and theories are 'in actuality' and activated in 'organized social relations' (Smith, 1997: 393).

It is not my intention here to engage in a systematic defence of these, or other, feminist standpoint theories, but rather to point out that problematizing experience is not the sole prerogative of postmodern feminists. Once everyday experience is understood as involving the reflexive construction of meaning, a practical form of theorizing, it is clear that foregrounding women's experience does not mean taking that experience as given. The interactionist and phenomenological traditions which inform the work of Stanley and Wise and Dorothy Smith also serve to demonstrate that some of the ideas associated with postmodernism – that the self is not a stable unitary inner essence, that meaning is not fixed in objects and events – have been in circulation among feminist social scientists long before postmodernism became fashionable (see Jackson, 1992). However, these perspectives differ from postmodernism in that their emphasis on the subject as actor – as a practical theorist and a reflexive negotiator of meaning – allows more space for individual agency than postmodernism's decentred subject.

Recent work on narratives has been inspired, in part, by interactionist and phenomenological perspectives, but also owes something to postmodernism, particularly to the tradition of discourse analysis. Discourse is a rather broader term than narratives. Discourse circumscribes what we can know and speak about, and how we can know and speak about it; it enables us to say and think some things rather than others, thus shaping our sense of social reality. A narrative, quite simply, is a story: a form in which we typically recount remembered events and experiences. Telling and interpreting narratives is a socially ordered practice, one means by which we interact with others and reflect upon our selves (see Stevenson et al., 1996). Narratives and discourses articulate with each other: we draw on discourses culturally available to us in order to construct narrative accounts, enabling us to tell particular stories at particular times. Hence there are often discursive regularities to these stories. An example, borrowed from Plummer (1995), is the 'coming out' story. The nineteenth-century construction of 'the homosexual' as an object of discourse ultimately made it possible for individuals to define themselves as such and, in a later era, to construct a counter-discourse in which 'gay' identity became a positive self-affirmation. As a result of changing historical circumstances and discursive shifts, the 'coming out' story could be told as a process of self discovery and liberation from the closet.

In recent years sociologists and psychologists from diverse theoretical backgrounds have become interested in narratives, in both telling stories and deconstructing them. For feminists, the collection of women's life histories and personal narratives began from attempts to challenge the androcentric bias of much academic work, to allow women's voices to be heard where previously they had been silenced. It became clear, however, that personal narratives were not merely a transparent record of women's experience, but also a source for understanding how women made sense of their experience (see Personal Narratives Group, 1989: 13, 99–102). At the same time, feminists became increasingly sensitive to the ways in which their own biographies intersected with those of the women they collected data from, leading to greater reflexivity about the process of intellectual production. Feminists have seen the need to locate ourselves in relation to our work, to make it clear where we are speaking from. Thus the conventional academic practice whereby writers sought to disguise their presence, to adopt a disinterested 'objective' voice, has been overturned in favour of rendering ourselves present in the texts we write.

Personal and academic storytelling

To bring personal experience into social scientific work used to be taboo. It was personal, subjective, anecdotal – in short 'unscientific'.

Yet while our own life stories were ruled out of order, other people's often provided the raw data we worked with. In conducting qualitative research – particularly semi-structured or unstructured interviews – we seek to elicit personal narratives from others. Feminists have favoured qualitative methodologies precisely because they privilege women's own accounts of experience. For example, feminist research on violence against women has allowed women themselves to define what counts as violence and what it means to them rather than imposing definitions upon them (Kelly, 1988).[2] Qualitative research presupposes that human, social action is meaningful, reflected upon by human individuals and rooted in their interpretation of their social milieux and relationships. Yet despite this emphasis on reflexivity and interpretation, the conventions of doing research still often assume that our subjects somehow communicate 'raw experience' – albeit meaningful experience – to us. Informants' stories are thus taken as a direct reflection of their subjective reality rather than as a form of representation. The relationship between the 'real' and the representation is never, however, this direct since constructing a narrative is itself a work of interpretation. Becoming aware of this produces a tension in feminist research between our desire to respect the accounts women offer us and the necessity of subjecting those accounts to critical scrutiny.

Moreover, in conducting qualitative research we are still positioned as expert 'knowers', drawing together the narratives that our informants provide and reshaping them into another, academic, narrative. Feminists have sought to break down this hierarchy between researcher and researched in a number of ways, thus challenging the dictates of scientific 'objectivity' which require us to be positioned 'outside' our data and which conceal the social and institutional locations from which we speak. One of the most innovative strategies has been to turn our analytical gaze on ourselves, either constructing critical self-reflexive individual autobiographies (Steedman, 1986; Walkerdine, 1990) or engaging in collective 'memory work' (Crawford et al., 1992; Haug, 1987a).

Drawing on our own or others' experiences in this way poses a number of questions. Can accounts of individual women's experiences be read at face value? Is there such a thing as 'experience' unmediated by language and culture? What happens to our experiences when we narrate them? Those engaged in the practice of feminist autobiographical work differ in the extent to which they confront these questions and the ways in which they seek to resolve them. In critically considering examples of such work, and in offering some narratives of my own, I will argue that telling stories can never communicate 'raw experience'. Narratives entail processes of representation, interpretation and reconstruction. Moreover, as feminist social scientists we have access to academic and feminist discourses which profoundly affect the stories we tell about ourselves and the ways in which we make sense of stories others tell us.

Feminist researchers are generally acutely aware that our ways of knowing differ from those of others. We have devoted a great deal of energy to challenging the version of the world constructed by traditional male-dominated social science. More recently, feminists – especially white, Western heterosexual feminists – have been forced to recognize that the alternative anti-patriarchal accounts which we have constructed often exclude the standpoints of other women. To take a now famous example, Susan Brownmiller's ground-breaking book *Against Our Will* effectively challenged the prevailing myths which defined rape as the work of a few psychopaths, arguing that it was a political crime against women, rooted in patterns of male domination (Brownmiller, 1975). Her account, however, was constructed from the standpoint of a white American woman and hence attracted criticism from black feminists such as Angela Davis (1982) and bell hooks (1982). It is less often noticed that Brownmiller also wrote from an unquestioned heterosexual location (see Jackson, 1997).

The existence of differences among women, and multiple feminist standpoints, should sensitize us to the ways in which narratives are shaped by the social location of their narrators and the cultural resources available to them. This is true not only of academic narratives, but of the lay narratives we all construct in our everyday lives. The stories we can tell vary historically and culturally and so too does the sense which their audience is able to make of them (Plummer, 1995). Once we begin to ask what stories can be told, when and by whom – and which stories are heard and found credible and which are unheard or discounted – we begin to move out from the analysis of subjectivity to consider wider social contexts and structures. Narratives do not float free from the material conditions of our existence, but are grounded in it. They are part and parcel of the everyday experience they help to construct. In short, stories are socially situated.

I am arguing, then, that experience is a reflexive, narrative construction, as is our sense of self. Using my own work on romantic love as an example, I will suggest our narratives of self depend on the interpretative devices and discourses culturally available to us. This in turn requires that we pay attention to the material and ideological conditions which shape our lives and the sense we make of them. Treating narratives of self as constructions is not to deny the material reality which structures women's experience, but does alert us to the ways in which this experience is made sense of through socially situated narratives.

Memory work as a research strategy

One of the purposes of subjecting our own memories to critical scrutiny is to understand how we come into being as subjects. Although some men writing on masculinity have drawn on their own experience (Jackson, 1990; Seidler, 1989), it was feminists who first brought their personal experience to bear on this issue and who developed the method of memory work (e.g. Crawford et al., 1992; Haug, 1987a; Personal Narratives Group, 1989). Those who have engaged in such work have primarily been white, Western women and while differences of class, and sometimes sexuality, have figured in their work, other differences have received less attention. For reasons of space I am concentrating here on four examples, two of collective memory work (Crawford et al., 1992; Haug, 1987a) and two individual reconstructions of the past (Steedman, 1986; Walkerdine, 1990). In what follows it should be borne in mind that the strategies and modes of interpretation these women have developed may well reflect their specific social locations.

The method of collective memory work was developed in Germany by Haug and her colleagues (1987a), and later elaborated by a group of Australian researchers (Crawford et al., 1992; Stevenson et al., 1996). It is an offshoot of consciousness-raising, the sharing of experience among women in order to politicize the personal and thus brings a political strategy into academic work. Sharing experience in consciousness-raising or collective memory work can make us aware of both commonalities and differences among us. The commonalities may tell us that we are not alone, that problems we thought of as individual may have social origins. Our differences might enable us to understand what has derived from each of our specific locations within the social structure in terms of class, ethnicity, nationality and so on – although this has yet to be a focus of memory work.

While having much in common, memory work and consciousness-raising differ in their strategies. Since the former is used as a research tool, it is necessarily a more formalized process. Whereas consciousness-raising usually involved verbal exchanges of experience in which women spoke in the first person (as 'I'), memory work begins from each woman in the group producing a written narrative in the third person (as 'she'). The memories are written to a specific cue or trigger (such as 'hair', 'telling lies' or 'danger') and must describe a specific event or episode, including inconsequential details, but without interpretation, explanation or autobiographical context (see Crawford et al., 1992: 43–52; Stevenson et al., 1996: 186). The narratives are then shared, discussed and theorized by the group – at which point each individual author re-emerges as an 'I' located within her own biography as her memories are further explained. Finally, the group as a whole reflects back on both the initial memories and the collective analysis of them, drawing together common themes which have emerged from the process.

This methodology is informed by a particular theoretical understanding of the self as reflexive – able to be both subject and object, to reflect upon itself – and intersubjective, constructed through our interactions with others. Hence the self is social and always in process.[3] Memory work itself is a highly reflexive and intersubjective method. Analysing our own memories makes us both subjects and objects of research and thus radically breaks with the hierarchical relationship between the researcher as 'expert' and the researched as object. As Crawford and co-authors put it when they first embarked on memory work:

> We were intrigued by the collapse of subject and object . . . by the idea of becoming our own subjects. We had the sense of taking a huge step, of working against the rules of empiricist method, of defying the imperatives of our training. (Crawford et al., 1992: 4)

Those who draw on their own memories, whether individually or collectively, do so from the assumption that our past has something to tell us about our present selves, about our individual subjectivities, about what made us what we are. As Valerie Walkerdine says of her 'ordinary childhood': 'There, caught in the threads of that ordinary life, is the basis for understanding what my subjectivity might be about' (1990: 162). Collective memory work is also concerned with understanding the construction of the self, understood as a process in which 'one engages with one's memories . . . responds to them' (Crawford et al., 1992: 39).

> In their attempt to wrest meaning from the world, persons construct themselves; and in their struggle for intelligibility they reflect. They remember what is problematic, which is itself socially produced, in terms of resolutions previously sought if not achieved. Memory work is thus intimately bound up with the uncovering of the processes of the construction of self. (Crawford et al., 1992: 39)

In collective memory work the emphasis is on scrutinizing the ways in which memories are recalled and narrated. The steps in the analysis are made explicit, 'autobiographizing' is barred from the initial stages of the process and individuals remain anonymous in writing up the analysis of memories.

In individual work of this kind, the methods by which the author arrives at her theorization of self are less transparent, embedded in the representation of herself which she constructs, and the final accounts are more explicitly autobiographical. Hence both Steedman and Walkerdine locate themselves within their specific biographical frame, as white (though this is unstated) academics from working-class backgrounds. Both see themselves as 'outsiders' in the 'middle-class world' of academia, yet their 'ordinary' backgrounds did not match the image of the heroic working classes struggling collectively against deprivation. They both seek to understand the specificity of their experience as working-class daughters upwardly mobile to the middle class. Hence both use the concept of class as an aspect of their representations of their childhoods.

As soon as we begin to develop such ideas we are moving beyond experience towards theorizing subjectivity and, in order to do so, we draw on explanations which do not derive directly from experience. For as soon as we begin to seek social explanations, to suggest that subjectivity is socially constructed, we have to admit that the totality of the social conditions of our existence cannot be grasped merely from our everyday 'lived experience'. If we see women's subordination as structural, then this is a fundamental issue and it means that we must somehow make links between social structure and human agency – between the structures which constrain us and ourselves as active agents within these structures. Frigga Haug uses the concept of 'subjectification' to capture this:

> The concept of subjectification can be understood as the process by which individuals work themselves into social structures they do not consciously determine, but to which they subordinate themselves. The concept allows for the active participation of individuals in heteronomy.[4] It is the fact of our active participation which gives social structures their solidity. . . . Externally, we are bound to a particular social location. Since we have at our disposal a whole range of interpretations for rationalizing this, we are blind to our shackles. (Haug, 1987b: 59)

This means that, in undertaking autobiographical work, we need interpretations of our memories which take account of constraints upon us of which we may not be consciously aware – and are unlikely to have been aware of at the time of the event we remember. This has prompted some writers, such as Steedman and Walkerdine, to draw on psychoanalytical perspectives. Participants in the two collective projects (Haug 1987a and Crawford et al.,

1992) while admitting the existence of an unconscious mind, draw more widely on a range of social constructionist perspectives. Introducing structural explanations whether deriving from an understanding of social class or from a psychoanalytical under-standing of familial, cultural and linguistic structures alters the sorts of stories we are able to tell. That such structural explanations sometimes do not suggest themselves out of our own experience, even to those of us trained to look for them, is something to which I can attest myself.

Narrating the self

I have recently been reminded by my mother of circumstances to do with my class background which I had known, but had not previously constructed into my memories – and which dramatically affects the stories I can tell about my childhood. In my final years of primary school and early years of secondary school I was relent-lessly bullied by other girls. In each case there was an identifiable leader of my tormentors, in the absence of whom others would leave me alone or even make friendly advances. I had always accounted for my victimization in individualistic terms, as a product of my emotional vulnerability; being easily provoked to anger and tears, I was a soft target. What has enabled me to re-tell this story of my past and re-position myself within it was my mother reminding me of where I and the bullies were located within a very rigid social hierarchy. My father was in the navy, but not an officer. The two girls who bullied me were daughters of naval officers. I and they were deemed 'bright' – but in both cases they did slightly less well at school than I did. In both cases, or so my mother told me, their parents gave them a hard time for 'letting a rating's daughter beat them'. As I searched my memories I recalled that most of these girls' actions were aimed at undermining my ability to succeed or were calculated to get me in trouble with teachers. My memory of being bullied thus came to 'make sense' in a new way: not as a story of my own individual inadequacy, but as an instance of class struggle in the classroom. In the process of reinterpretation I thus recon-structed the memory, and both my memories and my mother's were constructed into a new set of memories.

In writing this it becomes clear how complex and many-layered the construction of memories is. I am caught in the act of making and re-making memory and in the process of re-making my understanding of myself. I am using recollections of past memories (my own and my mother's) to construct new memories; I am drawing on memories about memories and about past theorizations of memories. I am not dealing with straightforward events which are simply filed in my memory awaiting recall. My narratives of my past are exposed as interpretative devices through which I effect a transformation of my past self.

Memories are not already there in story form, rather it is in story form that we construct and reconstruct our memories – and these stories are historically located and mediated. Conventional autobiographies and 'true confessions' stories in the media draw uncritically on a narrative form which is historically and culturally specific. Such narratives are sequentially ordered and assume a causal chain of events . . . because A occurred and I did X, B happened. This is, for example, characteristic of realist novels, but realism as a literary form is just that – a literary form. It does not, as is sometimes implied, simply reflect or portray a plausible version of the 'real' world, but helps construct our sense of reality and plausibility. The novel is of relatively recent (Western) invention and parallels the rise of the idea of the autonomous subject, the idea of subjectivity as inner being (see Errington and Gewertz, 1987). This modernist conceptualization of the self has also produced the idea of the self as a reflexive project to be worked on (Giddens, 1991). Hence we have notions of 'self discovery' and 'self improvement' which have produced so many 'self-help' manuals which provide yet another resource for constructing narratives of self (see Jackson and Scott, 1997). Narratives are not simply a form which we encounter in novels, magazines or films – they are part of everyone's cultural competencies. We learn to tell stories about ourselves (and to ourselves) very early in life, so that such narratives become a central part of the ways in which we routinely make sense of the world and our place within it. We compose narratives of self in the everyday practice of self-reflexivity.

Any form of autobiographical writing is necessarily a construction, a representation of the past. What differentiates critical, academic or feminist, autobiography from conventional autobiography is that writers of the former are aware of this. Of course the verisimilitude of the latter may be questioned – on the grounds that crucial events may be left out, glossed over or distorted. So some autobiographies are considered more 'honest', 'revealing' or 'true' than others. Critical autobiography pays attention to lacunae, silences, evasions. One of the processes involved in group memory work is that members of the collective challenge each other when they feel that something important may be left unsaid, and the reasons behind these 'unsaids' may themselves become the object of inquiry. Hence collective memory work can reveal 'the ways in which individuals construct themselves' (Crawford et al., 1992: 4).

Individuals, too, may reflect on the narratives they have constructed and produce new ones accounting for older silences. For
example, in an essay called 'Behind the painted smile', Walkerdine
returns to the themes she discussed in 'Dreams from an ordinary
childhood' (both in Walkerdine, 1990) and in particular the image
of herself – at three years old – as the bluebell fairy:

> When I wrote that piece it was as though I had said all there was to say,
> but I knew at one level then, and see more clearly now, that there are far
> more disturbing images to explore which are hidden and covered over by
> the erotic allure of the bluebell fairy. (Walkerdine, 1990: 147)

This is an image of herself she had previously described as one she
treasured, yet there was another, reviled, image in the story – an
older, fatter Valerie that she preferred not to dwell on. In the later
essay she claims that she no longer has the need to hold on to the
'bluebell fairy' image as a result of 'a set of moves made therapeutically' (1990: 148). In other words as a result of another form of
storytelling, another practice involving a narrative reconstruction of
self – although Walkerdine fails to note this. She is critical of the
story she has told before and, as a prelude to going back to what
she had previously failed to confront, she describes her previous
narrative as 'another set of fantasies':

> On one level, the idea that we are constructed in the male gaze is
> reassuring. We remain somehow not responsible for our actions. . . . I say
> that this is reassuring in the sense that the images of the bluebell fairy
> remained a treasured image; that is, they were an indication that I *was*
> feminine and attractive and loved. No matter how much we might take
> apart those fantasies as part of the male gaze, I think they prevent us
> from coming to terms with the negative emotions which are covered over
> by all this sugar and spice. Here I am referring to the fragility of the
> assumption of femininity and to the covering over of negative emotions.
> In other words, take apart *this* image as I might, this does not mean that
> I am prepared to look at the other one, the reviled image of me as fat. It
> strikes me as easier to take apart a beautiful image, blame patriarchy,
> and yet hold onto that image (Yes, yes I am that really) . . . than to
> examine what else may lurk beneath. (1990: 148–9)

However, more is at stake than absences and evasions. Memories
are seen here as a key to the past, in the hope of finding the origins
of the present in the past. Yet it is probable that rather than the
past determining the present, we are reconstructing the past to fit
our construction of ourselves in the present (Gagnon and Simon,
1974). In the case of the account Walkerdine gives us, this is a
therapeutically ordered present: in making sense of herself through

therapy she offers a new version of her past which fits the therapeutic model. She thereby implies that she is offering a truer version of herself, rather than simply another narrative reconstruction.

Collective memory work, less imbued with psychoanalysis, has more chance of avoiding this problem. Moreover, it assumes that it is the *way* in which we construct the past which shapes our sense of self. When Crawford and co-authors (1992) were doing memory work, other groups were founded, including a men's group, allowing some cross checks to be made on the ways in which memories become narratively reconstructed. For instance, in analysing memories of fear and danger, the men's stories focused on physical dangers encountered, for example, while swimming or climbing. The women's stories, on the other hand, tended to focus on interpersonal, and especially familial conflicts. Here the participants' current sense of themselves as masculine and feminine shaped both the stories which were told and ways in which they were told, the present thus significantly influencing the construction of the past.

Individual writers are not always unaware of this issue. Carolyn Steedman, for example, says of the project she undertakes in *Landscape for a Good Woman*:

> This book . . . is about interpretations, about the places where we rework what has already happened to give current events meaning. It is about the stories we make for ourselves, and the social specificity of our understanding of those stories. The childhood dreams recounted in this book, the fantasies, the particular and remembered events . . . do not, by themselves, constitute the point. We all return to memories and dreams like this, again and again; the story we have to tell of our own life is reshaped around them. But the point doesn't lie there, back in the past, back in the lost time at which they happened; the only point lies in interpretation. The past is reused through the agency of social information, and that interpretation of it can only be made with what people know of a social world and their place within it. (Steedman, 1986: 5)

This does not mean that the past has no impact on the present; rather it suggests that the ways in which our subjectivities are constituted involves a continual interpretation and reinterpretation of events, desires, emotions, and so on. It is not surprising, given this insight, that Steedman is more critical in her application of psychoanalysis than Walkerdine. While she uses the method of psychoanalytic case study, she simultaneously questions the narrative of childhood psychosexual development which psychoanalysis constructs. In particular, she points to the places where her story cannot be made to fit the Freudian plot, specifically her father's failure to take up his place in the oedipal triangle.

Steedman's use of the case study method means that she does not tell a continuous story of her childhood, but starts from particular memories which she analyses from her adult knowledge of class, gender and generational relations. She moves back and forth between memories and discusses the processes by which events remembered as a child were given new meaning as she grew to adulthood. She thus gives us a sense in which the memories we have are already worked over, re-remembered, reinterpreted. Hence in trying to examine the processes by which our subjectivities are constructed and reconstructed we are continuing that very process of (re)construction.

This suggests that our subjectivities are not fixed, but shifting, and this is recognized by most of those who engage in auto-biographical work. Much of what has been said already also suggests that our subjectivities do not form a unitary coherent whole. This again is where critical autobiographical work differs from conventional autobiography. The latter attempts to construct a coherent narrative of self, a tale of becoming, a life story which represents the 'I', the protagonist, as a fixed point, a unitary (usually rational and coherent) self who feels acts, achieves things and to whom things happen. We are presented with 'a life', a coherent whole. Critical autobiography challenges our temptation to produce coherent narratives of self which paper over the contradictions and discontinuities in our memories. Hence there is an avoidance of narrative conventions that produce such 'a life'. In Steedman we have the case study method and in collective memory work we have snippets of memory and are denied the tools which would enable us to link them together as stories about individuals.

None of this should be taken to deny that we remember real events – the point is that we give events meaning as we continually reinterpret them. This has consequences not only for autobio-graphical work, but for any research method that requires others to tell us stories about themselves and for any theoretical work which deals with issues of subjectivity and identity. From both standpoint and postmodern perspectives we can understand memory and subjectivity as constructions, but from a standpoint perspective these constructions are socially situated, located in material social contexts. I now want to go on to consider how these issues have figured in my own work on love and romance.

Love stories

My work on love is not empirical but conceptual and theoretical (Jackson, 1993a, 1993b, 1995). It can be characterized, in Mary

Maynard's terms, as middle-range feminist theorizing: theory which focuses on specific contextualized phenomena rather than seeking an overall explanation of women's subordination (Maynard, 1995). It is also empirically grounded in that it draws on past research from a range of disciplines. In seeking a means of theorizing love as a socially constructed emotion, I was looking for explanations which were consonant with existing research findings and which resonated with my own experience.

What remains carefully concealed in most mainstream research is the personal experience and political investment which lie behind a theorist's or researcher's intellectual endeavours. In the first paper I wrote on love and romance (Jackson, 1993a) I urged sociologists to draw on, rather than neglect, their own experience: after all, as the title of the paper announced, 'even sociologists fall in love'. What I did not feel able to say more explicitly in the pages of a mainstream academic journal was that the initial idea for the paper derived from a recent experience of 'falling in love'. The title was inspired by a friend's teasing: 'What, you mean even sociologists fall in love? Aren't you too busy analysing relationships to feel such things?' Writing the paper was a product of my capacity both to feel and to theorize, and suggests that 'feelings' are themselves understood through the everyday theorizing entailed in narrative construction.

Of course it was not only my personal experience of love which inspired the series of papers which followed, but also my awareness, as a feminist, that the personal is always political and therefore social. Moreover, love as a topic of inquiry also fitted well with my work on sexuality and raised some similar issues. Although I am a sociologist with a firm conviction that our lives are shaped by our location within material social structures and systems of inequality, I have always been interested in social-psychological issues, especially with the construction of sexuality at the level of individual subjectivity.

I began to think and write about love from the standpoint that subjectivity is socially constructed. It was easy enough to argue for the social construction of love at a macro-level of analysis. There were plenty of anthropological and historical sources pointing to the conclusion that a particular form of romantic love is a product of Western modernity, linked to culturally and historically specific notions of the self and to distinctive and particular forms of social relationship (see Jackson, 1993a). There was also a feminist literature directing me to the ways in which love was implicated in the maintenance of women's subordination and a few feminists had attempted to explore the subjective experience of love (Jackson, 1993a, 1993b). The challenge was to link individual experience to wider cultural understandings of love without falling into a simple reductionism which regards individual feelings as determined by society and culture.

I find it difficult to pinpoint how, exactly, the idea of love as a narrative construction came to me, except that the idea of narratives seemed to be 'in the air' in feminist circles at the time and had some congruence with interactionist perspectives I had drawn on in the past, with the idea that sexual behaviour is a product of 'scripts' learnt and negotiated through interaction (developed initially by Gagnon and Simon, 1974). This dramaturgical analogy is clearly close to that of storytelling. Moreover, as others have noted, there are parallels between the idea of sexual scripts and Foucault's later theorization of sexuality as discursively constituted (see Connell and Dowsett, 1992), except that scripts are more specifically located at the level of interpersonal interaction. Narratives are a form a discourse, and some feminists were already talking about understanding subjectivity in terms of locating ourselves within discourse (Hollway, 1984; Weedon, 1987). A key link was provided by Michelle Rosaldo's anthropological work on emotions,[5] specifically the following: 'Feelings are not substances to be discovered in our blood, but social practices organized by stories that we both enact and tell. They are structured by our forms of understanding' (Rosaldo, 1984: 143). I had also read Frigga Haug's work, and there is a clear link with memory work in my analysis of love. Just as we construct our sense of self though the memories we recount (to ourselves or others) so, in more general terms narratives are resources we draw upon in constructing our emotions. The various 'feelings' which make sense to us as being 'in love' could not be organized, made intelligible and understood in this way without the narratives culturally available to us which enable us to perform this interpretative activity.

This perspective also enables us to make sense of the much-reported differences between women's and men's expectations and experiences of love. It is not that men's lack of expressiveness is indicative of emotional inadequacy (however appealing that notion may be), but that discourses and narratives of emotionality are differentially available to and differentially deployed by women and men. This is clear in the discussion of men's and women's memories of fear and danger discussed above. Whereas women were drawing on an understanding of emotional *relationships* in their discussion of fear and danger, men abstracted 'fear' from social context, understanding it as a response to physical risk (Crawford et al., 1992). Growing up as a woman in modern Western societies involves learning a language of the emotions, a sensitivity to cues about others' feelings and a fluency in emotional storytelling. This is evident, for example, in the confessional culture of girls' and women's magazines (Jackson, 1996; Jackson and Scott, 1997). This happens in material social contexts; women's expressiveness can be taken as indicative of their location as carers and subordinates. Women are not only expected to care for and care about those they have intimate relationships with, they are also expected to take care of the relationship itself, to perform the 'emotional labour' necessary to ensure its continued viability (Delphy and Leonard, 1992; Duncombe and Marsden, 1993; Langford, forthcoming). Hence I have warned against uncritically valuing women's capacity for emotional fluency; it would be unwise to valorize what might be symptomatic of our subordination (Jackson, 1995).

I do not claim to have come up with a full theorization of love: there are still avenues which require further exploration. On the one hand, we need to account for the felt intensity of emotions such as love[6] and on the other, we need to link the construction of emotions, and subjectivity in general, to their material social context. This of course raises the intractable problem of the relationship between agency and structure. I believe, however, that the form of standpoint theorizing offered by Dorothy Smith (1987) and others may offer a way forward. If experience is always reflexively constructed, theorized and embedded in everyday material practices and social relations, and the means by which we make sense of ourselves is specific to the wider culture in which we live, then individual agency is always situated in a social context. In understanding our emotions, the insights from memory work offer more productive avenues of inquiry than psychoanalysis. Whereas the latter tends to accord causal priority to what is repressed, and hence banished from memory, the former emphasizes what we do remember as significant for our construction of self. It is not that the events recalled determine our subjectivities, but that memories themselves, conceived as a process of struggling to make sense, are central to the process whereby subjectivity is constituted.

Conclusion: the story is political

The idea of narratives of self is a means of taking personal experience seriously while recognizing that it is always and inevitably a construction. Experience has always been central to feminist politics as well as to theory. If the personal is political, so too are the stories we are able to tell about ourselves. Some narratives can be seen as supportive of the existing *status quo*; others have subversive potential. Hence narratives can be an arena of political struggle.

Narratives can be exclusionary, so that some variants of stories have more legitimacy than others. For example, narratives of love contribute to the pathologization of arranged marriages. Interestingly, arranged marriage is frequently contrasted with 'love marriage' rather than its more obvious binary opposite, marriage by choice. Choice, of course, is assumed to be motivated by love, by a magical force which transcends mundane quotidian reality – despite ample sociological evidence indicating that our choices are constrained by our social location and that romantic aspirations are tempered by more instrumental concerns such as economic security (see, for example, Gittens, 1986). Of course the love stories which are hegemonic in our culture are also specifically heterosexual. Hence gay and lesbian love stories have only recently begun to be heard and are still marginalized. Even when we are sceptical about such narratives, we may still remain in their thrall. I can be critical of love, of its exclusions and exclusivity, of its capacity to produce self absorption, of the ways in which it has served to perpetuate male-dominated heterosexuality, but none of this prevents me from falling in love or being moved by a romantic film.

Some narratives, however, have the potential to effect change, to bring about new ways of understanding the social world and ourselves. Feminist versions of the experience of rape, for example, challenged existing narratives which often told of women's provocativeness or individual male pathology. Nonetheless we continue to struggle for those stories to be heard against the continued influence of the older, patriarchal version. Our feminist understanding of the world is never secure. Attention has recently been drawn to the ways in which certain narratives of self can depoliticize that which we have brought into the political arena. For example, in relation to child sexual abuse, narratives of healing and forgiveness can displace feminist narratives of a struggle for survival against power and oppression (Armstrong, 1991; Davies, 1995). Another example of oppositional narratives being undercut by more conventional ones is provided by recent developments in gay politics, where the story of being 'born that way' is gaining ground once more. This is not only a means by which gay men (and some lesbians) construct a viable sense of self, but also it shapes political priorities; it is associated with campaigns for the right of inclusion into heterosexual institutions which precludes a critique of compulsory heterosexuality (see Whisman, 1996; Rahman and Jackson, 1997).

However, there is a problem if we think about these political developments only in terms of the stories currently circulating. If we are to avoid the relativist trap of treating one narrative as no more true than another, we need to pay attention to the politics of narratives and the extent to which they support or contest oppressive social structures and practices. We must also remember that there is a material world out there, that material social inequalities exist, that there are structures and institutions which perpetuate those inequalities. Narratives, however, remain important. If the only stories available to a majority of women (and other oppressed groups) are those which lead them to submit to, accept or buy into those dominant institutional structures, there is no hope of political change.

This brings me full circle to my point of departure: as feminists we need stories which challenge the taken-for-granted acceptance of the way things are, but which nonetheless resonate with women's everyday understanding of their experience in all its variety. This means that we can never again aspire to the feminist grand narratives through which we sought to explain women's subordination in the early years of second-wave feminism. But giving up on grand narratives, as postmodernists would have us do, need not entail giving up on any understanding of the structural inequalities which produce patterns of dominance and subordination. Rather, we should seek to develop situated knowledges from multiple standpoints which take account of the complexity of women's experiences and the differences among us.

Notes

1 Throughout this chapter I use first-person plural pronouns – we and our – in three contexts: when speaking of people or women as a generality (e.g. 'our cultural competencies'); when speaking of feminists and feminist theorists in general (as opposed to specific groups of theorists); to refer to narrower categories of feminists within which I am located myself (such as white, heterosexual feminists). I am aware of the problem of falsely universalizing this 'we', but in speaking about a political and theoretical context in which I am implicated I am uncomfortable with the distancing that 'they' and 'their' entails – especially in the context of discussing the use of personal narratives. Linguistically, in any case, they and their are equally susceptible to being deployed in universalizing ways. My use of 'we' and 'our' should therefore not be read as covering over difference. We – women and/or feminists – are by no means a homogenous group.

2 Feminists are, however, re-thinking quantitative methodologies, moving away from the idea that only qualitative research can be feminist (see Maynard, 1994). Liz Kelly and her co-researchers, for example, have recently used quantitative methods, arguing for their relevance in delivering data on the incidence of violence towards women and children (Kelly et al., 1992).

3   This analysis of the self can be traced back to the work of George Herbert Mead (1934), the founder of a perspective in social psychology which later came to be known as symbolic interactionism.
4   This is the translator's rendering of the German term *Fremdbestimmung*, literally 'alien determination' or 'determination by others', which conveys the sense of social relations being pre-patterned. Heteronomy means subject to external laws.
5   I am indebted to Jane Cowan for bringing this to my attention.
6   Here psychoanalysis is usually drawn on, but I remain sceptical of its utility (see Jackson, 1993b, 1995).

References

Armstrong, L. (1991) 'Surviving the incest industry', *Trouble and Strife* 21: 29–32.
Brownmiller, S. (1975) *Against Our Will*. London: Secker and Warburg.
Crawford, J. et al. (1992) *Emotion and Gender: Constructing Meaning from Memory*. London: Sage.
Connell, R.W. and Dowsett, G.W. (1992) '"The unclean motion of the generative parts": frameworks in Western thought on sexuality', in R.W. Connell and G.W. Dowsett (eds), *Rethinking Sex: Social Theory and Sexuality Research*. Melbourne: Melbourne University Press.
Currie, D. and Kazi, H. (1987) 'Academic feminism and the process of de-radicalization: Re-examining the issues', *Feminist Review* 25: 76–96.
Davies, M. (1995) *Childhood Sexual Abuse and the Construction of Identity: Healing Sylvia*. London: Taylor & Francis.
Davis, A. (1982) *Women, Race and Class*. London: The Women's Press.
Delphy, C. and Leonard, D. (1992) *Familiar Exploitation*. Cambridge: Polity Press.
Duncombe, J. and Marsden, D. (1993) 'Love and intimacy: the gender division of emotion and emotion work', *Sociology* 27 (2): 221–41.
Errington, F. and Gewertz, D. (1987) *Cultural Alternatives and a Feminist Anthropology*. Cambridge: Cambridge University Press.
Gagnon, P. and Simon, W. (1974) *Sexual Conduct*. London: Hutchinson.
Giddens, A. (1991) *Modernity and Self-Identity*. Cambridge: Polity Press.
Gittens, D. (1986) *The Family in Question*. London: Macmillan.
Haug, F. (ed.) (1987a) *Female Sexualization*. London: Verso.
Haug, F. (1987b) 'Memory work', in F. Haug (ed.), *Female Sexualization*. London: Verso.
Hekman, S. (1997) 'Truth and method: feminist standpoint theory revisited', *Signs* 22 (2): 341–65.
Hollway, W. (1984) 'Gender difference and the production of subjectivity', in J. Henriques, W. Hollway, C. Urwin, C. Venn and V. Walkerdine, *Changing the Subject: Psychology, Social Regulation and Subjectivity*. London: Methuen.
Hollway, W. (1989) *Subjectivity and Method in Psychology*. London: Sage.
hooks, b. (1982) *Ain't I a Woman: Black Women and Feminism*. London: Pluto Press.
Jackson, D. (1990) *Unmasking Masculinity*. London: Routledge.
Jackson, S. (1992) 'The amazing deconstructing woman', *Trouble and Strife* 29: 25–31.
Jackson, S. (1993a) 'Even sociologists fall in love: an exploration in the sociology of the emotions', *Sociology* 27 (2): 201–20.
Jackson, S. (1993b) 'Love and romance as objects of feminist knowledge', in M.

Kennedy, C. Lubelska and C. Walsh (eds), *Making Connections: Women's Studies, Women's Movements, Women's Lives.* London: Falmer.

Jackson, S. (1995) 'Women and heterosexual love: complicity, resistance and change', in L. Pearce and J. Stacey (eds), *Romance Revisited.* London: Lawrence and Wishart.

Jackson, S. (1996) 'Ignorance is bliss when you're just seventeen', *Trouble and Strife* 33: 50–60.

Jackson, S. (1997) 'Classic review: against our will', *Trouble and Strife* 35: 61–7.

Jackson, S. and Scott, S. (1997) 'Gut reactions to matters of the heart: reflections on rationality, irrationality and sexuality', *Sociological Review* (45) 3: 551-75.

Kelly, L. (1988) *Surviving Sexual Violence.* Cambridge: Polity Press.

Kelly, L., Burton, S. and Reagan, L. (1992) 'Defending the indefensible? Quantitative methods and feminist research', in H. Hinds, A. Phoenix and J. Stacey (eds), *Working Out: New Directions for Feminist Research.* London: Taylor & Francis.

Langford, W. (forthcoming) *The Subject of Love.* London: Routledge.

Maynard, M. (1994) 'Methods, practice and epistemology: the debate about feminism and research', in M. Maynard and J. Purvis (eds), *Researching Women's Lives from a Feminist Perspective.* London: Taylor & Francis.

Maynard, M. (1995) 'Beyond the big three', *Women's History Review* 4 (3): 259–81.

Mead, G.H. (1934) *Mind, Self and Society.* Chicago: University of Chicago Press.

Mills, C. Wright (1970) *The Sociological Imagination.* Harmondsworth: Penguin.

Personal Narratives Group (eds) (1989) *Interpreting Women's Lives: Feminist Theory and Personal Narratives.* Bloomington and Indianapolis: Indiana University Press.

Plummer, K. (1995) *Telling Sexual Stories.* London: Routledge.

Rahman, M. and Jackson, S. (1997) 'Liberty, equality and sexuality: essentialism and the discourse of rights', *Journal of Gender Studies* 6 (2): 117–29.

Rosaldo, M. (1984) 'Towards an anthropology of self and feeling', in R.A. Shweder and R.A. LeVine (eds), *Culture Theory.* Cambridge: Cambridge University Press.

Seidler, V. (1989) *Rediscovering Masculinity: Reason, Language and Sexuality.* London: Routledge.

Smith, D. (1987) *The Everyday World as Problematic.* Buckingham: Open University Press.

Smith, D. (1997) 'Comment on Hekman's "Truth and Method: Feminist Standpoint Theory Revisited"', *Signs* 22 (2): 392–8.

Stanley, L. and Wise, S. (1983) *Breaking Out.* London: Routledge.

Stanley, L. and Wise, S. (1990) 'Method, methodology and epistemology in feminist research processes', in L. Stanley (ed.), *Feminist Praxis.* London: Routledge.

Stanley, L. and Wise, S. (1993) *Breaking Out Again.* London: Routledge.

Steedman, C. (1986) *Landscape for a Good Woman: A Story of Two Lives.* London: Virago.

Stevenson, N., Kippax, S. and Crawford, J. (1996) 'You and I and she: memory work and the construction of the self', in S. Wilkinson (ed.), *Feminist Social Psychologies: International Perspectives.* Buckingham: Open University Press.

Walkerdine, V. (1990) *Schoolgirl Fictions.* London: Verso.

Weedon, C. (19897) *Feminist Practice and Poststructuralist Theory.* Oxford: Blackwell.

Whisman, V. (1996) *Queer by Choice.* New York: Routledge.

Part 2

DIVERSE POSITIONINGS

4

Women and Men Talk about Aggression: An Analysis of Narrative Genre

Corinne Squire

In this chapter, I am going to discuss some research I did in the early 1990s when I asked a number of women and men, students at a suburban New Jersey college, to talk about their experiences and expectations of aggression. Psychological research, popular media and our own everyday understandings connect aggression very closely to gender, especially to masculinity (Biden, 1993; White and Kowalski, 1994). My research explored how people's stories of aggression repeated yet also departed from that gendering, by examining the narrative forms used (Squire, 1994).

The study had a research procedure – collecting individuals' accounts – and a topic – aggression – that accord with feminist concerns about personal experience and gendered power and violence. The study investigated interviewees' language, a topic in which there has also been considerable feminist interest (Cameron, 1985; Lakoff, 1975; Spender, 1980; Thorne et al., 1983). However, the study's concern with narrative genre seemed to distance it in some ways from feminism. Focusing on narrative structures and their cultural significance, the study did not have experiential or immediate political resonance; it did not explain how oppressive gender relations are produced linguistically or socially, or how they may be changed; it even tended to emphasize the difficulty and unlikeliness of feminism. I want to argue that feminist psychology should be conceived broadly enough to include such research. In particular, such work may extend to our comprehension of gendered subjectivities, of their pleasures and dangers, and of the resistances and the possibilities of change that these subjectivities offer. The study I shall be reflecting on was an attempt to develop such tangentially feminist work.

The study assumes that it is important to listen to people talking about aggression in order to find out more about it. Such assumptions fit with those of 'feminist standpoint' research, a major perspective within contemporary feminist psychology. This perspective tries to ground objects, methods and theories in 'experiences and lives' (Henwood and Pidgeon, 1995: 14–15), especially of women, and aims to develop an analysis based in those experiences and lives (Harding, 1991: 269). Yet the study's concentration on narrative structure detached it somewhat from feminist standpoint concerns. At the same time, the study's interest in how narratives are shaped by cultural and social determinants of aggression accorded with feminist social constructionism, another widely adopted approach within current feminist psychology. This approach aims to understand gender's production by economic, political, social and cultural relations (Hare-Mustin and Maracek, 1988). Yet the study did not understand narrative solely as an artefact. Unlike much social constructionism, it assumed that the psyche is partly independent of social determination and has its own effects on narrative. I would suggest that the study's differences from feminist standpoint and constructionist work in psychology can be used to explore the problems such work faces.

Listening to gender: the content of the interviews

A portmanteau description of feminist psychology, taking in both standpoint and constructionist perspectives, could be that it aims to understand the complex 'experience and lives of women' within the power relations of patriarchy (Worrell and Etaugh, 1994: 444), and to change them. This aim can be pursued in various ways. One way is to investigate the *content* of gendered subjectivities. This mode of investigation assumes that a more or less 'true' content exists, and that we can achieve fairly reliable knowledge of it. Feminist psychological investigations of content measure or describe important aspects of gendered subjectivities, and differences between these subjectivities. When such investigations are qualitative, they often adopt a standpoint approach. Rather than silencing or ventriloquizing women, they try to give women's voices a feminist hearing. Such an approach may also involve 'listening' to men, though always from a vantage point that acknowledges their social power.

My interview study of aggression was, to some degree, a study of content that was compatible with the feminist standpoint perspective. I interviewed men and women about their experiences and expectations of aggression. Although at the beginning of the interviews I asked participants to talk about what they thought 'aggression' was, I then assumed that some consensus existed on this topic and how to talk about it. The interviews covered topics where aggression and its gendering are the focus of academic work and public commentary and, again, assumed a common understanding of them. These topics were the family, relationships and the domestic sphere; work and leisure, particularly sports environments; school and college; rural, urban and suburban environments, and the popular media.

The study's procedure was also compatible with a feminist standpoint approach. Sixteen women and seven men participated, partly a reflection of the gender imbalance among the psychology students I was recruiting, but also a deliberate skewing. Women are still most frequently represented in research on aggression as statistical victims of men: losers in the 'battle of the sexes', who do not speak (Harding, 1991: 121, 126; White and Kowalski, 1994). In response, the study focused on women's own narratives, and provided opportunities for them to tell stories of their and other women's resistance and active aggression. The skew towards women also produced some ethnic diversity among the female interviewees: two women self-described as African American, one as Latina, and one as (South) Asian, while all of the men self-described as white – including two who ticked 'Native American', though after questioning it appeared they did not identify as American Indian.[1] As most of the interviewees were part-time students, some were older than the college's average student and probably of lower socio-economic status, again increasing the range of voiced experience, especially female experience.

To a large extent, the participants directed the interviews. Interviewees could describe specific events, or they could speak generally. Although the same topics were always raised by the interviewer, participants could concentrate the interview on their own concerns. This semi-structured method could thus claim an accessibility, flexibility and unobtrusiveness (Henwood and Pidgeon, 1995: 9–10) that might let women's voices be heard. Moreover, the 'aggression' content of the interviews was counted in terms of narratives, each narrative being identified as a chronological and/or causal chain in the interview that centred on an incident of intentional harm. This 'story' basis for content assessment seemed especially apt for research with women, whose extensive use of narrative may often escape questionnaires or content assessments by semantic category.[2] A focus on narrative may also be helpful for women when they are discussing topics like aggression that are hard to speak about directly and denotatively. These advantages outweighed, I thought, the possibility that the method would create artefactual gender differences resulting from putative female facility and male unease with narrative.

The study yielded some results that were of potential value for a standpoint feminism trying to clarify the content of gendered subjectivities. Overall, women told many more stories than men of criminal male aggression against themselves: of sexual harrassment, sexual abuse, rape and physical violence. Four out of the seven male interviewees told such stories; only two of the sixteen women, both under 20, produced no stories of this kind. It was almost entirely women, too, who told stories of domestic violence by fathers, brothers and male partners. These latter stories were explicit about blaming the aggressor, described unambiguous and justified responses, and ended with safe, private, resolutions. The single male narrative of domestic violence, experienced in childhood by an interviewee from his father, was much more ambivalent, full of violent but apparently unresolvable hostility towards the aggressor.

The women interviewees described a narrow subjective zone of safety, sometimes comprising their street but often just their house or car, that did not necessarily circumscribe their movements, but that was the only area within which they felt secure. By contrast, men's safety zones typically encompassed their whole town or suburb. Women also lived with the possibility or, for some, likelihood, of a generalized male aggressor being present in public areas like the college campus, or a shopping-mall parking lot. Men, on the other hand, only postulated such an aggressor when they talked about 'the city'. Women's stories of being objects of aggression ended with effective but private solutions, never with public redress, while men's stories sometimes concluded with clear public retaliation, occasionally through the justice system.

The study suggested, too, that concepts of aggression are gender-differentiated. Women and men were equally likely to be aggressors in both sexes' stories of being aggressed against, but both sexes reported that their own defensive aggression was principally against men, and that their non-defensive aggression was mostly against women. This pattern suggests that men may be legitimated as targets of retaliation by their perceived aggressiveness, while women's perceived lack of aggression may render acts against them, almost by definition, offensive. Female interviewees nearly always framed their aggression towards men, even when it involved weapons, as defensive. They provided strong definitions of male verbal harrassment as 'aggression', but tended to describe them-selves as 'assertive' in arguments with men. On the other hand, men interpreted women's talk to them during arguments as 'aggressive', while their own talk was assertive or joking. But they never mentioned being physically aggressive to women and gave muted accounts of their verbal responses to female aggression. Bill (all interviewees' names have been changed), for instance, said of his mother's 'yelling' when he put things off, 'I, I fight back a little and then I realize that it's useless . . . I go and watch TV, just leave the room, do something else.' Of course, even men convicted of violence against women rarely mention these acts spontaneously and when they do talk of them, they tend to translate them into much milder ones. While the men in this study may have omitted or censored some narratives, it also seemed that for them, women were cultur-ally sanctioned targets of aggression only within the verbal realm.

At the level of content, then, the study can be read as providing further confirmation of the large amount of previous research indicating the ubiquity of male aggression against women and its far-reaching effects on women's lives (Dutton, 1992; Koss et al., 1994). Other characteristics that emerged, like women's chartings of narrower subjective zones of safety such as their house, street or car; their emphasis on personal solutions; their unconflicted morality tales about men's domestic aggression, and their fluent narratives of self-defence against male aggression, support prior findings about how women and men map 'aggression', and about women's public danger, private conflicts, and strategies of resistance (Ardener, 1991; Saegert, 1980; Ullman and Knight, 1993; White and Kowalski, 1994).

Relaying the voices of experience is not a straightforward process. Much feminist research on aggression is dominated by horrific records of abuse, but is such horror a direct transcription of experience? In this chapter and in other reports of my study, I decided not to retell women's many stories of sexual and physical violence. This decision was a risk. Without the women's words, perhaps the regularity and occasional extremity of male hostility in their narratives would be overlooked. My decision, however, aimed to resist the patronizing assumption that readers would only note such events if they experienced them vicariously, through women's autobiographical stories. The decision also aimed to forestall the common but illogical supposition that accounts of horrific events represent truth in a specially unmediated way. Finally, and perhaps most importantly within the context of social science research, the decision arose from a concern to address some less-studied issues that the narratives raised.

Despite the danger of underplaying the clearly gendered elements of the interview content, then, I am going to put them to one side and move on to aspects of content that have been less researched within feminist work on aggression. This move is not necessarily antithetical to the feminist standpoint approach. While the approach is often interpreted as embedded in women's experience, Sandra Harding, perhaps its most influential proponent, has emphasized its commitment to 'observations and theory' that merely start from women's lives (1991: 124). Standpoint theory values women's lives as neglected, potentially productive material, just as conventional social science values other such neglected material.

In this study, some content, not differentiated by gender, was differentiated in other ways, or problematized the notion of 'experience' itself. The feminist standpoint approach acknowledges such complexities. It does not suggest that all research findings will be gender-differentiated, that structural factors other than gender are irrelevant or that 'experience' will be easy to express or understand. However, its explanatory power derives from the principle that the gendering of human 'activity' and consequently 'vision' is ubiquitous, can be described, and is a division whose political moment has, with quasi-marxist inevitability, arrived (Hartsock, in Harding, 1991: 120; Harding, 1991: 132). Some interview content contradicted that principle.

First, much of the content was not clearly gendered. Men, like women, told on average ten stories per interview. As with women, two-thirds of the stories were about being objects of aggression. In these stories, both men and women explored their own role in the episode, a questioning that seemed closer to taking control of the event than to self-blame (Katz and Burt, 1988; Kristiansen and Guilietti, 1990; Phillips, 1996). Women, like men, told about one-sixth of their stories about being non-defensive aggressors. Often, for women and men, such stories of non-defensive aggression were bracketed by accounts of others' wrongdoing or hostility, but these justifications did not quite remove the active aggression from the succeeding action. Anna's story of how she turned a long-standing conflict physical when she responded to someone who 'said something', typifies both men's and women's stories in this category:

> *Anna*:   . . . once I used to be on the basketball team in my high school
> and one of the – I was really mad that we lost, whatever, and I
> never liked this one girl, and she never liked me, for no reason,

we just hated each other (laugh), and um, then the beginning of, and my team lost, and her brother was the coach and he had a ball, and he said something to me as I walked by, and I just like knocked the ball out of his hand, and sh – I turned round and all I heard was her screaming, and she like jumped on my back and started punching me (laugh).

From a standpoint perspective, it could be argued that similarity across genders – as here, in number and type of stories about active aggression – conceals underlying differences. Anna's aggression towards the brother of a girl who provoked her and later, towards the girl herself, would not 'mean' the same if we changed the sexes of the protagonists. While this argument makes sense on its own, it relies on some undeclared assumptions about the ubiquitous structure of gender relations. Standpoint research often seems to rely on such strong implicit theories of gender. These assumptions introduce a contradiction into a perspective that, only a few paragraphs ago, led us to take women's and men's different accounts of safety and danger zones at their word. Now we are saying, we value what the interviewees say, but we know, better than they themselves, what it 'really' means.

This switch points to a problem inherent in standpoint research: it wants to have and eat its epistemological cake. It grants women privileged knowledge by virtue of their 'oppressed', 'stranger' and 'outsider within' statuses, their involvement in everyday life, their less defensive personality structures and their ideological mediations, at the same time as it extracts what is useful for research and theory from women's raw accounts as any social scientist might, and accepts that 'women say all kinds of things' (Harding, 1991: 123).[3] Such a switch from one set of assumptions to another could be resolved if we assumed an understanding immanent in all women that coincides with the theorist's own – a rather arrogant assumption. Alternatively, we could accept that paying respect to 'women's lives' is a tactic that makes standpoint work more inclusive – and allows it to cite 'women' directly, but only when they agree with its underlying theories. If we make neither of these moves, then standpoint theory's epistemological sleights-of-hand introduce complications that I wanted to avoid.

Stories also varied greatly between same-gender interviewees. While some women talked about domestic physical and sexual abuse, other, younger women described themselves as 'protected' and talked mainly about their experiences of violence in sports, or campus safety issues. Women who lived in poorer and more urban areas talked much more than the other women about defending themselves against street and car crime. Young white women talking about the dangers of 'the city' seemed to be figuring that danger as black; sometimes, as in the case of Brooke, who said she visualized aggression in the shape of a large black man, this racialized expectation was explicit. Though all the male interviewees were white, their self-situating in terms of class and ethnicity inflected their accounts strongly. For instance, Alan was a young white man who decided, in what seemed a mixture of confusion and obstinacy, to tick 'Native American' on the demographics questionnaire. He recounted a long history of battles between his small town and Italian Americans from a neighbouring town whom he called, with a self-conscious laugh, 'Guidos'. Two other men, defining themselves respectively as middle-class and 'ordinary', related campus fights between themselves and, respectively, poorer and richer male students, that they related explicitly to class differences.

A feminist standpoint psychology would be sympathetic to a notion of multiple voices, articulating class and 'race' at the same time as gender. But the diverse social relations on display cast doubt even on the apparently clear gender differences in the interviews. How do we know when gender difference really is a gender difference, rather than a difference specific to the predominantly under-30s white women and men in this study – and should we be studying such differences anyway? (Baumeister, 1988; Eagly, 1987; Kitzinger, 1994; Unger, 1992). In stories of aggression between women or between men, too, gender often seemed of lesser or no importance beside other determinants. In such cases, the feminist standpoint perspective could argue for gender's concealed but underlying significance, analysing the male interviewees' emphasis on class as a playing-out of tensions within masculinity, for instance. But this resort to an undeclared interpretive frame would create an epistemological contradiction similar to the one mentioned above. Alternatively, the standpoint perspective could acknowledge that at times other 'standpoints' will foreground 'voices' based on class or 'race', thus propounding a sort of standpoint relativism, accepting different 'standpoints' as long as they all start from 'experience'. Such expanded standpointism is unable to integrate the different standpoints theoretically, and hence it is subject to a relativism whose good intentions do not resolve it.[4]

Often in this study, stories of non-defensive aggression contained elements of confusion or amnesia. These elements seemed idiosyncratic, yet powerful: not merely the result of embarrassment, and not reducible to women's self-doubt or men's self-censorship. Anna, for example, continued her basketball story:

Anna: I, I forgot about that (laugh), so like me forgetting. But um (pause).
Interviewer: What did you do?
Anna: I was like – I was shocked, I was like, what are you doing? (laugh). And then I saw my mother in the stand, I started yelling at her, 'get off me, get off me', and then somebody separated – like, I wasn't going to go after her because I was just, I couldn't believe that she did it, you know, so, but they had to grab her, her brother had to like tackle her, 'cause she was you know after me . . . I didn't like her because she was, like, a showoff, and she had a big attitude, and she didn't like me because (pause) um (pause) I don't know why (laugh). Um, I don't know, we just took an instant – we were very competitive against each other, so (pause).

The story's confusion about the cause of enmity, its vague pro-nouns that entangle Anna's mother and attacker, and its ambiguity about Anna's aggression (the other woman was 'separated' from her, not pulled off, and she protests, needlessly, that she didn't plan to 'go after' her) seem to arise from the flurry of events: from incredulity at a violated safe space, the school basketball court; but also from something unrepresented, perhaps unrepresentable, in the narrative. While a man makes the first aggressive move, the most significant hostility is between the women, and even if Anna remembered something about the hostility she did not want to say, it seemed she could not describe why it was so intense. Many inter-viewees' stories of their own aggression displayed this unrepresent-able intensity between people who were alike – usually female family members for men, and other women in general, for women.

Anna's confusions were perhaps partly the result of forgetfulness and lack of practice in telling culturally disregarded stories. From the standpoint perspective, though, when researchers have assayed their contradictory but frequently-made leap to a feminist theory of underlying meaning, they ought to be able to tell us what Anna's confusions 'really' meant. They might, for instance, try to read these confusions as signs of the mystifying and ambivalent symbioses induced between women by existing ideologies and practices of childcare and education. They might want to sort out these rela-tional dynamics theoretically, so they do not 'undermine other politically important projects' (Henwood and Pidgeon, 1995: 25). But in cases like Anna's, where voices are ambiguous or tail off, the dubiousness of containing them within a broad interpretive frame is, I think, especially clear.

All the interviewees also talked about media representations of aggression, often at length and sometimes in relation to their own experiences. While women described more emotional and identi-ficatory relations to representations, these concerns, again, were not straightforwardly gendered. There was convergence between women and men in the ways they retold and evaluated media represen-tations, for instance in their gleeful recounting of horror movie plots and in their assessments of images that shocked them or that were 'too much'. Again, this consistent lack of gendering does not fit well with the standpoint perspective. Moreover, a standpoint analysis's emphasis on 'lives' might lead it either to downplay these stories of representations, or to emphasize how such stories reflected or shaped interviewees' thoughts and actions.[5] The stories' content, however, only occasionally indicated direct resonance with everyday life, unless I was prepared to analyse content at an extremely general level, seeing for instance a woman's extensive account of a TV movie about domestic violence as a guide to her experience of the issue. Often there were contradictions between a woman's account of such a movie and stories from her own life. In this situation, I was not prepared to declare one kind of interview content, derived from life, better or truer than another kind of interview content, derived from representations. I did not want to say, for instance, that a woman showed a 'partial' understanding (Harding, 1991: 123) because she articulated a feminist perspective on domestic violence less in talking about her life than in describing a movie.

The complexity of narrative content in this study illustrates the dilemmas of making 'women's lives' the benchmark of feminism. Increasingly, feminist psychologists, including those sympathetic to the standpoint perspective, recognize these difficulties (Henwood and Pidgeon, 1995: 11, 15–16). Lives cannot be identified, accessed and communicated in an unproblematic way. Voicings of experience also always occur in a delimiting context of which the researcher is herself a part. The researcher can only 'listen' within a particular range of frequencies, and must speak in her own, usually more powerful voice, to re-present the voices she has heard. The power structures of interview research are complex (Bhavnani, 1990; Phoenix, 1991). A particular problem for the standpoint perspective is that it assumes a right of free passage across the gap between presentation and re-presentation, between the content and the meaning of a voice.

Gender as a construct

In the light of these qualifications, it made sense for the study to take on another perspective influential in feminist psychology: that of social constructionism. This perspective posits gender as a social construct, lived out in interaction with other social constructs like 'race' and class; shaped by cultural discourses as well as by the sexed bodies we inhabit (Hare-Mustin and Maracek, 1988; Worrell and Etaugh, 1994: 447). For social constructionists, gender forms one facet of subjectivity, rather than unifying and identifying it; and it structures the research process as well as the objects of research.

Social constructionism often seems, by its stress on the flexibility and mutability of gender, to oppose the standpoint approach with its relatively stable gender politics. Yet standpoint feminists also analyse gender as a construct, albeit using a conceptual vocabulary that relies less on postmodernism. Conversely, social construction-ism usually tries to preserve some political agency or 'standpoint' in its research programme. The 'concrete particulars of women's lives' that disrupt existing theory (Henwood and Pidgeon, 1995: 9) are starting points for it, as well as for standpoint feminists. There is, then, a convergence of theoretical assumptions and research pro-cedures between the two approaches (Henwood and Pidgeon, 1995: 22) – and, I shall argue later, a common theoretical failure in relation to subjectivity. Nevertheless, the difference in emphasis between the perspectives can be important.

It was a social-constructionist interest in the production of subjectivity by discourse that informed this interview study's focus on popular narrative genres. If language affects subjectivities at all, narrative genres are specially likely, given the ubiquitousness and high profile of fictional and documentary narratives of aggression in, for instance, movies and the news media, to produce effects. In addition, popular-cultural research has emphasized the possibilities for resistant readings that narrative genres can provide, possibilities that might also be apparent if such genres appear in spoken narratives of aggression (Ang, 1985; Radway, 1984; Tolson and Jenkins, 1995).

I have talked about 'narratives' but have so far addressed only their content, not their language. 'Narrative' is indeed an analytic category that often serves, paradoxically, to de-emphasize language. We all think we know what stories are. Psychologies of narrative frequently declare subjectivity to be structured by and as 'stories', thus suggesting that there is a single, universal pattern to narrative, and a synergy between that pattern and psychic life. Story is thus presented as serving psychological ends. This account renders the specific properties of narrative language, and differences between narrative forms, insignificant. And so, in order to examine narrative language and its effects on subjectivity, the study focused on par-ticular genres of narrative, whose specific structures are harder to overlook than is the case with 'narrative' in general (Sarbin, 1986; Squire, 1994).

The study examined interviewees' narratives as examples of the Gothic genre, in relation to what Kate Ellis in *The Contested Castle* (1988) calls Insider and Outsider Gothic. Ellis's characterization of the Gothic genre is one of many, but it proved appropriate for this study as it offered a way of linking narrative structure, popular culture and gender relations. Ellis describes Insider Gothic, typified by Ann Radcliffe's (1966) [1794] *Mysteries of Udolpho*, as stories in which a feminine protagonist ventures out of the domestic sphere only to encounter and resist danger, or else has to deal with such dangers at home. At the narrative's conclusion, the heroine either returns to or establishes a safe domestic sphere, or she dies. In the later Outsider Gothic genre, exemplified by Mary Shelley's (1988) [1818] *Frankenstein*, a masculine protagonist, cast out from a domestic eden, attempts to destroy it – and ends up vanquished himself, at least temporarily. Ambiguity is also part of the narratives' progressions. In Insider Gothic, Ellis notes, the protagonist is concerned about her own culpability for the problems she meets. The Outsider Gothic genre is more overtly ambiguous; the protagonist's destructiveness is intricately tied up with his exile and his efforts to recapture the paradise he has lost.

These two Gothic forms persist within contemporary popular culture, for instance within the horror, science fiction and action movie genres, and there were particular reasons for supposing that they might also appear within interviewees' spoken narratives. The interviewees were highly literate in the visual media. They talked analytically and at length about aggressive acts they had seen in movies, videos, television films and to a lesser extent in television news reports, and interspersed this talk with discussion of real-life aggression. Their narratives were also, as is probably the case with much contemporary storytelling, movie-esque, often sounding like a script written *post hoc*, after the events. The stories included elements of scene-setting; thumbnail character sketches; rapid, often present-tense delineations of action, and quick shifts from one scene to another. Given this filmic structure, and given the ubiquity and influence of film and television narratives of aggression, it seemed reasonable to analyse the spoken narratives in terms of the Insider and Outsider Gothic characteristics of popular visual narratives.

Most of the interviewees' stories, almost five out of six (around 190 out of a total of 240) were classifiable within the frame of Insider Gothic, if the narrator was the object of aggression; or Outsider Gothic, if she or he was the perpetrator. In the first category, interviewees produced narratives of being in safe, domestic places –

homes, neighbourhoods, workplaces, schools and recreation facilities. The narratives told of venturing out from these zones and running into danger, or of the safe havens themselves becoming dangerous. They traced how the protagonist returned to or re-established a zone of homelike security. In the second, Outsider Gothic category, interviewees told stories of their own hostility towards another. As with Anna's story of her barely provoked physical violence, the narratives traced the ambiguities of that hostility, through moments of similarity, self-doubt and incomprehension as well as difference and conflict. In these stories the object of hostility was usually female, a figuration of the domestic space. In the men's stories she was especially close to home, most often a mother or girlfriend.

At one level, using Ellis's (1988) classification of the Gothic allows the study to add cultural and historical context to its findings about gendered narrative content. Ellis suggests that the Gothic genres expressed cultural and individual concerns about the development in eighteenth-century Europe of gendered, 'separate spheres'. In the Insider Gothic genre, women eventually accept this ideology, but they struggle against and gain power over it in the course of the narrative. In the Outsider Gothic genre, men too accept the separate spheres ideology, but again, they continually rail against and try to overthrow it during the narratives.

Ellis's emphasis on the gendered history of the Gothic is not shared by all theorists of the genre. Her account is thus itself a kind of 'standpoint' feminism, enabling a devalued, popular and often female-associated literary form to be understood as an expression of and resistance to ideologies of gender. This understanding can help make sense of the interviewees' stories of aggression. We can, for instance, take women's stories of their limited, highly domestic safety, their self-questioning about responsibility for others' violence, and their resistance to limitations on their movements and to victimhood as examples of Insider Gothic narratives. With this reading, the stories' confusions appear, not as unresolved narrative contradictions, but as part of the necessary negotiations any woman must perform when navigating by a social map that still designates separate, gendered spheres. Similarly, men's ambivalent stories of domestic violence, reticent about their own role, and stressing women's hostility, can be read as instances of the Outsider Gothic. Such an approach makes them seem less like pathologies, rife with denial and paranoia, and more like a playing-out of how masculinity is constructed against and outside 'feminine' intimacy. The stories of conflicts with people very similar or close to you, for instance between women who are almost doppelgangers, like Anna and her nemesis, and men and their mothers, can, too, be read within the Gothic frame, as narrative inductions of subjects into a gendered order. This strand of the narrative analysis could also be seen as adopting a 'standpoint' approach. For although it focuses on the constructing interplay between narrative and subjectivity, not on experience, it concentrates on the feminist meanings of that construction. However, unlike the standpoint approach, this analysis declares a limited interpretive frame, rather than letting a universalized frame of interpretation function, often undeclared, across categories of content and language.

Other strands of the narrative analysis diverged further from the standpoint approach. While Ellis does not address factors like 'race', maternity or infantile sexuality, many texts on the Gothic and horror point to such factors (Carroll, 1990; Clover, 1992; Copjec, 1991; Creed, 1987; Dolar, 1991) and suggest ways of reading the narratives' construction beyond gender. They point, for instance, to the racialized as well as the gendered Other that may operate in such narratives. In male interviewees' stories about fights with similar yet markedly 'different' men, from another town or class or ethnicity, racial otherness seemed to be playing out within whiteness. A racial Other seemed also to lurk in the cities and shopping malls in young white women's tales of the generalized male aggressor they expected to encounter there. This reading of the racial Other within the Gothic also adds another level of narrative complexity, a double ironization, to the Insider Gothic stories of domestic aggression told by the four female interviewees who were African American, Latina and Asian. These women's narratives cast a figure of cultural terror and neglect, the woman of colour, as the virtuous protagonist. At the same time, they subverted the convention in every twentieth-century work by US writers of colour, particularly men, of picturing the domestic sphere as a sanctuary, 'inside of all the pressure, away from it, separate from it' (Himes, 1986 [1945]: 169).

From a social-constructionist perspective, the uncertainty introduced into narratorship as a result of Ellis's and other characterizations of the Gothic, suggests that ambiguities and confusions in interviewees' narratives, as in Anna's account of her basketball fight, express the ambiguities of a constructed subjectivity, including its gendered aspects. Though we speak as if we know who and what gender we are, our 'selves' are inevitably contextualized. They are situated at, or in stronger accounts put together by, the intersection of a set of historically and socially specific discourses.[6] The inevitable imperfections in knowledge of such 'selves' often show through.

This constructionist perspective on the uncertainty of identity also helps make sense of some other aspects of the study. The reticence of some female interviewees, for instance, need not be judged against the deeply confessional style of others, only as signs of lack of engagement or poor listening. They can also partly be understood as the products of social differences and similarities in age, ethnicity, nationality and class between them and me. When Alan spoke to me about 'Guidos' he assumed that, across different nationality but shared whiteness, I knew and tolerated what he meant. When Brooke told me, with a small laugh, that her symbol of urban danger was a large, probably black, man, she was making the same assumption, shored up by gender similarity. The women of colour were less likely than the white interviewees to assume similarity – they were prone to include explanations of economic and social geography in their narratives, for instance. When, as often happened, male interviewees asked whether I believed that all men were aggressive towards women, this meta-engagement with the research was constructed partly by their own heavily gendered concerns about male aggression, played out on me; partly also by their resistance to the imbalance of power inherent in the interview situation.[7]

Some of what Ellis says about the Insider and Outsider Gothic forms, and some of what emerged from interviewees' own Gothic narratives, does not, however, seem to fit well with a social-constructionist account. Narrators of the two Gothic forms can, Ellis points out, be of either sex. Among the interviewees in the study, men and women used both genres, depending on whether they were telling of being objects or subjects of aggression. It was as if using a narrative culturally recognized as feminine allowed both sexes to talk about safety and danger, and their own negotiation of a life between the two. Similarly, the Outsider narrative, recognized as masculine, let both women and men explore the ambiguous pleasures of aggression. Unlike the content, the narrative genres seemed adaptable in their gendering. Interviewees used, in an ungendered way, forms that are, in Ellis's argument, of a specific cultural and historical gender; and so they seemed to 'slip' between genders. The genres may, as Ellis argues, resist the ideology of separate spheres, but the interviews suggest they perform this resistance for everyone, undiscriminatingly, which makes them valueless for explaining broader gendered social patterns.

At this point, my account may appear to be losing all vestiges of feminism in its social constructionism. How much use to a feminist analysis is a narrative structure that, when the diverse contents are removed, appears the same, and with the same frequency, across narratives of women's rape, men's street fights, and men's and women's scuffles on the sports field? Were there, perhaps, different *uses* of the genres, depending on gendered content in and around the story, or the gender of the narrator? Perhaps the Insider Gothic narrative 'worked' differently when it told the story of a young man attacked during a basketball game than it did telling the story of a woman's rape, or, indeed, of a young woman attacked during a basketball game? In the first case, for instance, the 'feminine' genre might mask active aggression, while in the second and third cases it might offer a reassuring structure for understanding and controlling aggression narratively. To pursue this analysis I would need to return to content. I could hypothesize, for example, that there would be more aggressive content in or near to the men's than the women's Insider Gothic narratives, in the form of explicit denials of aggression perhaps, or closely associated Outsider Gothic narratives. Or I could investigate whether broad discourses to do with managing aggression were associated more often with the women's than the men's Insider Gothic stories.

There are two problems with this analysis of gendered genre use and content. First, I was unable to find content that suggested gendered uses of the genres. But if I had adopted a stronger feminist theory of what functions 'must' be served by the narratives, perhaps I *could* have found gendered uses. Feminist constructionist psychology often does resort to such theory when, as here, its findings have no clear political implications. There seems to me nothing wrong with this procedure, as long as you are explicit about it. Often though, such analyses present themselves as data-driven – paradoxically, when they are resistant to mainstream psychology's reverential approach to the empirical (Squire, 1995). Then, as with the standpoint approach, feminist constructionism is claiming a privileged understanding of the data, and is switching from one epistemology to another – from a focus on language, for instance, to a feminist grand narrative (Widdicombe, 1995). I wanted to avoid such sophism if possible.

My second and more fundamental objection to looking for gendered 'uses' of genre was that the focus of the study was narrative genre itself. To attend to the functioning of genre, and to return to content, is to detract from this focus. Such a move itself again replaces the declared object of study, narrative, with another, undeclared one: language use as it has been theorized by feminists. This analysis would once more collapse language into a general psychologism. Language would become part of gendered subjectivity, with none of its own specificity.

If a social constructionist account of the interview does not adopt any of these solutions, if it accepts that the narrative genres in the interview simply tell us a bit about how women and men talk about aggression, then the account runs another risk. It may start to look like that relativist exploration of endless differences which many feminists in and outside psychology associate with social constructionism and 'postmodernism', and see as feminism's nemesis.[8] I would suggest however that when a study is, like this one, of limited scope, a description of how gendered genres work within men's and women's interviews constitutes, not terminal relativism, but theoretical restraint and political respect (Nicholson, 1995: 15).

A further problem arises from social constructionism's putting into question of identity, in this case, the identities of the interviewees. Feminist constructionists in psychology either assume an active subject who acts within the constraints of social determination; or they assume that the 'subject' is the sum of its construction, an artefect of the collision of discourses. But accounts of Gothic genres often take the notion of the construction of identity further, finding at the heart of the Gothic an uncanniness that replicates the lacunae in subjectivity itself (Dolar, 1991). These accounts draw on Freud's (1974) [1919] description of the uncanny as literally, in German, 'unhomeliness', a disturbance in the familiar domestic order. The doppelgangers in the interviewees' Outsider Gothic stories, figures with whom the narrator has uneasily close and hostile relations, are, such accounts of the uncanny would suggest, characters in a more individual and unknowable story than that of the social construction of gendered, separate spheres. The triad of Anna, the opposition team's coach, and his hated sister – or, in many other women's stories, the narrator, a boyfriend and another girl – is not a formation that could be erased by changing gender relations. Rather, such accounts would claim, this formation is unavoidable, and indissoluble. Each revisiting of it is an attempt to excavate an unknowable psychic substratum, a powerful but indescribable 'unhomely' family romance.

Some of the men's stories about their aggression, centred on the domestic sphere, support this contention more directly. Bill, for instance, defined aggression as 'hatred'. When asked to speak about a recent experience of aggression he talked at length, with many pauses and repetitions, about his own aggression towards his mother, and hers towards him:

> *Bill:*   . . . an actual situation where I feel hatred, um (4 sec) I guess (4 sec) actually I guess, um, towards my mother, it's a, a few things, she's just (2 sec) she'd just start yelling at me about, ridiculous things and I was just, because I was, I'd stayed home for three days over the

weekend, and um, sometimes she just drives me nuts now because we're just different types of, of people. (Inaudible) she's very conservative, and like she wanted me to get flowers for my grandmother, like, Saturday night, and I was getting them Sunday morning, which I saw as no big deal, and um, it took me ten minutes to get them and she yelled at me for like an hour, and just you know, Easter morning, it was just ridiculous you know . . . she just yells and yells and yells, that's just my mother and er, I guess I always feel aggressive every time she yells about something completely ridiculous. You know, she wants me to do things in advance, I just, I guess, do 'em at the last minute just to try and spite her you know, half of the time, you know (laugh), I guess. She feels aggression towards me and I feel it towards her . . . I, I fight back a little and then I realize that it's useless . . . I go and watch TV, just leave the room, do something else. (3 sec) I guess in other situations if it's not your mother I'd stay there and fight a little longer, you know you can't really fight the woman who's paying all your bills too much (laugh) so . . . a lot of times my dad also reminds me that it's completely useless to fight, and just, just ignore her basically.

Such a story can be read along Outsider Gothic lines as a narrative deploying a male-associated form to negotiate masculine distance from and dependency on the domestic sphere. Yet it is also a more individual account of intimacy and tension. Only some of the men told such stories, and the ambivalence of the stories brings them closer to stories like Anna's than to other men's more straight-forward accounts of conflicts with their mothers. In stories like Anna's and Bill's, the object of aggression is close to or knows the narrator. She is also dangerous, slightly mad and quite powerful, and so she can get the narrator where it hurts. The man – the brother, the father, the boyfriend – seems incidental to the story, but it is as if he has to be there as a third point. Such narratives cannot be explained fully as constructs of gendered ideologies any more than they can be heard simply as the voices of women and men under patriarchy. Some other account has to be added. But if it derives from a psychoanalytic notion of triangulation and separation, it carries a strong risk, for many constructionists as well as standpoint theorists, of being unhelpful. If it is too 'embedded in psychoanalysis' (Hare-Mustin and Maracek, 1989: 1333) it may share the misogyny that is conventionally attributed to psychoanalysis by feminism, or, at the least, it may divert attention from feminist politics. While this suspicion of psychoanalysis seems consistent with the standpoint approach's rationalism, it is at odds with the philosophical lineage of social constructionism, which takes many ideas from a poststructuralism itself heavily inflected by psychoanalysis.

A social-constructionist account of the procedures in the aggression study comes up against similar limits in the individual and unreachable histories of interviewees and interviewer. A female interviewee disclosed childhood sexual abuse for the first time and said she did not want to talk about it again after the interview. A male interviewee became angry with me about having talked too much about his family. Over a 45-minute interview, I tried reformulating questions many different ways but was unable to get one young woman to describe any specific experience of aggression. There are a variety of ways to explain such moments of openness, enmity and frustration, but the language of transference and countertransference seems especially suited to their intensity and particularity. Again, though, this psychoanalytic language would make some feminist psychologists suspicious.

The missing subject

A social-constructionist analysis could try to address the interviewees' cross-sex uses of gendered genres, the psychoanalytically inflected aspects of their subjectivity that evade notions of gender construction, and the presence in the interviews of other, less-gendered narrative genres. Would such an analysis dissipate all traces of feminism in the relativism and the abdication of agency that many see as social constructionism's failing?

The posing of a problematic dualism between theory and politics is very common in feminist research in social sciences and the humanities. In psychology, the problem is enhanced by the discipline's powerful bias towards science. This bias seems to encourage a feminist psychology highly critical of science and committed to explicitly political research. 'Good', politically responsible research, that listens to what women are 'really' saying, then itself takes on the epistemological status of science, uncovering underlying truths. This feminism, broadly identifiable with the 'standpoint' approach, also often articulates an insistent social determinism (Hollway, 1994) that, contradictorily, has the effect of erasing the active subject assumed by the standpoint. Conversely, feminist constructionism in psychology interprets most phenomena – the subjectivities of women and men in violent relationships, for instance – as produced within patriarchal gender relations. But, in violation of this explanatory principle, it tends to attribute a relatively unproblematic agency to women who resist patriarchy, such as women who leave violent relationships. In this account, then, while we occupy multiple, sometimes contradictory subject positions, as soon as we take feminist action we seem to attain an essential subjecthood. This dualism has been fairly exhaustively pursued in feminist considerations of discourse analysis, which set concerns about the infinite regress involved in discourse analysis's attention to language, against a determination not to take language's meanings and ownership for granted. While, for example, these considerations do not assume that language is transparent or easily identifiable as pro- or anti-feminist, they also suggest that there is a point where researchers have to 'explain and justify the basis for their readings or analyses' (Gill, 1995: 182).

A commonly proposed antidote to these dualisms in feminist psychology is an alternation between the two positions, aptly described by Henwood and Pidgeon as a '"flip-flop" between ideas and research experience' (1995: 19). This seems an accurate description of what research should, and often does, look like, as it negotiates between theoretical positions. But the description does not engage with the continuing theoretical omission that renders the dualisms such a problem: the omission of the subject.

What feminist-psychological dualisms have in common is an inattention to the concept of the subject: through an assumption of an agentic subject in the 'standpoint' case; and through a similar assumption, or a dissolution of the subject, in the social-constructionist case. Both strategies can be problematic. The standpoint analysis assumes an Enlightenment subject, unified, rational and effective. The operation of this 'standpoint' subject becomes clearer if we think about Anna's and Bill's stories. In standpoint terms, Anna is expressing the aggression of a woman turned against other women by the separate spheres ideology, while Bill's story of irritation with his mother exemplifies how men are distanced from and hostile to women within that ideology. Implicitly, these explanations assume an originally or potentially coherent and logical human subject to which patriarchy has given a false consciousness. Through political struggle, 'we can begin to see beneath the appearances created by an unjust social order to the reality' (Harding, 1991: 127).

The feminist-constructionist account, too, does not rid itself of the epistemologically crucial subject if it simply declares the subject a construct. When, as usually happens, such accounts assume that some active and efficient feminist subjectivity is possible, the same Enlightenment subject returns, by default. From a 'strong' social-constructionist perspective, 'Anna' and 'Bill' can be explained as the intersections of specific sets of determinants – of gender, 'race', class and age, for instance. If, though, this constructionist account iso-lated the more agentic moments in the stories, like Anna knocking the ball out of the coach's hand, or Bill's semi-deliberate goading of his mother, it would be likely, again, to explain them by assuming an active, unified subjective identity, perverted into false consciousness by patriarchy.

This unregarded subject is what Wendy Hollway tries to engage with when she uses psychoanalytic concepts derived from Klein and object relations theory to map what she calls the 'psychological' space that feminist psychology needs to engage with (1994: 544; see also Henriques et al., 1984; Hollway, 1995). Without a theoretical consideration of the subject, both standpoint and constructionist feminist psychologies are fields with missing objects: in an important sense they fail to be psychologies at all. What is valuable in Hollway's project is the interest it has in the idiosyncratic history of each gendered subjectivity, in, for instance, Anna's implication of her mother in her story, or her self-conscious comments on her amnesia; or in Bill's direct and intense chronicling of his conflict with his mother. At the same time, Hollway's project is usefully general in that it does not tie gendered discourse, even feminist aspects of it, to biological sex. Anna's story of active yet ambivalent aggression can be acknowledged to be as much masculine-identified Outsider as feminine-identified Insider Gothic. Yet taking this 'psychological' approach, we need not view Anna as coopted by dominant gender relations, or strain to interpret her antipathy as a kind of protofeminist resistance.

This 'psychological' approach is not and should not try to be rigorously psychoanalytic, for brief spoken texts cannot be evidence of unconscious processes. However, they can generate helpful suppositions about such processes. In the case of Anna's and Bill's stories, and other Outsider Gothic narratives produced by the male and female interviewees, for instance, ambivalent aggression seems to relate to a more infantile kind of hostility that is hardly accessible in consciousness or narrative (see also Walkerdine and Lucy, 1989).

Conclusion: aggression as a genre

The emphasis in Hollway's work on Kleinian descriptions and how these have been developed in feminist directions by Nancy Chodorow (1989) and Jessica Benjamin (1990), makes this psychological approach relatively congenial for feminist psychologists since it says less about sexual difference than work that takes a more Freudian or Lacanian stance. Despite the advantages of Kleinian concepts for dealing with aggression, however, a problem remains in regard to the untheorized subject. The Kleinian processes discussed by Hollway (1994, 1995) for instance, at times seem separate from and subsequent to a pre-existing subject who operates them. My approach with the aggression study drew more on work within the humanities (Butler, 1993; Cornell, 1991; Mulvey, 1975) that has used other psychoanalytic concepts, again quite loosely, that keep the subject in question. Though these concepts place more stress on sexual difference's place in subjectivity, their use does not fatally compromise feminism. Moreover while the concepts tie subjectivity and its uncertainties to language, this emphasis does not lead to relativistic paralysis. A variety of 'flip-flops' like those Henwood and Pidgeon (1995) advise have been developed to resist the possibility of, for instance, a strategic, even metaphorical essentialism about the category of 'women' (Cornell, 1991: 58; Spivak, 1996). Within cultural studies, a stress on how the productivity of textual meanings is limited by conditions of consumption can check interpretive excess (Morris, 1988). Within social theory, the concept of the person as a citizen, as well as a subject, allows for a provisional agency that does not rest only on psychological assumptions (Mouffe, 1995).

In feminist psychology, an emphasis on language, though always prone to shift towards what the language means rather than staying with the language itself, remains, I think, potentially valuable as a way of keeping the subject in question. In the interview study discussed here, this focus meant taking note of small, symptomatic aspects of the narratives, like Anna's verbal fumblings and pauses; or the lexical repetitions in Bill's story that insist on a 'yelling' and 'ridiculous' mother whom Bill must 'fight', and that mirror the mother's agitation. More importantly, this interview study deployed a feminist literary analysis of genre (Ellis, 1988), a deliberate appropriation from another, language-centred discipline. Coming from literary theory, the analysis was clearly one of many possible ones, and brought with it its own polemical, explicitly feminist 'standpoint'. But that standpoint was not, as in psychology, encumbered by a quasi-scientific claim to truth. At the same time, this tactical import from literary theory helped guarantee a concentration on language, and some remove from the strong and specific presuppositions about subjectivity that are built into psychology. It turned the subjectivity of aggression into a genre: not a bad thing, when popular discourse and academic psychology alike seem assured of so much incontrovertible knowledge about how aggression feels and how it is gendered. Without the genre analysis, Anna's and Bill's narratives would have been poor, unclear, self-contradictory examples of aggression's gendering. With it, they turned into hints and foreshadows of the complexity of that gendering.

Notes

1 This misunderstanding, sometimes accidental and sometimes deliberate, seems fairly common among white people completing ethnic monitoring and affirmative action questionnaires in the United States.

2 Gilligan's (1982) work provides a general frame for understanding gendered 'voice' differences. White and Kowalski (1994) provide a relevant discussion of the methodology of gender and aggression studies.

3 Thus Harding's notion of 'strong objectivity' both involves stripping knowledge claims as far as possible of the power relations within which they are embroiled – a perfectly conventional scientific aim – and a *combination* of 'nearness and remoteness, concern and indifference' (1991: 269–70, 124). Her notion of subjective objectivity, as in a researcher being explicit and reflexive about her own involvement in the research (in Pidgeon and Henwood, 1991), seems to belong securely in the first category.

4 Harding (1991: 152ff.) remarks that charges of relativism are used to defend existing power structures, but relativism also characterizes the liberal understandings that fail to challenge those power structures (as Gayatri Spivak comments of Catherine MacKinnon's invocations of matriarchal tribal law, 1996: 251). The finessing of these issues that is achieved by describing the feminist standpoint as keen to 'include the voices of marginal groups' (Hartsock, in Harding, 1991: 182), or by saying liberatory perspectives need to 'permeate' each other, seems to me inadequate (Harding, 1991: 156).

5 While the emphasis on language's relationship to lives is important, research along these lines suggests that language's effects are complex and hard to identify (e.g. Lamb and Keon, 1995).

6 Benhabib's (1992) endorsement of a 'weak' postmodernism around agency, compatible with a Habermasian hermeneutics, seems to me close to what goes on, less carefully theorized, in most social constructionist psychology. The stronger position that sees subjectivity as a social product is sometimes adopted in a dramatic way that leads rapidly to big problems about agency. In the more theoretically nuanced work (Henriques et al., 1984) the strong position holds the polarity between agency and determinism together rather than trying to resolve or balance it, often deploying psychoanalysis to do this, in ways that parallel similar moves within feminist theory (Riley, 1988; Spivak, 1996). 'Strategic essentialism', though a good description of what goes on, has not proved really helpful theoretically. For some it still seems to underplay agency (Benhabib, 1992), for others it implies there are still agentic subjects who strategize.

7 If this question was asked during the taped interview, I responded with summarizing sentences on both sides of the issue: 'Some people think . . . But other people argue . . .'. If the question was asked during the debriefing at the end, I gave the same summaries but said that I did not think aggression was entirely or intrinsically determined by gender.

8 Outside psychology, Benhabib (1995) and Fraser (1995) serve as moderate and informed critics, while Butler (1995), Cornell (1995) and Rattansi (1995) suggest that these two, and others, are partial readers of postmodernism and poststructuralism.

References

Ang, I. (1985) *Watching Dallas: Soap Opera and the Melodramatic Imagination*. London: Methuen.

Ardener, S. (1991) *Women and Space*. London: Croom Helm.

Baumeister, R. (1988) 'Should we stop studying sex differences altogether?', *American Psychologist* 43: 1092–5.

Benhabib, S. (1992) *Situating the Self*. New York: Routledge.

Benhabib, S. (1995) 'Feminism and postmodernism: an uneasy alliance', in S. Benhabib, J. Butler, D. Cornell and N. Fraser, *Feminist Contentions*. New York: Routledge.

Benjamin, J. (1990) *The Bonds of Love*. London: Virago.

Bhavnani, K.-K. (1990) 'What's power got to do with it? Empowerment and social research', in I. Parker and J. Shotter (eds), *Deconstructing Social Psychology*. London: Routledge.

Biden, J. (1993) 'Violence against women: the Congressional response', *American Psychologist* 48: 1059–61.

Butler, J. (1993) *Bodies that Matter*. New York: Routledge.

Butler, J. (1995) 'For a careful reading', in S. Benhabib, J. Butler, D. Cornell and N. Fraser, *Feminist Contentions*. New York: Routledge.

Cameron, D. (1985) *Feminism and Linguistic Theory*. London: Macmillan.

Carroll, N. (1990) *The Philosophy of Horror*. London: Routledge.

Chodorow, N. (1989) *Feminism and Psychoanalytic Theory*. London: Yale University Press.

Clover, C. (1992) *Men, Women and Chainsaws*. Princeton, NJ: Princeton University Press.

Copjec, J. (1991) 'Vampires, breast-feeding and anxiety', *October* 58: 25–43.

Cornell, D. (1991) *Beyond Accommodation*. New York: Routledge.

Cornell, D. (1995) 'Rethinking the time of feminism', in S. Benhabib, J. Butler, D. Cornell and N. Fraser, *Feminist Contentions*. New York: Routledge.

Creed, B. (1987) 'From here to modernity: feminism and postmodernism', *Screen* 28 (2): 47–67.

Dolar, M. (1991) '"I shall be with you on your wedding night": Lacan and the uncanny', *October* 58: 5–23.

Dutton, M. (1992) *Empowering and Healing the Battered Woman*. New York: Springer.

Eagly, A. (1987) 'Reporting sex differences', *American Psychologist* 42: 756–7.

Ellis, K. (1988) *The Contested Castle: Gothic Novels and the Subversion of Domestic Ideology*. Urbana: University of Illinois Press.

Fraser, N. (1995) 'Pragmatism, feminism and the linguistic turn', in S. Benhabib, J. Butler, D. Cornell and N. Fraser, *Feminist Contentions*. New York: Routledge.

Freud, S. (1974) [1919] 'The Uncanny', *Standard Edition of the Complete Works of Sigmund Freud* (Vol. 9). London: Hogarth Press and the Institute of Psycho-Analysis.

Gill, R. (1995) 'Relativism, reflexivity and politics: interrogating discourse analysis from a feminist perspective', in S. Wilkinson and C. Kitzinger (eds), *Feminism and Discourse: Psychological Perspectives*. London: Sage.

Gilligan, C. (1982) *In a Different Voice*. Cambridge, MA: Harvard University Press.

Harding, S. (1991) *Whose Science? Whose Knowledge? Thinking from Women's Lives*. Milton Keynes: Open University Press.

Hare-Mustin, R. and Maracek, J. (1988) 'The meaning of difference: gender theory, postmodernism and psychology', *American Psychologist* 43: 355–64.

Hare-Mustin, R. and Maracek, J. (1989) 'Thinking about postmodernism and gender theory', *American Psychologist* 44: 1333–5.

Henriques, J., Hollway, W., Urwin, C., Venn, C. and Walkerdine, V. (1984) *Changing the Subject: Psychology, Social Regulation and Subjectivity*. London: Methuen.

Henwood, K. (1998) 'Feminist consciousness and complex subjectivities: a qualitative case study of adult mother–daughter relationships'. Unpublished manuscript.

Henwood, K. and Pidgeon, N. (1995) 'Remaking the link: qualitative research and feminist standpoint theory', *Feminism and Psychology* 5: 7–30.

Himes, C. (1986) [1945] *If He Hollers Let Him Go*. London: Pluto Press.

Hollway, W. (1994) 'Beyond sex differences: a project for feminist psychology', *Feminism and Psychology* 4 (4): 538–46.

Hollway, W. (1995) 'Feminist discourses and women's heterosexual desire', in S. Wilkinson and C. Kitzinger (eds), *Feminism and Discourse: Psychological Perspectives*. London: Sage.

Katz, B. and Burt, M. (1988) 'Self-blame in recovery from rape: help or hindrance?', in A. Burgess (ed.), *Rape and Sexual Assault II*. New York: Garland.

Kitzinger, C. (ed.) (1994) 'Should psychologists study sex differences?', *Feminism and Psychology* 4: 501–46.

Koss, M., Heise, L. and Russo, N. (1994) 'The global health burden of rape', *Psychology of Women Quarterly* 18: 509–37.

Kristiansen, C. and Giulietti, R. (1990) 'Perceptions of wife abuse', *Psychology of Women Quarterly* 14: 177–89.

Lamb, S. and Keon, S. (1995) 'Blaming the perpetrator', *Psychology of Women Quarterly* 19: 209–20.

Lakoff, R. (1975) *Language and Woman's Place*. New York: Harper & Row.

Morris, M. (1988) 'Banality in cultural studies', *Block* 14: 15–26.

Mouffe, C. (1995) 'Feminism, citizenship, and radical democratic politics', in L. Nicholson and S. Seidman (eds), *Social Postmodernism*. Cambridge: Cambridge University Press.

Mulvey, L. (1975) 'Visual pleasure and narrative cinema', *Screen* 16: 6–18.

Nicholson, L. (1995) 'Introduction', in S. Benhabib, J. Butler, D. Cornell and N. Fraser, *Feminist Contentions*. New York: Routledge.

Phillips, L. (1996) 'Power asymmetries in the construction of adolescent girls' experiences'. Paper presented at the International Congress of Psychology, Montreal, Canada, August.

Phoenix, A. (1991) 'Social research in the context of feminist psychology', in E. Burman (ed.), *Feminists and Psychological Practice*. London: Sage.

Pidgeon, N. and Henwood, K. (1991) 'Qualitative methods and subjectivity in psychological research'. Paper presented at the Second European Congress of Psychology, Budapest, Hungary, July.

Radcliffe, M. (1966) [1794] *The Mysteries of Udolpho*. Oxford: Oxford University Press.

Radway, J. (1984) *Reading the Romance*. Chapel Hill: University of North Carolina Press.

Rattansi, A. (1995) 'Just framing: ethnicities and racisms in a "postmodern" framework', in L. Nicholson and S. Seidman (eds), *Social Postmodernism*. Cambridge: Cambridge University Press.

Riley, D. (1988) *'Am I That Name?' Feminism and the Category of Woman.* Minneapolis: University of Minnesota Press.

Saegert, S. (1980) 'Masculine cities and feminine suburbs: polarized ideas, contradictory realities', in C. Stimpson (ed.), *Women and the American City.* Chicago: Chicago University Press.

Sarbin, T. (1986) *Narrative Psychology.* The Hague: Mouton.

Shelley, M. (1988) [1818] *Frankenstein.* London: Macdonald.

Spender, D. (1980) *Man Made Language.* London: Routledge & Kegan Paul.

Spivak, G. (1996) 'Diasporas old and new: women in the transnational world', *Textual Practice* 10 (2): 245–69.

Squire, C. (1994) 'Safety, danger and the movies: women's and men's narratives of aggression', *Feminism and Psychology* 4 (4): 547–70.

Squire, C. (1995) 'Pragmatism, extravagance and feminist discourse analysis', in S. Wilkinson and C. Kitzinger (eds), *Feminism and Discourse: Psychological Perspectives.* London: Sage.

Thorne, B., Kramerae, C. and Henley, N. (1983) *Language, Gender and Society.* New York: Harper & Row.

Tolson, A. and Jenkins, H. (1995) *Science Fiction Audiences.* New York: Routledge.

Ullman, S. and Knight, R. (1993) 'The efficacy of women's resistance strategies in rape situations', *Psychology of Women Quarterly* 17: 23–38.

Unger, R. (1992) 'Will the real sex difference please stand up?', *Feminism and Psychology* 2 (2): 231–8.

Walkerdine, V. and Lucy, H. (1989) *Democracy in the Kitchen: Regulating Mothers and Socialising Daughters.* London: Virago.

White, J. and Kowalski, R. (1994) 'Deconstructing the myth of the nonaggressive woman: a feminist analysis', *Psychology of Women Quarterly* 18: 487–508.

Widdicombe, S. (1995) 'Identity, politics and talk: a case for the mundane and the everyday', in S. Wilkinson and C. Kitzinger (eds), *Feminism and Discourse: Psychological Perspectives.* London: Sage.

Worell, J. and Etaugh, C. (1994) 'Transforming theory and research with women', *Psychology of Women Quarterly* 18: 443–50.

5

Voice and Ventriloquation in Girls' Development

Lyn Mikel Brown

Wash the white clothes on Monday and put them on the stone heap;
wash the color clothes on Tuesday and put them on the clothesline to dry
. . . don't walk barehead in the hot sun; cook pumpkin fritters in very hot
sweet oil; soak your cloths right after you take them off; when buying
cotton to make yourself a nice blouse, be sure that it doesn't have gum
on it, because that way it won't hold up well after a wash . . .

(Jamaica Kincaid, 'Girl', pp. 3–4)

From the age of three and four, sociolinguists tell us, girls tend to
shift speech style depending on whether they are talking to boys or
to other girls. Girls, Amy Sheldon (1992) suggests, are more likely
to use 'double-voiced discourse' (Bakhtin, 1981) than are boys.
Three- and four-year-old girls' conflict talk, Sheldon explains, has 'a
dual orientation in which the speaker negotiates [her] own agenda
while simultaneously orienting towards the viewpoint of [her]
partner' (Sheldon, 1992: 95). Such a capacity, she argues, is a
strength of little girls' talk and conflict negotiation, a capacity to be
assertive in the context of relationship. But Sheldon also notes the
value-laden language others use to interpret gender differences in
young girls' talk. She says: 'To say that boys are more forceful [that
is, better] persuaders hides the important work that mitigation does
to further self-assertion in the conflict process' (1992: 98).[1]
One might ask what it means that girls as young as three years
old already know that what persuades other little girls does not
persuade little boys, but like Sheldon I would argue that this
question cannot be disconnected from the ways in which girls'
discourse and actions are situated and interpreted by powerful
others. 'The word', Valentin Volosinov reminds us, is always 'a two-
sided act . . . it is determined equally by *whose* word it is and *for
whom* it is meant' (1986 [1929]: 86). Girls' thoughts and feelings,
their actions, their experiences, cannot be separated from their

audience – from the relationships that sustain and support them, or from the patriarchal lens through which they are filtered.

It is precisely this act of interpretation, of relationship between action and reaction, that I want to address in this chapter. Specifically, I explore adolescent girls' active struggle to stay with their own experiences and to create space for their own voices in the presence of alternative voices or truths held by those with the power to name, to reconfigure, their reality. I do so by considering the relationship between voice and ventriloquation – two concepts that are central to the work of Russian philosopher and literary theorist, Mikhail Bakhtin (1981, 1986; see also Day and Tappan, 1996; Holquist, 1990; Tappan, 1991; Wertsch, 1991). My aim is to initiate a dialogue between this theoretical perspective, grounded primarily in semiotic, linguistic and literary analyses, and the feminist research programme in which I have been engaged, focusing on girls' psychological development and highlighting girls' relationship with a dominant culture in which inequality and oppression are woven into the fabric of daily discourse.

The feminist research programme to which I refer is grounded in a notion of voice as a relational, discursive phenomenon – linguistically constituted, socially constructed, physically embodied and, thus, by definition, polyphonic, layered, infinitely varied, often contradictory, fragmented, and rich with intentions (Brown and Gilligan, 1991, 1992; Brown et al., 1988, 1989, 1991; Gilligan, 1982, 1990; Gilligan et al., 1990). Adopting such a perspective, I thus assume subjectivity is constructed, often unconsciously, within ongoing power relations and acknowledge power as historically, socially and personally contingent.

And yet, while I assume 'the plurality of language and the impossibility of fixing meaning once and for all', and question 'the sovereignty of subjectivity as the guarantee of meaning', hallmarks, if you will, of feminist poststructuralism (Weedon, 1987: 85–6), my research carries the tension between such a view and an appreciation of the *experience* of an authentic self to which the girls I listen to subscribe. In other words, while I acknowledge subjectivity as a process, I also acknowledge the agentic power of the felt experience or phenomenology of an integrated, conscious, more or less continuous, permanent subjectivity. Because I am concerned not only with understanding and describing what girls from different social and material locations know and say in particular social situations, but also the ways they resist or comply with normalizing views of femininity, such appreciation and documentation of this tension is necessary. It has been my experience that girls who express confidence about what they know to be true from their experiences, who feel they are genuine or true to their thoughts and feelings in particular times and places, are more likely to critique and resist norms of what it is to be a 'proper' woman.

Authenticity, in this research programme, is thus not meant to connote essentialism, but to convey girls' experiences of feeling genuine, to document those places where girls feel safe, at home with themselves and in the world. From such a subjectively powerful reference point, I follow girls to those places where they feel foreign, false and out of relationship, insecure and unsafe; I can move with them and hear their various culturally grounded understandings of femininity, note their strategies for resistance, witness their performances. Such a way of listening reveals new possibilities and contradictions, and challenges the legitimized fictions (Walkerdine, 1990) of idealized femininity.

Ventriloquating voices

Discourse about 'appropriately' – that is, culturally sanctioned – gendered behaviour interlace children's everyday experiences. Consider, for example, the following story of sexual harassment of poor and working-class seven-year-old girls in an all-white, rural Maine primary school.[2] The principal, a woman aged about 35, described the scene to me:

> [W]e had these girls go to a teacher after lunch-time and they were upset, visibly upset. And they said the boys were saying some words to them that were scaring them and they didn't like it. . . . The boys started to say, 'Well, you're my girlfriend. And I'm gonna marry you and . . . we're gonna have sex.' And . . . the little girl . . . said, 'Oh, I know you. You just want to tie us up and have sex with us.' And the little boy went on and on and pretty soon two other boys joined in, until there were . . . four boys . . . and it got pretty aggressive and real loud and pretty soon there were lots of things coming out from all the boys: 'Yeah, we're gonna have sex with you,' and 'Yeah, we're gonna rape you; we're gonna kill you.' And 'Yeah, 'cause you're our girlfriend.' And then one boy said, 'I'm gonna put an engagement ring on you 'cause that's what you do when you love someone, but I'm gonna NAIL it on 'til the blood comes out!' And another boy said, uh, 'Well, I'm gonna . . . put an ax in your head 'til blood comes out your eyes.'

Talking with the children after this incident, the principal became convinced that they did not fully understand what they were saying – didn't know, for example, what the word 'rape' meant – but were repeating things they had heard elsewhere. The one little girl who spoke back to the boys said she had overheard junior high students reading the opening scenes from Stephen King's novel, *Gerald's Game*, on the school bus. The novel begins with a man tying his wife to their bed, enacting his sexual fantasy. The boys spoke of repeating comments they'd heard on afternoon TV magazine shows like *Hard Copy* and *Current Affair*.

But while they may not have fully understood the words or comprehended the overlay of violence on female–male sexual relationships, the boys and girls evidently understood the incident at the level of feeling. The boys felt powerful using hostile language they knew would strongly affect the girls; the girls, including the more assertive child, felt uncomfortable, frightened, angry and upset.

In Bakhtin's terms, these children are engaged in the very natural process of *ventriloquation* – a process, that is, 'whereby one voice speaks *through* another voice or voice type' (Wertsch, 1991: 59). Like the ventriloquist's dummy who speaks only the words of the ventriloquist, we sometimes speak only the words of others. More often we 'appropriate' these words and make them 'our own'. Prior to this moment of appropriation, however:

> the word does not exist in a neutral and impersonal language (it is not, after all, out of a dictionary that a speaker gets his words!), but rather it exists in other people's mouths, in other people's contexts, serving other people's intentions: it is from there that one must take the word, and make it one's own. And not all words for just anyone submit easily to this appropriation, to this seizure and transformation into private property: many words stubbornly resist, others remain alien, sound foreign in the mouth of the one who appropriated them and who now speaks them; they cannot be assimilated into [her] context and fall out of it; it is as if they put themselves into quotation marks against the will of the speaker. Language is not a neutral medium that passes freely and easily into the private property of the speaker's intentions; it is populated – overpopulated – with the intentions of others. Expropriating it, forcing it to submit to one's own intentions and accents, is a difficult and complicated process. (Bakhtin, 1981: 293–4)

Others' words, language and forms of discourse enter and become part of the inner dialogue that constitutes the psyche as a result of a difficult and complicated *developmental process* that Bakhtin calls the process of 'ideological becoming' (1981: 341). 'One's own discourse', Bakhtin argues, 'is gradually and slowly wrought out of others' words that have been acknowledged and assimilated, and the boundaries between the two are at first scarcely perceptible' (1981: 345). Others' words come, quite simply, from the different speaking voices that a child hears in the context of her various social relationships and social interactions – voices engaged in the ongoing dialogue that constitutes the culture in which she lives. A child hears (and interacts with) a multitude of voices: the voice of her mother (as in the case of Kincaid's 'Girl'), her father, her grandparents, her teacher, her baby-sitter, her friends, characters and personalities on television, popular musicians, and so forth. Moreover, these voices, more often than not, represent competing points of view. Thus the process of ideological becoming, according to Bakhtin, results from an 'intense *struggle* within us for hegemony of various available and ideological points of view, approaches, directions, and values' (1981: 346).

The importance of struggling with another's discourse cannot be overestimated, argues Bakhtin, in understanding how and why a person ultimately comes to her or his own sense of 'ideological consciousness':

> One's own discourse and one's own voice, although born of another or dynamically stimulated by another, will sooner or later begin to liberate themselves from the authority of the other's discourse. This process is made more complex by the fact that a variety of alien voices enter into the struggle for influence within an individual's consciousness (just as they struggle with one another in surrounding social reality). All this creates fertile soil for experimentally objectifying another's discourse. A conversation with [another's] word that one has begun to resist may continue, but it takes on another character: it is questioned, it is put in a new situation in order to expose its weak sides, to get a feel for its boundaries. (1981: 348)

The difficult transformation of public language into private consciousness is most apparent under conditions of struggle; that is, not only when, as Bakhtin suggests, words 'stubbornly resist' appropriation, 'remain alien', 'sound foreign in the mouth of the speaker', but also when persons actively resist pressure to appropriate others' words, language and forms of discourse (Bakhtin, 1981: 294). Indeed, as I have been suggesting, issues of power are central to a critical understanding of girls' development.

At early adolescence girls speak about, struggle with, and often resist the reconstruction of their experiences (Brown and Gilligan, 1992). The boundary line between girls' experiences and others' expectations is exposed to view for a brief time as girls negotiate the pressures they feel to re-voice and re-vision their reality. For a time they seem caught between contradictory realities; living the fragmented, homeless lives of double agents. Against an increasingly simplistic and pessimistic rhetoric of psychological loss and capitulation in more popular interpretations of educational reports (AAUW, 1991, 1992) and psychological studies (e.g. Pipher, 1995), I have become interested in tracking these moments, when meaning shifts from what feels genuine or authentic, to what tastes bitter and foreign; to articulate girls' active and conscious struggle against what feels alien to their experience.

Listening to working- and middle-class girls' voices

In order to understand and interpret the meaning of a person's words one has to ask (and answer) two interrelated questions: 'Who precisely is speaking, and under what concrete circumstances?' (Bakhtin, 1981: 340.) In addition, it would seem, one must also ask: 'Who is listening and what is the nature of her relationship with the speaker – especially with respect to power?'

Responding to such questions demands a method that is responsive to the polyphonic nature of voice, the non-linear, nontransparent interplay and orchestration of feelings and thoughts, as well as sensitive to the issue of power and to the fact that 'positionality weighs heavily in what knowledge [and in what ways of knowing] comes to count as legitimate in historically specific times and places' (Lather, 1991: 116). In my attempts to understand how girls negotiate the borderline that lies between childhood and adolescence, I rely on such a method – a voice-centred 'Listener's Guide' – that illuminates my own positionality and regulatory power with respect to the girls with whom I work. The Listener's Guide offers a way to trace the movement in girls' understanding of themselves and others as they take in the words, the voices around them, 'appropriating' and resisting 'alien' viewpoints, as well as different perspectives on relationship (Brown and Gilligan, 1991, 1992; Brown et al., 1988, 1989, 1991).

Over the course of a year I videotaped two focus groups, one consisting of middle-class girls from Acadia, a mid-size city in Maine, and one consisting primarily of girls from working-class and working poor families who live in Mansfield, a small rural Maine town. The 19 girls who participated in these groups range in age from 11 to 14; all are white (see Brown, 1998). Because I planned to explore the relationships among the girls' understandings of themselves, their expressions of resistance, their views of conventional femininity and their social and material location, these girls were chosen for their outspokenness and strong opinions, and in some cases their critical perspective on and their behavioural resistance to dominant societal expectations of femininity. The groups met weekly in their state schools to discuss their feelings about themselves, their relationships with each other, their families, their teachers, and their reactions to pressures to accommodate to 'appropriate' femininity. At the end of the year I revisited these issues in individual interviews.

The Listening Guide requires one to attend to a person's narrative at least four separate times, each time listening in a different way. In this study, I listened to (and watched, in the case of the videotapes) each interview and group session five times. First, I attended to the overall shape of the dialogue or narrative and to the research relationship – that is, I considered how my own position as a white middle-class academic with a working-class childhood affected the girls' perceptions of me, our interactions, and my interpretations of their voices. During this listening, I documented my struggle to remain ever conscious of the fact that, as an observer and a narrator of these girls' lives I become, in Foucault's terms, a 'Surveillant Other', not simply listening, watching and describing 'but also producing a knowledge that feeds into the discursive practices regulating girls' voices and class consciousness' (Walkerdine, 1990: 195).[3]

The second time, through the tapes and interviews, I attended to the girls' first-person voices, to the ways they spoke for and about themselves. Since, as Anne Campbell (1987) has illustrated, much of our sense of who we are, our identity and individuality, arises from who we believe we are not, I listened also to the girls' gossip and put-downs of their peers and siblings to establish who they considered 'Other' and why. In the third 'listening' I attended to the girls' discussions of anger: what people, events or experiences provoked their anger and critique? How and to whom did they express their strong feelings? What form did their anger take? Who or what forces constrained their expressions of these strong feelings?

The final two times through the girls' conversations and interviews, and most pertinent to the present analysis, I focused on the ways the girls accommodated to and resisted conventional (i.e. white, middle-class, heterosexual) notions of femininity. More specifically, in the fourth listening I identified ventriloquized voices of conventional femininity – that is, I document the girls' expressions of voices, characteristics and qualities of feminine behaviour idealized or denigrated by the dominant culture. Such attention to cultural intentions and meanings moves one to consider who is speaking and for what purpose.

In the fifth listening I attend to the ways the girls resist such conventions of femininity; that is, I document ventriloquized voices of strength, fluidity, irreverence and creativity and explore the ways these voices interact to attenuate the pull of convention. Here class and culture, relevant throughout the various listenings, take centre stage as the voices and values of the girls' immediate communities come into conflict with those of the dominant culture, particularly as they are inculcated in the school classroom. Here also any notion of identity development as unitary or linear is called into question as the girls struggle with different voices, some clearly more publicly legitimized than others, and as they learn the power of context and audience and the necessity of performance and impersonation.

The Listener's Guide thus provides a way to elucidate the struggles these two groups of girls experience as they negotiate and contest the contradictory voices and visions vying for their attention and allegiance. Attuning to the girls' voices in this way reveals not only the 'fragmented and reactive nature of their self-definition[s]' (Campbell, 1987: 452), but also the contextual and community voices inherent in their different material and structural positions; voices that undergird their understandings of themselves and that encourage a struggle for personal integration.

Class accents

Speaking in and through patriarchy

As the Mansfield and Acadia girls discussed themselves and their relationships, talk of other girls and women emerged spontaneously and frequently. Attending to these 'others', revealed through the girls' gossip and put-downs, offers a guide to ventriloquized voices of conventional femininity; that is, to the appropriation of dominant, patriarchal understandings, definitions and categories of the feminine that the girls most fear or reject in themselves.

There is a common belief, expressed repeatedly, among the working-class girls that 'other' girls are, by nature, indirect and deceitful, that they talk behind people's backs and have a propensity for breaking confidences or telling secrets. Such girls are 'two-faced' and untrustworthy, and make private conversations public out of revenge or to seek attention. Often, the Mansfield girls complain in voices full of anger and disgust, these are the same girls who are 'stuck on themselves', 'who think they're the best', who want to be 'the centre of attention', and who 'strut around' all 'stuck-up', with 'an attitude problem'. Such girls will do anything for attention – lie, steal other girls' boyfriends – and are therefore deceitful and traitorous, perhaps two of the oldest character flaws associated with femininity.

Such associations and opinions instigate perhaps the most clear and striking examples of ventriloquation of patriarchal voices: the ways in which the Mansfield girls appropriate sexist, misogynistic and homophobic language to tease or poke fun at each other and, more pointedly, to denigrate those girls, mothers, grandmothers, aunts and women teachers whom they feel have betrayed or hurt them in some way. 'She was a bitch', Stacey says of a teacher who treated her badly the day before. Later in the same session she exclaims: 'My mother's a cheap ho!'[4] 'I called Dawn a ho', Rachel admits, explaining why she was in trouble with one of her teachers. She and her friend can't 'be together' with another girl, Susan laughingly explains, 'Not unless she's a lezzie'. Like a Greek chorus, the girls shout derogatory comments about other girls and women. Terms like ho's, bitches, lezzies, accompanied by 'Maybe it's PMS' or 'She's such a cow', and 'What a bag', assault those others the girls feel have let them down or betrayed them.

Such misogynistic terms and phrases seem funny to the girls; on the surface they are playful in a threatening sort of way; a linguistic sign of their insider status with the group, sometimes a verbal test of toughness. When asked why they say these things, they deny that such words mean anything significant. 'That's just joking around', Amber protests when asked if girls' feelings are hurt when they are called 'ho's'. The other girls interrupt each other in their eagerness to dismiss the significance of the word. 'Ho?' they shout in practised voices. 'It's a garden tool!' 'It doesn't hurt me', Angela insists. 'Everybody does that!' 'We just fool around.'

The Mansfield girls' denigration and put-downs of other girls and women signal their momentary alignment with conventional views of women and understandings of femininity. That is, they speak about girls and women in a language drenched in a patriarchal history of women's oppression. In this sense, their language or forms of expression forge an unexamined truce with the prevailing social order that polices the borders of appropriately gendered expression and activity and ultimately situates girls and women, to the degree that they express such 'feminine' qualities, in subordinate positions relative to boys and men.

Forswearing their connections to other girls and aligning or bonding with male views of femininity requires that these girls, if they are to be strong and wilful and direct, distance themselves from anything explicitly feminine. This means both vulnerability and bitchiness, but also homosexuality. By using terms like 'fag' and 'lezzie' to put down others, as they do often, the girls participate in a conventional sex/gender system that normalizes oppressive structures and categories.

Acting tough, talking trash, giving the camera the finger, pushing and pinching each other, shouts of 'Shut the hell up!' or 'He's a jerk-off!' 'She's a bitch!' invite Bakhtin's questions: 'Who precisely is speaking, and under what concrete circumstances?' Such actions and discourse distance the girls from the traditionally feminine and align them with the observed behaviour and discourse of boys and men they know. Talking about 'really cool', 'really funny' guys at a party, for example, the girls are quick to put down another girl who was, as Stacey says, 'playing hard to get. The bitch.' When the boys begin to bet on whether this girl 'would do it' with the boy she was with, some of the girls try to join in.

> *Stacey*: Yeah, he goes . . . he said . . . he told her to 'Come on, I've got five bucks riding on this!' . . . He said that to her. Cause him and Charles had a bet.
> *Rachel*: Yeah, they did. And I did too, but I didn't have enough money, so they wouldn't let me bet.
> *Stacey*: Yeah, me neither. I only had eleven cents.
> *Diane*: Well, who was betting who?
> *Stacey*: Charles and Jon. Charles won.
> *Rachel*: He's so nice. He's really cool.

In this instance the girls fully accept the boys' reading of the reluctant girl's refusal to have sex at the party – she is 'a tease' and 'a bitch' – and identify with their behaviour by trying to join in on the joke. They further align themselves with these 'cool' boys who were 'sitting there swearing in the car', bragging about who 'could kick the piss out of' who, by insisting they too, as Rachel says, 'swear all the time'.

In other instances, as they talk about sexual and physical abuse they have experienced or witnessed, the girls struggle with how to understand such experiences, see-sawing between the evidence of their own senses and identifying with the perspectives of the abusers. Donna, who has been physically assaulted by her father, talks in one session about how she learned that 'no-one deserves to be hit', and in another session rejects her father's girlfriend's accusations of rape – 'He wouldn't do that. He don't rape. He doesn't do that', she insists – even as she ventriloquates her father's justification for assault:

> Anyway, he said that . . . when she asks dad something and dad doesn't answer back . . . he's mad or something – he like walks away and she runs after him and wants an answer from him. And dad, when he gets mad he just walks off, and he wants to deal with it on his own, and she runs after him and tries to get answers and so he got mad and hit her. . . . She had a bruise right here (pointing to the side of her face), and a bruise

on her forehead and he threw her . . . and she hit the top of the door thing and broke it, broke the door.

While the working-class girls distance themselves from other girls and women on the basis of relational treachery and vulnerability read by them as signs of feminine weakness, the Acadia girls struggle with rigid categorical divisions long mapped on to white middle-class conventions of femininity, predominantly opposing good girls with bad. Good girls, nice girls, with whom they identify, are kind and considerate, selfless, they always care, listen, do not hurt others, do not get in trouble, do not express anger directly or publicly, they don't cause scenes, are well behaved, do not feel or at least express sexual desire and are not sexually active. Nice girls try to meet others' expectations, do well in school, are involved in various activities, don't brag or call attention to themselves.

Bad girls, on the other hand, those the Acadia girls talk about and distance themselves from, are obsessed with appearing physically beautiful, but are not too smart or at least don't reveal they are smart; they are false and superficial; they act and speak in ways that garner male attention; some are sluts who wear tight, provocative clothes or act in sexual ways to please boys; such girls are promiscuous, out of control, make gross comments, throw themselves at boys. Bad girls speak too much or too loudly, they are obnoxious, sharp, shrewd, controlling, in-your-face types, who bully, push, or intimidate other girls. They are girls who brag about their accomplishments or who are simply too aggressive.

There is little space between these carefully constructed and policed categories for the Acadia girls to imagine or envision themselves as complicated, whole, interesting young women. They are always in danger, it seems, of being misunderstood, their behaviours and motivations misinterpreted: in wanting to be noticed for their accomplishments they risk being seen as selfish or too self-invested; in expressing their strong opinions they risk being viewed as aggressive, a bitch, or worse, an angry feminist.

While the Mansfield girls appropriate misogynistic language to ridicule each other and distance themselves from other girls and things feminine, the Acadia girls appropriate historically weighted conceptions of girls and women as superficial, false and trite, and speak through these conceptions to denigrate other girls. In twelve-year-old Robin's terms such other girls are 'mindless airheads', always 'hee, hee, heeing', or, as Lydia says, they are 'whiners' and 'complainers' always expecting to be the centre of attention, or they are deceitful backstabbers who constantly whisper and conspire against each other, especially when there is a possibility of advancing their social standing. Against these 'feminine' qualities, the girls admire and identify with historically masculine characteristics such as independence and autonomy, rationality, creativity, intelligence and cleverness. And yet they struggle a good deal with the fact that these qualities, when embodied by 'nice' girls, have a different resonance, are less visible or recognizable, are invested with less power, are likely to be misread. Here they are caught in a bind. Good girls do not demand things, certainly not recognizability and privilege, earned or not. And yet their longing to break out, to claim their space, is palpable. 'Boys', Jane explains, are 'supposed to be more outgoing and they're supposed to be brighter. . . . So far, I would like to be outgoing sometimes, because boys who are outgoing get their way. . . . It might be nice', she adds, 'to just . . . let it go.'

The Acadia girls thus struggle a good deal with the contradictory relationship between the white middle-class feminine voices they take in, voices that are always nice and self-deprecating, and the radical individualism, the demanding, competitive characteristics they admire that seem to serve the boys so well. Speaking through such conventionally masculine characteristics, they also, by association, denigrate opposing, feminine qualities as mindless, weak and superficial. I want to suggest that distancing themselves from girls who, they say, are obsessed with appearance and their bodies, who are stupid, deceitful and fake signifies the Acadia girls' ventriloquation of such a gendered polarity.

As these adolescent girls, working- and middle-class, move into the culture, struggle 'to make the language of others [their] own', they confront the voices and definitions and accents of femininity and masculinity historically legitimized and sanctioned by the dominant culture. Their acceptance of the dichotomization of gender, admiration of 'masculine' characteristics and distance from more 'feminine' qualities, their misogynistic and homophobic language all signal their gradual appropriation of these voices and accents; a sign they are trying on pre-existing definitions and categories. Labelling other girls naturally deceitful, needy of attention, shallow, false or traitorous, I want to argue, are examples of girls' experiences and observations sifted through a white middle-class masculinized culture. By disconnecting the girls from other girls and women, and thus from themselves, such a discourse serves to reconfigure and depoliticize the anxiety they feel in the face of their own abuse, betrayal or self-interest. The justified fear of those in subordinate positions who depend on loyalty and know the dangers of division or abandonment, is thus buried beneath such an explanatory framework.

Renegade voices

The Acadia and Mansfield girls' ideological struggles reveal the complex relationships between discourse and power, language and domination. They also reveal, what bell hooks (1994) calls the possibility of 'outlawed tongues, renegade speech'.

> Like desire, language disrupts, refuses to be contained within boundaries. It speaks itself against our will, in words and thoughts that intrude, even violate the most private spaces of mind and body. . . . Words impose themselves, take root in our memory against our will. (hooks, 1994: 167)

The Mansfield girls find strength in the renegade voices and outlawed tongues of those who refuse to be narrowly contained in or made invisible by the language and categories and expectations of conventional white middle-class femininity. These working-class girls convey their parents' mistrust of and irreverence for authority derived solely from material wealth or status, reiterate their parents' stubborn refusal to be dismissed, their predilection for expressing strong opinions openly. Her courage to speak out and criticize the way the school is run and the values it espouses, Susan says, for example, 'comes from my parents. They always taught me if I had something to say, just say it.'

Echoing their parents and other adults in their community, the Mansfield girls resist the white middle-class notions of femininity espoused at their school. Speaking through their fathers and mothers, many of whom work more than one part-time job, the girls talk of the practical necessity of hard work and their willingness to do menial jobs and endure long hours of physical labour to achieve their dreams of having enough. Qualities fostered at home such as toughness, boldness, straightforward expressions of thought and feeling which often label them as difficult and disruptive at school, connect them with each other, their families and their community. Such qualities and behaviours hold different meanings and intentions. Reprimands from teachers and administrators for such behaviour, in turn, invite open critique and anger from their parents. Dana's mother is notorious at the Mansfield school for her support of her children's right to protect themselves physically or to fight for a just cause, for example, and has been to the school a number of times in Dana's defence. Dana and the other girls openly admire her for such physical and psychological toughness, qualities Dana, in particular, imitates.

In fact, Dana's pride in and love for her mother become apparent as she ventriloquates her mother's belief in self-protection and the defence of those weaker or less powerful, and enacts her devotion to her family, their sense of humour, and their beliefs about what it

means to be a woman. For the Mansfield girls, other women too –
aunts, cousins, friends – embody and give voice to the possibility
for an economically successful, healthy, self-propelled, contented life
against the dire predictions they read in many of their teachers'
faces and reactions.

So, too, over the course of the year, does a woman teacher, Diane
Starr, provide a language and course of action for the girls to resist
unfair school practices they encounter. The girls take in Diane's
bold commitment to them, a commitment which interrupts the
prevailing discourse in the school about themselves as difficult,
'stupid', with 'dim' futures, and complicates also the girls' too
simplistic descriptions of all teachers and all administrators as
uncaring, unpredictable and unjust. Channelling the girls' strong
feelings and opinions into constructive avenues, Diane facilitates
what becomes a formidable group of resisters over the course of the
year.

Renegade voices from diverse sources thus enter and take root in
the Mansfield girls' minds and bodies. Their over-sized T-shirts and
baggy shorts, their slang – references to each other as 'ho's' and
'bitches' – read negatively in one light, and also loosely identify
them with the sexuality, boldness, resistance and the marginalization
of the black rappers they listen to and watch on MTV, particularly
their favourites, Salt n' Pepa. Within strictly heterosexual para-
meters, these white girls play on and reappropriate the particular
sexualized audacity of Salt n' Pepa, as well as more general
stereotypes of black women as sexy and dangerous. Taken in and
taken on by these white working-class girls, such voices, gestures
and ways of dressing become highly contradictory, heightening their
resistance to white upper-middle-class feminine ideals of niceness
and sexual purity, as well as their tension with the relentless
expressions of material abundance relayed through television –
particularly the MTV shows the girls watch, such as 'The Real
World', 'House of Style' and the popular but short-lived 'My So
Called Life'.[5] Such tensions and contradictions among voices and
viewpoints open the Mansfield girls to an indeterminacy of meaning,
to creative possibilities, alternative values, feelings and thoughts,
and also give voice to longings and desires that contrast sharply
with their material realities.

The Mansfield girls occupy that liminal space between childhood
and adulthood where intentions are questioned, meanings are
indeterminate. In their struggles for personal truth and self-
definition, in their desires to make the different voices they hear and
take in coherent and understandable, to make them their own, they
ferret out, expose and wrestle with the contradictions, the

limitations, the hypocrisies in their lives. In their anger, expressed throughout their interviews and group sessions, they react stubbornly to the constraints white middle-class femininity, indeed, the traditional category 'girl' or 'woman', places on their personhoods, and to the frustrations they experience as they search for words to describe their difference, to speak what they know and who they might become.

There is, in this struggle, the possibility of an opening, of creative alternatives; the possibility that the languages they inherit and voice can be 'possessed, taken, claimed as a space of resistance'. Within the comfort and intimacy of their group sessions, for example, such alternatives to the dominant discourse emerge in the way the Mansfield girls interrupt conventional meanings and definitions of femininity, or playfully reappropriate such words as 'slut' or 'ho', and also in the way they collectively question their middle-class women teachers' interpretations of their experiences and behaviours.

But these girls struggle to know and trust these openings when they are in the public arena of school, where it seems always necessary to translate their teachers' commands and expectations to their lived experiences, and where their potentially creative moves, born of the interface of two disparate and sometimes contradictory realities, risk misunderstandings and confusion. And, too, their distrust of their teachers and the lessons, the language and behaviours promoted in school sits uncomfortably beside their desire for adult love and approval and for the future successes such lessons, well learned, promise. Against such contradictions the Mansfield girls publicly voice their anger and frustration, distancing their teachers from the intimate group space that is creatively their own.

The Acadia girls, too, occupy this liminal reality; they too struggle with and against the gendered boundaries pressing upon them. But unlike the Mansfield girls, they embrace their education as the medium for refusal and resistance. The ease with which they play within and manipulate the conventions of language speaks to their comfort with, indeed their pleasure in, the privileged middle-class world of school they occupy. Experiencing the limits of 'appropriate' speech and behaviour, they create new unofficial ways of expressing themselves and their reactions. Robin, for example, introduces new words, as yet unpopulated with the intentions and meanings of the dominant culture, as a way to express her strong feelings and to carve out room for those pieces of her experience unfit for the public world of her classroom: 'Teachers would be horrified by my opinions', she says, 'they are very descriptive and colorful – even purple'. 'Purple', to Robin and her friends means:

It's kind of really open. It's really flat out kind of sleazy. You know, not something too many people would like to hear . . . colorful in a way. I mean it definitely gets attention, but sometimes negative attention. A lot of times people don't want to hear it. It might offend somebody . . . I have a lot of fun with the guys that would say really nasty stuff, and I'll make some smart little retort. . . . And it's like 'ROBIN O'BRIAN!' If you can talk like that, so can I!

Robin's 'purple' language allows her to play with, to have 'fun' with, the passions she feels, to interrupt notions of her as a nice, sweet white middle-class girl. Using this language to shock the boys – especially to claim her right to out-'nasty' the 'guys' – disturbs the boundaries of 'normal' gendered expression. In doing so, she claims a new space; her intent, it seems, is less to be like the boys than to be unlike the girl others imagine her to be.

Both groups of girls know the power of words to affect their teachers and their peers. But while the Mansfield girls appropriate socially unacceptable terms and endow them with their own meaning, the Acadia girls create new words. And while the Mansfield girls speak a 'double voiced discourse', simultaneously assuring a level of intimacy and trust with their friends and keeping their teachers at a distance, they often do so loudly and directly. The Acadia girls, on the other hand, tend to cultivate their creative language and shocking personas among themselves, in the active underground.

While Robin does not bring her strong feelings or 'purple' language into the public world of the school, her subterranean expressions hold a place for another identity, for another Robin. And anger, although not often seen above ground, is critical to such disruption of the ideal, to such possession and reclamation. Throughout her interview, Robin's anger is focused; her feelings intense. Anger is a justified emotion that permeates her life: 'I express [anger] in my writing and in my art and stuff like that. And in my general personality', she says. 'I mean I express a lot of anger at society and everything because a lot of this is – a lot of what makes me mad is a society that ideals (sic) the perfect woman. It really makes me mad.'

For Robin and her classmates, white middle-class girls living in a postmodern world, the picture of what the good life for a woman consists of is no longer certain, no longer a given that over deter-mines their life-course. While such indeterminacy creates situations where these girls find themselves moving between categories and, as Robin says, 're-evaluating all my roles and what I was thinking', their anger serves as a kind of touchstone, a sign that something is wrong or off in the relational surround (Gilligan, 1990: 527). While

Robin is sometimes shaken by the intensity of others' reactions to her 'difference', for example, her anger moves her to question, to respond, and to judge others' attempts to define her in ever narrower terms.

As with the other Acadia girls, much of Robin's anger is directed at expectations that she will meet dominant middle-class fictions about femininity; much of her resistance is against being regulated and constrained by these fictions. In these moments of struggle, Robin calls on other voices, 'outlawed tongues' that have 'taken root in her memory': the voices of her mother, who sometimes 'thinks I'm too opinionated', but who nonetheless listens to and supports Robin, allows her daughter's 'weirdness' – her dyed hair, unusual dress, her 'multiple personalities' and 'imaginary friends' ('It helps with acting and everything', she insists); the voices from the different cultures she travelled to when her mother was married to a military man; the voice of her anti-establishment uncle, who's 'really, really funny', who 'paints', and who defends her actions to her parents when she wanders too far off the beaten path. Against the conformist voices of many of her classmates, the 'wannabes' and the 'posers', Robin hangs on the margins with her friends and listens to the 'unusual music' of Prince, John Lennon and Kurt Cobain; against boys' desires that she be appropriately submissive and attentive, she draws from 'tough women' like Janice Joplin and Courtney Love: 'She's a very strong person. She's very talented, you know. She hasn't free-loaded off her [late] husband's fame or anything; she's just a strong person.' Against the constraints of 'nice and feminine' voices, she draws from the bolder images of MTV and voices from magazines like *Skateboarder 90*, where, she says, she picks up 'good views of the world', views that are 'insightful' and 'candid'. She listens to the voices of friends who, like her, claim their difference, and to the older actors in the city theatre group to which she belongs. And she listens eagerly to the outlaw voice of a woman teacher who is funny and eccentric, sometimes embarrassingly original, but 'cool', who 'doesn't lie to us. She tells us the truth.'

Like Robin, the other middle-class girls play with, appropriate, resist and adapt to their own intentions, a language constructed to serve the interests of more powerful others. In their certainty of social place and simple ease of movement they underscore their privilege, for such successful play and manipulation necessitates an insider's understanding of the rules of the game. Their creative, often indirect, resistance too, hints at their astute observations and understanding of the thin line between what is appropriate and acceptable and what is out of bounds.

In some cases, as Robin illustrates, being a girl who speaks like a boy itself creates new accents and possibilities, but more often these girls delight in disturbing expectations and meanings: they look words up in the dictionary, question their semantic and expressive intentions, break down or reconfigure their original meanings until, in their transformed context, they mean nothing at all. During a conversation about the names popular boys call them, for example, Jane jumps up and grabs the dictionary to look up the word 'skid', a derogatory appellation aimed at the less than popular kids. The definition causes her to shriek with laughter:

Theresa: Is it funny?
Jane: Kind of, in the way that they use it. It's a log or plank for
             supporting something above ground (everyone is laughing). . . .
             Any device that slows up or retards movement . . . or the act
             of skidding, slide . . .
Lydia: We can tell them, 'Oh, you mean a plank?'
Jane: 'You're calling me a sad plank?'
Lydia: 'You're calling me a sad sliding movement?'

Subverting language with language, outwitting the popular kids at their own game, the Acadia girls signify their cultural and class privilege through their expressed power to more 'appropriately' or 'correctly' interpret and also, then, to undermine social conventions. Subverting power from the 'inside', they are backed by their families, friends, and at least some of their teachers. Their greater fluency in the meanings and terms of white middle-class experience allows them to play with, manipulate, laughingly reject the very language that would define and contain them.

In this way the Acadia girls question and resist expectations and understandings of what it means to be a girl, engage in an active struggle to be 'ourselves' against categorical entrapments and assumptions. 'I don't want to be just like anyone', Kirstin insists. 'I want to be myself.' She knows this struggle to 'mean it' brings her into conflict with 'people who have a hard time dealing with changes', who 'have a grudge against women having power . . . because when they were young women were lower and they've just remembered that way'.

Thus, against different expectations and pressures and in quite different ways, the Mansfield and Acadia girls create space in language and culture for their expression of thoughts and feelings and for alternative versions of themselves. Experiences of struggle, ambiguity and contradiction reveal the differing voices and identities these girls try on and sometimes embrace on the way to their own ideological becoming. Their ability to play and experiment allows for movement between categories of girl and woman and their perceptiveness, as well as their anger and resistance and desire for personal space and self-protection, motivates them to shift about, to experiment, to resist and, at times, to mirror what others desire and want from them. Whatever else these girls are, they are not deluded by, passive to, or easily indoctrinated with cultural prescriptions. On the contrary, their responses to the pressures they feel and the expectations they encounter from different people and in different contexts give their lives the feel of creative, active performance.

Conclusion

Listening to these working- and middle-class girls in this way raises profound questions about what happens when the words of others carry the force of the dominant culture, of cultural prescription. What is the effect of legitimized, privileged, or valorized discourses, of controlling categories or normative behaviours, on the development of persons who live on the margins, who stand outside the dominant cultural frameworks of white, middle-class, heterosexual and male? How do those on the margins resist, retain voice, engage in genuine, mutual dialogue where they have the possibility of being heard, much less of defining and redefining the language and assumptions of the *status quo*?

The process of ventriloquation, as I have argued, is by no means simple or fluid – girls often valiantly struggle against and resist appropriation. Moreover, as the Mansfield and Acadia girls evidence, social, cultural and material location have profound effects on what voices, fictions and fantasies of femininity are ventriloquized and they provide a sense of how different, often contradictory, voices interact to affect girls' feelings about themselves, their interactions with other girls and women, and their resistance to social separations and internal divisions.

Ventriloquation can be 'a powerful strategy of silencing, of speaking on behalf of another, of disrupting the boundaries of a propertied utterance', argues Elizabeth Harvey (1992: 142), and has long been used in patriarchal culture to mute or shape feminine speaking by calling into question the gender of the voice that speaks and the power (or lack of power) a given voice therefore possesses. Women and girls who speak through male voices do so in part to appropriate the power these voices have in the world, and yet the voices they speak carry with them the marginalization of the feminine and the attenuation of female power, both personal and political. Such ventriloquation of conventionally feminine voices thus unwittingly reflects and contributes to a larger cultural silencing of women.

And yet while ventriloquation can be a powerful strategy of silencing, it can also be a strategy and process of creation, holding within it the possibilities of disruption, infiltration, the potential to interrogate and contest conventional categories and frameworks, offering up new discourse and language. Such creativity is evident in the subtle forms and strategies of resistance the Mansfield and Acadia girls employ in the face of pressures to not speak; the ways they play with, in and around the boundaries of appropriate expression to interrupt and disrupt the social construction of gendered reality and to invent spaces and possibilities for themselves. Such resistance and refusal does not deny the power of dominant cultural expectations and expressions of white middle-class femininity on the Acadia and Mansfield girls' sense of themselves. On the contrary. But it does give back to girls the power of their *response*, the deep feeling, the frustration and anger, the cleverness, the potential for a different outcome that is rightfully theirs.

But if girls struggle so, what keeps this definition of the proper in place and why is it so difficult to resist? As Foucault reminds us, 'What makes power hold good, what makes it accepted, is simply the fact that it doesn't only weigh on us as a force that says no, but that it traverses and produces things, it induces pleasure, forms knowledge, produces discourse' (1980: 119). Certainly the costs of refusing conventional femininity – the hostility, ostracism, ridicule, even violence – as well as the rewards – acceptance and love, a seamless move into the dominant culture, good grades, promises of security and safety – entice girls to take in, to ventriloquate, to psychologically embrace such notions of the ideal. In this sense one might ask whether femininity might best be construed, in Valerie Walkerdine's terms, as 'a defense against the frightening possibility of stepping over the gender divide?' (1990: 143). Do girls and women assert and reassert such idealized images for fear that they are not true? Does the paranoia of the powerful and the anxiety of the powerless keep such truths in circulation? Or do girls use the construction of 'proper' femininity as a protective cover for their power, a way to safe-guard 'a different set of desires and organization of pleasures from those which can either clearly be articulated at the moment or are sanctioned' by such legitimized fictions? (Walkerdine, 1990: 144).

'Where the notion of "proper" operates, it is always and only improperly installed as the effect of a compulsory system', Butler

(1991: 21) argues. Femaleness is voiced and mimed throughout girls' lives, but as girls move into the dominant culture, the conventional gender/sex system and its intimate connection to idealized femininity becomes heightened, narrowed, more regulated and controlled. Girls to varying degrees conscious and unconscious of such control and regulation, react – comply and resist. How they experience such attempts at socialization and also how they respond depends on where they are positioned *vis-à-vis* the dominant culture and also on the competing and contradictory voices and experiences they take in.

The edge of adolescence thus constitutes a key developmental and political moment in girls' lives, a critical period if you will, for possibility and potential. Girls' struggles with the push and pull of often contradictory, fragmented voices telling them who, as young women, they are or should be, provide an opening, a juncture in the life cycle where the incongruity between the personal or experiential and the 'externally authoritative' (Bakhtin, 1981) comes into focus and where the processes of ideological becoming are salient and pronounced. In their struggle with varying conceptions of what it means to be female, adolescent girls destabilize the categories of girl and woman, revealing them to be what Judith Butler (1991) calls 'structures of impersonation', exposing the fact that gender is performative, a construct, 'a kind of imitation for which there is no original', a phantasmatic idealization of what a woman is supposed to be in a given culture (1991: 21). In their resistance to increased attempts to regulate or train their voices and actions, girls at this developmental juncture call attention in different ways to this idealization, and to the demands and costs of female impersonation. Their strong feelings and their questions are disruptive of the way things 'naturally' go and anxiety-provoking for those who like such things the way they are.

Notes

I would like to thank the editors, Chris Griffin, Karen Henwood and Ann Phoenix, for their very helpful comments and suggestions. A special thank you to Betty Sasaki for her wise counsel.

1 Brackets are mine.
2 I conducted this study with Mark Tappan at the request of the school principal who was concerned about the students and how they were making sense of this incident. We observed the children over the course of a week and interviewed each individually, along with a number of their classmates, about a range of topics.
3 Such vigilance to power relations meant early adjustments to my research plan. For example, while I identified with the working-class girls' experiences and

knowledge – their mistrust of authorities, their forms of resistance – I had to acknowledge, with a good deal of disappointment, that they perceived me primarily as a middle-class academic and that this perception produced particular performances for my benefit, even as it silenced certain patterns of interaction. 'No amount of humanistic seeking', to quote Walkerdine, would move these working-class girls to 'see in me a . . . girl "like them"' (1990: 196). As a result, I gave over the facilitation of this group to Diane Starr, a teacher's assistant that the girls knew and trusted. I also identified with the middle-class girls' efforts to be seen and heard and their struggle to integrate limiting constructions of femininity with their new-found language of autonomy and individuality. Unlike the working-class group, however, these girls perceived me to be more like them. While the relationships we forged were often easier in this sense, with these girls I struggled to make conscious my own judgements of their privileged girlhoods (quite different from mine) and their unqualified faith in the workings of a system designed in many ways to benefit them and those like them. I attempted to track these feelings and struggles in my documentation of the first listening.

4   'Ho' is an idiomatic reference to 'whore' that the working-class girls have appropriated from popular Black rap music they listen to. It is a term that has its own popular cultural manifestations within this music genre – a genre still considered, like the working-class girls, somewhat marginal and problematic within dominant white middle-class culture. The term is polyvalent to the girls, and their use of it depends on the person they are talking about, the situation and the audience. While their use of 'ho' is not fully disconnected from its popular cultural meanings, it has its own power and significance within their group and community. The girls appropriate its misogynistic overtones when they use the term as a form of threat or to denigrate other girls and women they dislike. (In other words, the girls use 'ho' much the way Sue Lees (1993) describes boys' use of the term 'slag'. Thus, in these moments, they speak through or ventriloquate male voices.). The term is also used playfully, however, and can serve as a linguistic marker of intimacy; i.e., a word whose layers of meaning are understood by only the initiated (hence their response to Diane Starr, the adult group facilitator, when she queries them about the term: 'Hoe? It doesn't mean anything. It's just a garden tool.') 'Ho' can also be used to threaten those who have been disloyal to the group or may indicate the girls' rejection of someone who has, in some way, challenged their understanding of what is appropriate treatment of those in the group or of appropriate behaviour for girls like them. Hence the term is drenched in intentions, some parodic and some subversive.

5   This show is a favourite of the girls. Because MTV in the USA continuously re-runs the episodes, the girls know each episode nearly by heart.

References

American Association of University Women (1991) *Shortchanging Girls, Short-changing America*. Washington, DC: AAUW Educational Foundation.
American Association of University Women (1992) *How Schools Shortchange Girls*. Washington, DC: AAUW Educational Foundation.
Bakhtin, M. (1981) *The Dialogic Imagination* (M. Holquist, ed., C. Emerson and M. Holquist, trans.). Austin: University of Texas Press.
Bakhtin, M. (1986) *Speech Genres and Other Late Essays* (C. Emerson and M. Holquist, eds, V. McGee, trans.). Austin: University of Texas Press.

Brown, L.M. (1998) *Raising Their Voices: The Politics of Girls' Anger*. Cambridge, MA: Harvard University Press.

Brown, L.M. and Gilligan, C. (1991) 'Listening for voice in narratives of relationship', in M. Tappan and M. Packer (eds), *Narrative and Storytelling: Implications for Understanding Moral Development* (New Directions for Child Development, No. 54). San Francisco: Jossey-Bass.

Brown, L.M. and Gilligan, C. (1992) *Meeting at the Crossroads: Women's Psychology and Girls' Development*. Cambridge, MA: Harvard University Press.

Brown, L.M., Argyris, D., Attanucci, J., Bardige, B., Gilligan, C., Johnston, K., Miller, B., Osborne, R., Tappan, M., Ward, J., Wiggins, G. and Wilcox, D. (1988) *A Guide to Reading Narratives of Conflict and Choice for Self and Relational Voice* (Monograph No. 1). Cambridge, MA: Project on the Psychology of Women and the Development of Girls, Harvard Graduate School of Education.

Brown, L.M., Debold, E., Tappan, M. and Gilligan, C. (1991) 'Reading narratives of conflict and choice for self and moral voice: a relational method', in W. Kurtines and J. Gewirtz (eds), *Handbook of Moral Behavior and Development: Theory, Research and Application*. Hillsdale, NJ: Lawrence Erlbaum.

Brown, L.M., Tappan, M., Gilligan, C., Miller, B. and Argyris, D. (1989) 'Reading for self and moral voice: a method for interpreting narratives of real-life moral conflict and choice', in M. Packer and R. Addison (eds), *Entering the Circle: Hermeneutic Investigation in Psychology*. Albany: State University of New York Press.

Butler, J. (1991) 'Imitation and gender insubordination', in D. Fuss (ed.), *Inside/out: Lesbian Theories, Gay Theories*. New York: Routledge.

Campbell, A. (1987) 'Self-definition by rejection: the case of gang girls', *Social Problems* 34 (5): 451–66.

Day, J. and Tappan, M. (1996) 'The narrative approach to moral development: from the epistemic subject to dialogical selves', *Human Development* 39: 67–82.

Foucault, M. (1980) *Power/Knowledge: Selected Interviews and Other Writings, 1972–1977* (C. Gordon, ed., C. Gordon, L. Marshall, J. Mepham and K. Soper, trans.). New York: Pantheon.

Gilligan, C. (1982) *In a Different Voice*. Cambridge, MA: Harvard University Press.

Gilligan, C. (1990) 'Joining the resistance: psychology, politics, girls, and women', *Michigan Quarterly Review* 29: 501–36.

Gilligan, C., Brown, L.M. and Rogers, A. (1990) 'Psyche embedded: a place for body relationships and culture in personality theory', in A. Rabin, R. Zucker, R. Emmons, and S. Frank (eds), *Studying Persons and Lives*. New York: Springer.

Harvey, E. (1992) *Ventriloquized Voices*. New York: Routledge.

Holquist, M. (1990) *Dialogism: Bakhtin and His World*. London: Routledge.

hooks, b. (1994) *Teaching to Transgress*. New York: Routledge.

Kincaid, J. (1983) *At the Bottom of the River*. New York: Farrar, Straus & Giroux.

Lather, P. (1991) *Getting Smart: Feminist Research and Pedagogy with/in the Postmodern*. New York: Routledge.

Lees, S. (1993) *Sugar and Spice: Sexuality and Adolescent Girls*. Harmondsworth: Penguin.

Pipher, M. (1995) *Reviving Ophelia*. New York: Ballantine.

Sheldon, A. (1992) 'Conflict talk: sociolinguistic challenges to self-assertion and how young girls meet them', *Merrill-Palmer Quarterly* 38: 95–117.

Tappan, M. (1991) 'Narrative, authorship, and the development of moral authority', in M. Tappan and M. Packer (eds), *Narrative Approaches to Moral Development*. San Francisco: Jossey-Bass.

Volosinov, V. (1986) [1929] *Marxism and the Philosophy of Language* (L. Matejka and I. Titunik, trans.). Cambridge, MA: Harvard University Press.

Walkerdine, V. (1990) *Schoolgirl Fictions*. London: Verso.

Weedon, C. (1987) *Feminist Practice and Poststructuralist Theory*. Oxford: Basil Blackwell.

Wertsch, J. (1991) *Voices of the Mind*. Cambridge, MA: Harvard University Press.

6

Researching Marginalized Standpoints: Some Tensions around Plural Standpoints and Diverse 'Experiences'

Harriette Marshall, Anne Woollett and Neelam Dosanjh

In this chapter we draw on feminist standpoint theory and post-structuralism to discuss research in which we have been involved on childbirth, motherhood and childcare in the multi-ethnic context of East London. We take a poststructuralist view of language as fully implicated in the construction of experience and outline the uses of discourse analysis in challenging dominant discourses of motherhood in 'professional' texts. A poststructuralist perspective on experience as neither fixed nor unified poses the question *how* to put into practice feminist standpoint stipulations to work from marginalized 'experiences'. We discuss some conceptual and political tensions with the notion of 'diversity of experience' in relation to our research with 'Asian' women in the course of considering how to disrupt dominant psychological and health construals of parenting, as well as how to transform oppressive psychological and health care 'advice' offered to mothers. In tackling these tensions between utilizing poststructuralist challenges while retaining a political agenda, we align ourselves with other feminist researchers who have argued for a 'feminist politics of articulation' (Wetherell, 1995:14; see also Wetherell and Edley in this volume). We reflect on the ways in which our standpoints as researchers were/are centrally implicated in the representation of the 'experiences' of our research participants. In this respect we resist the claims of some feminist standpoint theorists to having privileged access to *real* social reality.

The research project

Our research had three focal points; the accounts of motherhood and childcare in (i) 'professional' texts, (ii) Asian women and (iii) health carers. The project had a number of starting points, one being that an interest in motherhood and mothering had not been central to a psychological agenda until the late 1980s. Developmental psychology had focused attention on mothers largely as caregivers and on their relationships and interactions with their children. The growth of feminist critiques from the late 1970s turned attention to the mother in her own right and opened up a concern with issues relating to the identity of women as mothers as well as to women's feelings and views on childbirth and childcare (Chodorow, 1978; Eichenbaum and Orbach, 1985; Oakley, 1981; Phoenix et al., 1991). This shift in focus is slowly making its mark on a psychological agenda.

Our research topic has been positioned within psychology but also in health research. Traditionally health and ethnicity have been linked around 'problems' of 'ethnic minorities' *vis-à-vis* health. In post-Thatcher Britain discussions around the provision of 'professionalized' health care which is 'user friendly' take centre stage. This has led to some concern for the experiences of women as consumers, including women from ethnic minority communities. As we were hoping to 'make a difference' in both camps, our research could be seen as part of a wider feminist agenda of pointing to women's ideas and needs as different or in conflict with those of medical staff (Oakley, 1981, 1993).

These academic and political interests can be viewed in relation to wider socio-cultural changes whereby in Western societies there has been a growing professionalization of motherhood and childcare. The practice of health care professionals has a key impact on most families. The academic psychological literature is sometimes used to inform decisions about health care practice and treatment offered to mothers. At the same time there has been an increase in mass media interest in pregnancy, baby care and parenting with popularized manuals, videos and leaflets written and produced by various 'experts', often journalists but also doctors, health professionals and psychologists. This offers advice on 'equipment you'll need' and 'emotional preparation for parenthood' through to 'helping children to be sociable and popular' (Spock, 1988). This material is widely available, some is distributed in ante-natal clinics, and it is consulted and read by a large number of mothers. The texts which formed the basis for our first research focus included childcare and parenting manuals and leaflets produced by the then Health Education Council (now Authority).

The second research focus was concerned with 'viewing' motherhood and parenting from the perspective of women's lived experiences as mothers. We carried out 32 in-depth interviews with women of South East 'Asian' origin living in East London, comprising in the main South East Asian peoples who migrated to London from the Indian subcontinent during the 1950s and some women who came from East Africa in the early 1970s as ex-colonial subjects (Bhachu, 1985; Clarke et al., 1990). They are located in a poor area of inner London where they faced and face high levels of unemployment, poor housing and education. At the time of interview 13 women who participated in this study had lived in Britain all their lives, four had been resident for over ten years and the remaining 15 had arrived in Britain as adults and resided in the UK between one and ten years. The interviews were broad based in scope and included questions about pregnancy, childbirth and hospital care, post-natal depression, the transition to motherhood, parenting and childcare. A further 43 shorter interviews were carried out with non-Asian women in hospital ante-natal clinics as they waited for their appointments. For the third research focus on health professionals, we interviewed 15 midwives and health visitors, mainly white but also from a variety of ethnic communities working in East London, primarily about their ideas regarding the changing nature of their work and about 'good practice'. We located their accounts in relation to the emphasis in contemporary British health policy on the implementation of 'individualized care' and 'culturally sensitive care' as constitutive of good practice (Dobson, 1988; Horne, 1988). In a number of publications we have juxtaposed the accounts from the Asian women with health care policy and practice.

Analysis of professional advice to parents

The poststructuralist interests in subjectivity, language, social organization and power were implicit in the first research focus on professional accounts. These analyses are presented in detail elsewhere (Marshall, 1991; Woollett and Marshall, 1997). In line with poststructuralist theories of language we have explicitly utilized a discourse analytic approach which stresses language as constructive and implicated in the maintenance of power relations (Burman, 1990; Gavey, 1989; Malson and Ussher, 1996; Weedon, 1987).

So, for example, in these analyses we have pointed to the rhetoric used in bolstering the advice offered by the experts over the accounts of 'old wives'. We have detailed the particularity of constructions of women as mothers, initially as 'foetus containing vessels' and later as responsible not only for the child's 'normal' development but more extensively for the maintenance of an 'egalitarian' marriage and 'happy' family. We have noted the absences in the texts, the silence around the influences on a child's development beyond an individualistic focus on the mother–child dyad and the exclusion of any discussion of parenting in *various* 'family' structures and circumstances, except as 'not good enough' parenting. The consequences of what could be characterized as a unitary, homogenized, medicalized construal of women as mothers reproduced in these 'professionalized' accounts is of concern given the Western privileging of both science and medicine. These 'dominant discourses' serve to define pathological/abnormal mothering and to regulate the practices which are taken as 'good mothering'.

In engaging in these discourse analytic and hence poststructuralist tasks we have been expressly concerned with the ideological effects of a particular and powerful version of motherhood in these texts and considered specifically the potential consequences for *women* as a general category. We have explored the various assumptions and prescriptions written into the manuals and subjected to critique the apparently seamless account which gives little attention to the complexity and diversity of experiences of mothering.

Our research can also be considered as poststructuralist in so far as we have emphasized that our analyses have to be taken as partial, not definitive deconstructions. But also, in placing a priority on the impact and possible consequences for *women* of these constructs of motherhood, our research could be said to work with a feminist agenda. We view these analyses as feminist (and therefore political) in their intent to disrupt academic understandings of motherhood and to direct attention to diverse and alternative discourses of motherhood in order to transform the iniquitous advice offered to women and prescriptions for 'good' mothering (Fine, 1992; Woollett and Phoenix, 1996). Yet we have paid less attention to other aspects of the texts implicated in the reproduction of various inequalities. So, for example, while we have given some consideration to the socio-economic values and Anglo-American/Eurocentric assumptions in these texts, we have not focused on constructions of the child in advice/psychological texts. The attention to alternative foci of inequality would not necessarily stand in contradiction to Hartsock's (1987) writings on feminist standpoint theory in that she suggests that there are many standpoints which share subjugated status, from which analyses of universalizing theories can be mounted. However, there is a potential problem here *if* an analysis which foregrounds a particular standpoint, for example a woman-centred one, prematurely shuts off a full explication from other critical positions, for example a child-centred position (see Owens, 1994; Stainton Rogers, 1996). Further, it is not clear what to do if challenges to dominant constructions posed from diverse marginalized positions produce incompatible analyses of inequalities and consequently radically different agendas for emancipatory politics. The discourse analyses that we conducted of these professional texts might be said to share a concern of feminist standpoint research as that which 'builds in an analysis of power relations, describing dominant conceptual schemes as the outcome of knowledge produced exclusively from the social activities of the powerful in society (typically though not necessarily, men)' (Henwood and Pidgeon, 1995: 14–15). However, the understanding of power relations merits further attention and presented problems with respect to the ways in which we proceeded with the research project.

In setting a political agenda for research, feminist standpoint theorists have directed attention to the processes of data collection. One central contention is that a more complex basis for knowledge than that produced by positivist social scientists can be found by starting from the perspective of women's experiences and lives and other social groups ordinarily excluded from the dominant social order. This stipulation raises further conceptual and political issues regarding the uses of poststructuralism and feminist standpoint theory which we will discuss by reflecting on various dilemmas and decisions that faced us as researchers throughout the research process.

Working with Asian women's accounts of parenting and childcare: commonalities and differences in researcher standpoints

Central to the second research focus and to our consideration of how to approach the collection of accounts from women as mothers were discussions within feminism that the category 'woman' should be scrutinized as to its inclusiveness and concern be given to diversity (Riley, 1988; Spelman, 1988). Mainstream psychological theorizing about normal/good parenting has drawn almost exclusively on findings from research on white, middle-class families and with first children (Phoenix et al., 1991). We aimed to extend this 'data base' and in so doing to challenge the universalization of psychological ideas based on particular data sets. Our reasons for this were theoretical and political. As members of the research team, Anne and Harriette were employed as full-time academics and Neelam as a full-time research assistant at a university in East London, UK. The student population was diverse, including students who were parents as well as those who were childless, from a broad spread of ethnic backgrounds. They, as well as we, challenged the appropriateness of psychological models and theories based on limited samples. Working in East London also meant that the local population was ethnically diverse and largely working class. We shared the view that it was of central importance to bring the experiences of parenting of Asian families to the centre of our research. In addition, we shared and share a feminist perspective that could be described as materialist, prioritizing issues around lived experiences, racism, socio-economic factors, and the context of the East End of London. This perspective marks the research as different than, for example, if we had taken a feminist psycho-dynamic approach and focused attention on attachment and subject/object relations (Benjamin, 1988).

While we shared certain commonalities as researchers, we differed in many respects, including our ethnic backgrounds: Anne and Harriette are white British/English and Welsh, Neelam is of Punjabi Indian origin. We have different histories and statuses as researchers and had varying involvements with the project when collecting the 'data' (Neelam taking responsibility for conducting all the interviews with 'Asian' women and Harriette those with health professionals) through to writing up the research (Neelam has subsequently moved on to practise as a clinical psychologist and consequently has been less involved in 'writing up'). Our academic concerns vary, so too our theoretical and methodological 'knowl-edges' and preferences which in turn inevitably shape(d) our ideas about how best to transform social inequalities and practise feminism (Marshall and Woollett, 1997). Our varying positions and relationships with the research from start to finish, pose questions about the ideas of a singular feminist *standpoint*. In addition, the above (partial) representation of our positions raises the issue that standpoints can be analysed in partial ways (which is in itself problematic for standpoint theory).

Conceptualizing ethnic diversity

Many psychologists have noted the longstanding exclusion of ethnicity from psychological agenda (Graham, 1992), although others have argued that 'race' and ethnicity *are* present almost always in terms of an undisclosed whiteness (Wong, 1994). With respect to research on parenting, the unstated practice has been to focus almost exclusively on white families in theorizing 'normal' development unless the concern is with dysfunctional families, in which case ethnic minority families have often become the central and explicit concern (Phoenix, 1990). We did not want to reproduce ideas of difference as deficiency (or as exotic), but instead to work towards including Asian women's accounts as part of a normative developmental model.

Most usually when mainstream psychology has engaged explicitly with ethnicity it has been in terms of building in ethnicity as a variable. As such, ethnicity is taken as static, clearly bounded and separate from other variables. The assumption is that an ethnic category such as 'Asian' can be treated as fixed and the 'content' taken as homogenous. If we had taken a conventional psychological approach, the first step would have been to counter the previous lack of attention to Asian women by conducting interviews with an aim to 'find' an account of 'Asian' mothering and childcare and *add* it into existing theorizing. Additionally, in mainstream psychology, ethnic *differences* have often been taken as self-evident and their identification taken as a main reason to study ethnicity. Psychology has therefore repeatedly set up research settings where the aim is to 'discover' and document differences and in so doing has played its part in uncritically reproducing such differences.

This approach to difference is problematic and feminists (working from both poststructuralist and standpoint positions) have argued against taking such an approach on both conceptual and political grounds (Anderson and Collins, 1995; Bhavnani and Haraway, 1994). They argue powerfully that additive approaches leave untouched mainstream assumptions and models and fail to engage with the intricate interrelationships and particular ways in which various configurations of gender, ethnicity and class shape experience.

We wanted to bring the accounts from Asian women face to face with the professional and academic texts in order to make a challenge to the partiality and veiling of diversity in the latter texts. In so doing there were various considerations that shaped the ways in which we approached and later analysed the interviews, which problematize both conventional psychological treatments of ethnicity *and* also feminist standpoint theory.

Reading 'Asian' experience

Analyses of the interviews expose problems for both Nancy Hartsock's (1983) and Sandra Harding's (1987) discussions of feminist standpoint theory, specifically concerning how to work from 'experience' (here regarding *Asian* experience(s) of parenting). The following extracts from the interviews illustrate how women made reference to varying aspects of ethnicity which, in some cases, are used to explain certain childcare and parenting beliefs and practices. Some of the women use the term 'Asian' whereas others draw on varying 'ethnic' terms to represent and identify themselves and others. They move between referring to religion, culture and/or being Westernized/Indian in pointing to alignments and divisions *within* the category 'Asian'.

(1)   I don't think I'm very Westernized because I value my culture very much and my religion. I wouldn't like to be called Westernized. I have adopted a lot of the ways [Westernized] but only those that are not against my religion and my culture. . . . I think religion is very important although I think that my children will be more Westernized than myself obviously. . . . I don't want to forget my image or my culture living in a Western society. I think they [children] should accept it and they do. There are so many Asians here in Newham.

In this first extract the complexity of ethnicity is apparent. Identification is made with Indian culture and religion, although the speaker says that she has adopted certain Westernized practices. Ethnicity is represented not as fixed, but as fluid, and reference is made to a shifting sense of ethnicity which is discussed as resulting from living in Western society, specifically in an Asian community in Newham, London and as a consequence of having children. The complexity of ethnicity emerges again in the following extracts.

(2)   All my family is in India. We never used to eat meat but we do now, not my in-laws though. We wear Indian clothes, nothing fashionable. We live more within our family and relatives. When we have time we go to the gurdwara. If our children don't want to go to the gurdwara, we insist that they do so, so that they'll learn about their religion. We don't like our children mixing too much with the Western culture because the English live a different style.

(3)   A lot of women, or Gujurati women today, don't want many children. They would like to have two or three but the Muslims have five or six, especially the Bangladeshi . . . but I can't speak for all Gujurati women.

In extract 2, having a family in India, Indian dress and upholding religion are all mentioned in relation to ethnicity. English is constructed as 'different', contrasted with Indian/Sikh *culture* and used as a basis to inform parenting practices. It is taken as beneficial for children to retain their sense of ethnicity 'so they'll learn about their religion' and for them not to mix 'too much' with Western culture. In the third extract, consideration is given to different ethnic groupings within the 'Asian' community (Muslim – a religious grouping, Gujurati – a grouping based on language/location, and Bangladeshi – a grouping based on location). The speaker, while representing the views of 'a lot of women' concerning the desirability of a small family, qualifies this in terms of 'Gujurati women' although she states clearly that she cannot represent the views of all women in this ethnic grouping. A contrast between Muslim and Gujurati families is set up with links made between ethnicity and family size.

However, when the last extract is considered alongside an interview where a Muslim woman discusses her own fulfilled wish to have a large family, seemingly reinforcing a 'Muslim' standpoint as outlined by the previous speaker, she points out that there are other factors to be considered as well as/beyond Muslim beliefs and that links between the practice of having several children with ethnicity (Muslim) have to be made with caution as education, religion and lack of knowledge around family planning also play a part.

> (4)   These days women tend to have two or one [child(ren)]. So I wanted more than most people. I've had more than most people. Four these days is unheard of. I would say it's unheard of, even among Asians two or three is maximum.
>
> > *Interviewer*:   Does that idea of having a big family exist more in Muslim families?
>
> > Yes, I think so, yes, those that I know yes, but again those who are uneducated, education comes into it again. And those from back home and don't know about family planning or think it's against their religion, which it is not, will tend to have more even if they cannot afford it.

As discussed earlier, poststructuralism expects diversity of experience as constituted in language, renders impossible 'knowing' experience outside discourse, and problematizes the task of empirically researching 'experience'. But we had decided to collect 'data' as part of the project partly because of the status accorded 'empirical' research over conceptual/theoretical debate in both mainstream psychology and health domains (see Gergen, 1992; Griffin and Phoenix, 1994). So, we have used extracts such as those above as a means to displace constructions of 'Asian women's experiences' in the mainstream literature. In so doing we have challenged attempts to make a straightforward link between ideas about parenting and parenting practices with ethnicity or aspects of ethnicity, whether religion, culture, language or length of time in Britain. Therefore, we have argued that any attempt to take up a traditional psychological treatment of 'ethnicity' as a variable, isolated for examination, or to establish a one-to-one mapping of parenting practices on to ethnicity is flawed. But, in addition, the more fluid, complex nature of ethnicity makes it impossible to talk about 'Asian' experience (in the singular) or indeed of *the* experience of particular religious and cultural groupings within the broader term 'Asian', as indicated by those women who stated their reticence in speaking for others. It was not possible to establish an authentic version of 'Asian'. Instead we were presented with diversity and had to make certain decisions concerning what to do with it – and here our original political and research aims took priority. Although Sandra Harding and Nancy Hartsock in recent writings grapple with the charge of 'essentializing women' and the need to engage with 'fractured identities', the issue regarding how feminist standpoint theorists should proceed empirically and politically remains unresolved and would seem to have no easy resolution (Harding, 1986, 1990; Hartsock, 1990).

The above extracts illustrate how certain tensions emerge between feminist standpoint and poststructuralist accounts, most noticeably around the concept of 'experience'. Our position would be aligned with poststructuralism in problematizing any notion of a monolithic 'women's experience' or singular 'Asian women's experience', and instead would view experiences as ordered through a plurality of socially and historically specific discourses.

The reading of diversity was a central concern to our research project in other respects. While the extracts above were used to point to diverse meanings of ethnicity and the complex links with childcare practices, alternative readings are possible. Once again poststructuralist theory, in suggesting that it is always possible to read a text in different ways, 'fits' the extracts. But this in itself raises political dilemmas. The representational move from text to 'reality' is not straightforward and attention needs to be given to why women's accounts were previously excluded from the mainstream (the centre) (Bhavnani, 1990). When the reading of diversity is located in the broader socio-historical context, the tendency of the 'centre' (both mainstream psychology and health practices) can be seen to have made sense of 'differences' such as those in the extracts above, as indicative of deficiency or problem. For example, in extract 4 the expression of a desire to have more than two children and agreement with the characterization of Muslim families wanting five or six children, *if* read as a generalized account of 'Asian' parenting, can be taken as confirmation of the stereotype that 'Asian women have too many children' (Marshall, 1992; Phoenix, 1990). The statement that Indian parents do not want their children to mix with English children can be read as a 'refusal to integrate' into 'British culture', as can the wish not to forget culture. Our political strategy with regards to the representation of difference in this respect, geared to a (mainstream) psychological audience, was to impose a reading which refused to utilize the accounts in comparison with an assumed 'white norm'. However, this does not guarantee a progressive reading where the reader has invested in a framework where ethnic difference means deficiency.

We have been strategic in our consideration of when and how to represent diversity (and when to consider commonality) in ways which relate to the intended purpose of this research. So, for example, in going about the analysis and publication of papers based on the interviews we have sometimes engaged in an exploration of diversity and variability *within* the accounts. For example, there were many different reactions to pregnancy. The variation in accounts was not all reducible to individual subjective experience as there was some evidence of certain patterning in the accounts. For example, while not mapping on to ethnicity in a one-to-one fashion, women's accounts around ante-natal care and parentcraft classes did relate to parity, fluency in English, and/or family structure. We have drawn attention to these and other differences in the accounts for theoretical purposes. Additionally, with regards to our third research focus on health carers' accounts, we have addressed differences in publications likely to be read by health professionals to enable the development and implementation of practice which engages with the complexity of cultural beliefs and practices within any ethnic group (Marshall, 1992; Woollett et al., 1995). In drawing attention to diversity *within* Asian women's accounts, we have attempted also to point to experiences which would seem to be shared by Asian and non-Asian women. In each case we struggled to ensure that diversity was contextualized historically so as to explicate how and why the accounts from women in our sample have not carried equal status with the professional accounts and the ways in which power and privilege continue to be denied in these accounts.

So far in this chapter we have stressed the challenges to an homogenized conceptualization of 'Asian' and the instability of ethnic boundaries and practices. However, a continual focus on diversity can result in a political impotence, which offers the possibility of only a momentary critical vision (Burman, 1990; Maynard, 1994). In the setting of a feminist and 'critical' audience it has been possible (and perhaps safer although no less problematic) to explore diversity, drawing on debates around the politics of representation regarding ethnicity. For the most part these debates have been more thoroughly rehearsed *outside* psychology (Brah, 1996; Hall, 1989; hooks, 1992). However, increasingly they are being raised as issues within feminist psychology (see the special issue of *Feminism and Psychology, Shifting Identities, Shifting Racisms* (1994) and the special feature in *Feminism and Psychology, Representing the Other* (1996)). Further, in taking a poststructuralist line which poses challenges to the 'truth' claims of the mainstream, one frequent charge is that of relativism, an absence of any discussion of value regarding the diverse discourses around gender, ethnicity and 'race'. In this respect we find useful Gill's characterization of a position of 'politically informed relativism' which in turn relates to Hall's call for a 'politics of articulation' (Gill, 1995; Hall, 1988). While the scrutiny of variability and diversity is needed, the researcher has also to halt deconstruction at certain points to focus strategically on commonalities and community in order to secure a call for unity to enable political action. We might characterize ourselves, as researchers, as thoroughly immersed in making decisions around representation. We are in agreement with other feminist researchers who have suggested that a politics of articulation offers the potential to bring together feminist politics and poststructuralism (Gill, 1995; Wetherell, 1995).

Placing an analytic focus on intra-ethnic commonalities

Our crucial concern with the representation of 'experience' can be illustrated further with reference to the occasions and ways in which our reading of the accounts of childbirth, ante-natal and post-natal care has sometimes been with an eye for commonalities *within* Asian women's accounts and differences between Asian and non-Asian women. While these views are differentiated by class and tradition, and may be shared by other groups of women, we considered it important to report certain views as widespread among South East Asian women. For example, in representing views of post-natal care we have pointed to the importance some Asian women place on rest and recovery after labour, as illustrated below.

> (5) The whole family stayed with my mother-in-law for three weeks. After three weeks I came home. The reasons you shouldn't do anything for five or six days is because you haven't got the strength and you need all the rest. All this is supposed to be good for you.

The emphasis on resting after labour was particularly evident in the accounts of women who self-reported as being traditionally Asian and who upheld the custom of letting other female relatives take care of them and give them a rest from other childcare demands and work loads (Woollett and Dosanjh, 1990). However, current hospital practice, which places an importance on early mother/child bonding and attachment and encourages mothers to take responsibility for their children soon after delivery, clashes with

Asian women's views about the need to rest as reported in the following extract.

> (6)   After having such a big operation (Caesarean) I was in need of rest, I was left to look after my child. Doctors said you mustn't go home, you need rest. But I would have got more rest at home. When it came to eating, they want you to go to the dining room, but I didn't have the strength to get up. You are expected to get up and get whatever your baby needs. . . . My state was really bad at night. I couldn't sleep. I would ask the nurse to take the baby for a while so I might get some sleep. They would say: 'No, it's your child, you look after it'.

From placing a focus on commonalities in the accounts of Asian women around aspects of post-natal care and reporting the negative consequences resulting from a clash in different cultural beliefs and practices, we have built a case for the need for health professionals to ensure that maternity care recognizes and respects the diversity of cultural practices that exist in British society and women's own wishes, in the recognition that this constitutes 'good practice'.

In other publications our analytic concern with commonalities has been used to point to ways of putting policy into practice. For example, the characterization of good maternity care in both health policy documents and from midwives and health visitors talking about 'good care' has been in terms of 'individualized care' where the health carer not only respects but responds to the wishes and needs of women, *as* individuals (Marshall, 1992; RCM, 1987; UKCC, 1986). Therefore, in order to consider the interrelationship between policy and practice we have examined and reported the shared negative experiences of childbirth and ante-natal care resulting from communication problems as discussed by a number of women.

One obvious consequence of a failure of communication between the health carer and the mother in her care is the obstruction of the realization of good maternity care, defined as individualized care for all women. In some analyses, we reported the shared experience around communication problems to reiterate the importance accorded to interpreters and advocates in hospital settings (Marshall, 1992). In other publications we have focused on and explained commonality in terms of the shared experience of oppression from being negatively racialized. Here, as researchers, we read and represented the accounts through an interpretative framework derived from academic analyses of inequality. We 'fixed' the accounts with reference to the socio-economic circumstances of racism in Britain. This was very much our particular representation of the accounts because few of the women themselves made explicit reference to racism in the interviews or took up the invitation to do so when given.

> (7)   There was another lady [patient] and she had problems with her stitches which opened. . . . They [nurses] told her to sit in a bath, but then again sometimes the nurses used to be pretty bad. They weren't always considerate. If the mother was in the bath they wouldn't always check the baby. The baby used to cry and I thought the coloured ladies were really tight. They didn't help them much, like the lady who complained about the stitches and wanted painkillers, but all they said was 'Stop complaining, you can't have painkillers any more'. Sometimes they think that because you're Asian they can push you around.

> (8)   *Interviewer*:   How do you feel about the ways pregnancy and childbirth are managed here?

> It depends, some nurses are all right, like the English, and there are some who are not so nice. When I went into hospital a black nurse said 'Oh, not again'. I went in at midnight and she probably thought she's got one already, why does she want another. Some nurses are good and some are always angry and the way they talk to you, you remain upset all the time. Some will say 'So many children'. . . . If you want painkillers they'll say 'You've had so many already'.

We have used accounts such as these to point to the consequences of failing to implement 'individualized care' and resorting to care where the woman is viewed and treated on the basis of ethnic grouping (Marshall, 1993). But additionally, in these extracts there is a singling out of black nurses. This raises the issue of what to do when working with marginalized accounts which themselves reproduce prejudicial viewpoints and evaluations. Our decision to date has been not to report these aspects of the accounts. (Leaving silenced aspects of the accounts that we do not want to hear?) An alternative approach would be to represent these experiences through an interpretive framework which makes sense of the accounts in terms of there being no guarantee that oppressed groups will share standpoints, nor align with others who are also on the receiving end of racism. These tensions around the representation of 'experience' were and are central for us as researchers. In adjudicating between what and what not to write up we could be accused of taking the political/moral highground, a position somewhat contradictory with our earlier critique of 'professional' analyses although in accordance with a 'politically informed relativism'. But, in addition, this sort of 'suppression' results in a misunderstanding of power, social relationships and inequalities, and hence, prevents opportunities for countering oppressions which currently exist.

The research process: the researcher and the researched

These issues concerning the representation of ethnicity (and experience) are relevant and partially constitutive of the research process, specifically our relationships with the women we were researching and the status accorded to their accounts. Here, further problems with feminist standpoint theory emerge with respect to the experiences elicited in the interviews. Bearing in mind the argument that 'groups unequal in power are correspondingly unequal in their ability to make their standpoint known to themselves and others' (Hill Collins, 1990), it is crucial to reflect on the interviewing process. Taking a poststructuralist stance, we would view the accounts as produced to address the questions as posed in the immediate circumstances of the interview and *in relation to* the interviewer rather than as 'repositories of a unitary truth' (Phoenix, 1994).

In the second research focus of the project, the researcher/researched relationship was raised by the women themselves at an early stage. As interviewer, when initially contacting interviewees, Neelam was often questioned closely about herself, her position, her involvement in the research and the purpose of the interviews. Consequently, many participants had often established a particular perception of Neelam as a researcher prior to the interview which varied between that of expert, friend or stranger/outsider. Sometimes Neelam thought that she was accepted as being similar to the interviewee on the basis of shared ethnic background, education, age, religion and/or as being equally 'Westernized', whereas in other instances she was viewed as very different. These varying perceptions would seem to have shaped the form and content of the interview. For example, on occasions there is little or no explanation of certain views, possibly because the interviewee assumed a shared perspective and took-for-granted that as interviewer Neelam already understood what was being said. Sometimes the perception of similarity resulted in an easy interaction between interviewer and interviewee where Neelam was asked about her life, opinions and ideas. On other occasions the positioning of Neelam as educated and an expert led to a more formal interaction where Neelam was asked for information and advice.

Women's accounts varied in length, amount of detail and explanation. This might have happened for a number of reasons. Sometimes the brief responses and sparse discussion suggest a reticence on the part of the interviewee or an unfamiliarity with certain topics. This was especially the case around childbirth, labour and delivery which were shorter than might have been expected, given our experience of interviewing white women and from findings of other research (e.g. Oakley, 1980). But the accounts of post-natal experiences were fuller and more detailed than might have been expected on the basis of previous research, suggesting a reticence about the topic rather than reticence generally. At other times the presence and pressures from others during the interview, whether young children, husbands or other family members, resulted in shorter, more rushed interviews where the abrupt responses would later preclude any detailed exploration of fluidity and complexity. The pertinent point is that these accounts have to be viewed as spoken within the constraints of our interview questions, in relation to Neelam as interviewer, in the context of the interview and according to the perceived purposes of the research. Clearly there were many aspects of experience which, for various reasons, remain unvoiced in the interviews.

The analyses of these accounts point again to the partiality of the processes of 'knowledge' production and accordingly to our reticence in claiming a privileged status as researchers having access to the 'reality' of Asian women's experiences. In all cases the analysis was carried out by the research team, two of whom had not carried out the interviews nor been involved in the translations with women whose interviews were not conducted in English. These two researchers were somewhat 'distanced' from the interviews. The 'knowledge' we, as researchers, created of these women's experiences was a particular one. At the very least the experiences were 'filtered' through our various frameworks as researchers. These are some of the reasons why we would endorse the reservations of Liz Stanley and Sue Wise that 'feminist researchers have a privileged access to *real* social reality' or that 'a single and unseamed social as well as physical reality exists "out there"' (Stanley and Wise, 1993: 189). An interrogation of the representational processes inherent in the research process problematizes these assumptions.

Throughout this chapter we have found useful certain poststructuralist ideas regarding the centrality of language and the adoption of discourse analytic approaches, especially in relation to 'experience' taken as constituted variously through language. We have also taken up poststructuralist arguments about knowledge and power, giving recognition to a plurality of 'knowledges' where 'professional' and academic constructions no longer retain a privileged 'truth' status over others. These various poststructuralist concerns problematize aspects of feminist standpoint theory. Specifically, we have directed attention at our own differing standpoints as researchers which would suggest that we need to talk about feminist *standpoints* (in the plural). In reflecting on some of our positionings as researchers we have argued that these are inevitably constitutive of the accounts of 'experiences' presented in the research setting. In pointing to the partiality of such accounts we question their investment as a sounder knowledge base as suggested by feminist standpoint theorists.

However, in contesting the notion that feminist standpoint is the key to understanding marginalized experiences and the priority accorded to feminist researchers' viewpoints, we would not want to lose the political impetus offered by feminist standpoint theory but not by poststructuralism. In our attempts to reconcile poststructuralism and feminism we have centred our discussion around representational issues. Accordingly, in considering ourselves as researchers making strategic decisions around when to explore diversity and when commonality, in order to build a politics around challenge and resistance, we have characterized our approach as engaging with a 'politics of articulation' (Hall, 1988). While aligning with this agenda Gayatri Chakravorty Spivak adds a caution against *fixing* the 'unities' or 'communities' that have been settled for the purposes of political action: 'Deconstruction does not say anything against the usefulness of mobilising unities. All it says is that because it is useful it ought not be monumentalized as the way things really are' (Spivak, 1991: 65). Along with other feminist psychologists we would see this as a way of permitting the retention of a feminist politics which aims to understand oppression and take action to redress it, while taking up certain poststructuralist challenges, notably in not taking for granted or 'monumentalizing' the experiences of a 'community' of women for all time (Wetherell, 1995).

References

Anderson, M. and Hill Collins, P. (1995) *Race, Class and Gender*. California and London: Wadsworth.

Benjamin, J. (1988) *The Bonds of Love*. New York: Pantheon.

Bhachu, P. (1985) *Twice Migrants: East African Sikh Settlers in Britain*. London: Tavistock.

Bhavnani, K.-K. (1990) 'What's power got to do with it? Empowerment and social research', in I. Parker and J. Shotter (eds), *Deconstructing Social Psychology*. London: Routledge.

Bhavnani, K.-K. and Haraway, D. (1994) 'Shifting identities, shifting racisms', *Feminism and Psychology* 4 (1): 19–39.

Brah, A. (1996) *Cartographies of Diaspora: Contesting Identities*. London: Routledge.

Burman, E. (1990) 'Differing with deconstruction', in I. Parker and J. Shotter (eds), *Deconstructing Social Psychology*. London: Routledge.

Chodorow, N. (1978) *The Reproduction of Mothering*. Berkeley: University of California Press.

Clarke, C., Peach, C. and Vertovec, S. (1990) *South Asians Overseas: Migration and Ethnicity*. Cambridge: Cambridge University Press.

Dobson, S.M. (1988) 'Transcultural health visiting: caring in multi-cultural society', *Recent Advances in Nursing* 20: 61–80.

Eichenbaum, L. and Orbach, S. (1985) *Understanding Women*. Harmondsworth: Penguin.

Feminism and Psychology (1994) Special Issue, *Shifting Identities, Shifting Racisms*. London: Sage.

Feminism and Psychology (1996) Special feature, *Representing the Other*. London: Sage.

Fine, M. (1992) *Disruptive Voices: The Possibilities of Feminist Research*. Ann Arbor: University of Michigan Press.

Gavey, N. (1989) 'Feminist poststructuralism and discourse analysis: contributions to feminist psychology', *Psychology of Women Quarterly* 13: 459–75.

Gergen, K. (1992) 'Toward a postmodern psychology', in S. Kvale (ed.), *Psychology and Postmodernism*. London: Sage.

Gill, R. (1995) 'Relativism, reflexivity and politics: interrogating discourse analysis from a feminist perspective', in S. Wilkinson and C. Kitzinger (eds), *Feminism and Discourse: Psychological Perspectives*. London: Sage.

Graham, S. (1992) 'Most of the subjects were white and middle class', *American Psychologist* 47 (5): 629–39.

Griffin, C. and Phoenix, A. (1994) 'The relationship between qualitative and quantitative research: lessons from feminist psychology', *Journal of Community and Applied Social Psychology* 4: 287–98.

Hall, S. (1988) 'The toad in the garden: Thatcherism among the theorists', in C. Nelson and L. Grossberg (eds), *Marxism and the Interpretation of Culture*. Urbana: University of Illinois Press.

Hall, S. (1989) 'New Ethnicities', in K. Mercer (ed.), *ICA Documents 7: Black Film, British Cinema*. London: ICA Publications.

Harding, S. (1986) *The Science Question in Feminism*. Milton Keynes: Open University Press.

Harding, S. (ed.) (1987) *Feminism and Methodology*. Milton Keynes: Open University Press.

Harding, S. (1990) 'Feminism, science, and the anti-Enlightenment critiques', in L. Nicholson (ed.), *Feminism/Postmodernism*. London: Routledge.

Hartsock, N. (1983) 'The feminist standpoint: developing the ground for a specifically feminist historical materialism', in S. Harding and M. Hintikka (eds), *Discovering Reality: Feminist Perspectives on Epistemology, Metaphysics, Methodology and Philosophy of Science*. Dordrecht: Reidel.

Hartsock, N. (1987) 'The feminist standpoint', in S. Harding (ed.), *Feminism and Methodology*. Milton Keynes: Open University Press.

Hartsock, N. (1990) 'Foucault on power: a theory for women?', in L. Nicholson (ed.), *Feminism/Postmodernism*. London: Routledge.

Henwood, K. and Pidgeon, N. (1995) 'Remaking the link: qualitative research and feminist standpoint', *Feminism and Psychology* 5 (1): 7–30.

Hill Collins, P. (1990) *Black Feminist Thought: Knowledge Consciousness, and the Politics of Empowerment*. London: Unwin Hyman.

hooks, b. (1992) *Black Looks: Race and Representation*. London: Turnaround.

Horne, W. (1988) *Ethnicity and Health* (Vol. VII of the Ethnicity and Public Policy Series). Madison: University of Wisconsin Institute on Race and Ethnicity.

Malson, H. and Ussher, J. (1996) 'Bloody women: a discourse analysis of amenorrhea as a symptom of anorexia nervosa', *Feminism and Psychology* 6 (4): 505–22.

Marshall, H. (1991) 'The social construction of motherhood: an analysis of childcare and parenting manuals', in A. Phoenix, A. Woollett and E. Lloyd (eds), *Motherhood, Meaning, Practices and Ideologies*. London: Sage.

Marshall, H. (1992) 'Talking about good maternity care in a multi-cultural context: a discourse analysis of the accounts of midwives and health visitors', in P. Nicolson and J. Ussher (eds), *The Psychology of Women's Health and Health Care*. London: Macmillan.

Marshall, H. (1993) 'Analysing discourse: qualitative research and the helping professions', in R. Bayne and P. Nicolson (eds), *Counselling and Psychology for Health Professionals*. London: Chapman and Hall.

Marshall, H. and Woollett, A. (1997) 'Researching Asian women's accounts of parenting and childcare: some conceptual and methodological concerns', *Changes* 15 (1): 42–6.

Maynard, M. (1994) '"Race", gender and "difference" in feminist thought', in H. Afshar and M. Maynard (eds), *The Dynamics of 'Race' and Gender: Some Feminist Interventions*. London: Taylor & Francis.

Oakley, A. (1980) *Women Confined: Towards a Sociology of Childbirth*. Oxford: Martin Robertson.

Oakley, A. (1981) *From Here to Maternity: Becoming a Mother*. Harmondsworth: Penguin.

Oakley, A. (1993) *Essays on Women, Medicine and Health*. Edinburgh: Edinburgh University Press.

Owens, C. (1994) 'Some notes towards "Standpoint"', *Manifold* 1 (3): 45–52.

Phoenix, A. (1990) 'Theories of gender and black families', in T. Lovell (ed.), *British Feminist Thought*. Oxford: Blackwell.

Phoenix, A. (1994) 'Practising feminist research: the intersection of gender and "race" in the research process', in M. Maynard and J. Purvis (eds), *Researching Women's Lives from a Feminist Perspective*. London: Taylor & Francis.

Phoenix, A., Woollett, A. and Lloyd, E. (1991) *Motherhood, Meaning, Practices and Ideologies*. London: Sage.

Riley, D. (1988) *Am I That Name? Feminism and the Category of 'Women' in History*. Basingstoke: Macmillan.

Royal College of Midwives (1987) *The Role and Education of the Future Midwife in the United Kingdom*. London: Royal College of Midwives.

Spelman, E. (1988) *Inessential Woman: Problems of Exclusion in Feminist Thought*. London: The Women's Press.

Spivak, G. (1991) 'Reflections on cultural studies in the post-colonial conjuncture', *Critical Studies* 3 (1): 63–78.

Spock, B. (1988) *Dr Spock's Baby and Child Care* (40th anniversary edition). London: Allen.

Stainton Rogers, W. (1996) 'Review of deconstructing developmental psychology by Erica Burman', *Feminism and Psychology* 6 (2): 320–3.

Stanley, L. and Wise, S. (1993) *Breaking Out Again: Feminist Ontology and Epistemology*. London: Routledge.

United Kingdom Central Council for Nursing, Midwifery and Health Visiting (1986) *Project 2000: A New Preparation for Practice*. London: UKCC.

Weedon, C. (1987) *Feminist Practice and Poststructuralist Theory*. Oxford: Blackwell.

Wetherell, M. (1995) 'Romantic discourse and feminist analysis', in S. Wilkinson and

C. Kitzinger (eds), *Feminism and Discourse: Psychological Perspectives*. London: Sage.

Wong, L.M. (1994) 'Di(s)-secting and dis(s)-closing "Whiteness": two tales about psychology', *Feminism and Psychology* 4 (1): 133–54.

Woollett, A. and Dosanjh, N. (1990) 'Pregnancy and ante-natal care: the attitudes and experiences of Asian women', *Child Health Care and Development* 16: 63–78.

Woollett, A., Dosanjh, N., Nicolson, P., Marshall, H., Djhanbakhch, O. and Hadlow, J. (1995) 'A comparison of the experiences of pregnancy and childbirth of Asian and non-Asian women in East London', *British Journal of Medical Psychology* 68: 65–84.

Woollett, A. and Marshall, H. (1997) 'Discourses of pregnancy and childbirth', in L. Yardley (ed.), *Material Discourses of Health and Illness*. Hemel Hempstead: Harvester Wheatsheaf.

Woollett, A. and Phoenix, A. (1996) 'Motherhood as pedagogy: developmental psychology and the accounts of mothers of young children', in C. Luke (ed.), *Feminisms and Pedagogies of Everyday Life*. New York: State University of New York Press.

7

Shameful Women: Accounts of Withdrawal and Silence

Irene Bruna Seu

Shame, Remorse and Misery are three Furies in whose hands women
inevitably have to fall as soon as they cross the boundaries.

(Balzac, 'Gobsek' in Wumser, 1981: 60)

This chapter discusses some of the central analyses conducted as
part of a research project on women and shame and focuses on two
questions. The first, one of the core questions in this book asks
whether poststructuralism is compatible with feminist struggles and
research (Burman and Parker, 1993; Soper, 1990). The second
question stems from my own interest as a clinical practitioner and
from the concern of those feminists who conduct mutual interrogations between feminism, poststructuralism and psychoanalytic
theory (Flax, 1990). In particular it explores some of the benefits
and shortfalls of employing a classical psychoanalytic reading while
carrying out research from a feminist standpoint.

My argument starts from the belief that poststructuralist theories
of discourse can coexist with a feminist approach and be instrumental to it in many crucial ways. First, it forces us to question the
use in our research of unitary and cohesive categories, like that of
'woman', and an intrinsic privileged access to women's experience.
Furthermore, by instilling a radical and liberating scepticism
(Wetherell, 1995), it forces us to a more critical reflexivity on the
ideological underpinnings of our work. Finally, but crucially, as I
will endeavour to show, interrogating feminist theories from a
poststructuralist, discursive angle, can reveal how they might subtly
corroborate stereotypes of female identity.

As far as the second point is concerned, I claim that psychoanalysis still has a great contribution to make to feminism, particularly to poststructuralist feminism, not only in the attention
given to the internal reproduction of dynamics of oppression, but
also because of the space, otherwise absent in poststructuralist

discursive analyses, allowed for extra-discursive dimensions in the analysis of subjectivity. On the other hand, an interrogation of classical psychoanalysis from a poststructuralist point of view is also necessary. In this chapter I will show how the individualistic ideologies underpinning some psychoanalytic theories are detrimental to women in making a socially constructed issue into an individual problem, thus contributing to women's isolation, self-blame and suffering.

My main concern, as a feminist, a clinician and a researcher, is precisely women's suffering. Once we agree that we are studying subject positions because of their real implications for people's well-being and sense of self (Burman and Parker, 1993), then it is no longer a question of choosing between psychoanalysis, feminism or poststructuralism. We don't have a choice. We need them all to understand, counteract and prevent people's suffering and oppression, albeit through a process of continuous, mutual interrogation.

Women's accounts of shame is the subject of investigation in this chapter. There are a number of reasons why I chose shame as the subject of inquiry. The most important is that although everybody experiences shame in ways that are peculiar to them as individuals, I believe there are specific ways in which women experience shame due to being women in a patriarchal society (Anthony, 1981; Bartky, 1990). The shame I am referring to has the existential flavour of uncertainty about oneself, a sense of inadequacy and low self-esteem. My feminist motivation behind the project was the sense that women's suffering and ways of improving women's lives should feature firmly on the psychological agenda. My political aim in investigating shame, then, is to identify the processes through which oppression becomes internal regulation and self-discipline; in other words to explore the self-oppression involved in taking the subject position of shameful.

Initially, the specific research questions were framed psycho-analytically, concerning the function of protective activities to prevent the exposure of the shameful self. However, as the research evolved, issues such as the multiple and contradictory meanings of shame, their negotiation in relationships with others, and the practical ideologies associated with the subject position 'shameful woman' increasingly came to centre stage. Hence, the resulting analyses reported here exemplify a set of contemporary analytic practices involving the mutual interrogation of interpretations drawn from feminism, psychoanalysis and poststructuralist theory.

The main project consisted of semi-structured interviews conducted with 18 women about their shame experiences. The participants were between the ages of 25 and 36, with the exception of one who was 47. Two participants were black, six were not-British, three of whom came from non-English-speaking countries. All of them were able-bodied and when talking about their sexuality, exclusively made reference to themselves as heterosexual. Although some of the participants were from a working-class background, their various occupations (two social-workers, an art therapist, a musician, an accountant, a clerk, a journalist, a film-maker and a teacher), indicated a level of education typical of the middle classes. All the others were post-graduate students, mainly in psychology. The interview consisted of two parts: the first focused on the woman's life, sense of self and self-esteem. The second focused more on shame. No definition of shame was given to participants, and whatever they told me I took to be what they understood shame to be. Although I had a list of questions, I tended to let the women take the lead in directing the interview. Some women told me about recent events, others talked about their past, most reported from both.

One striking commonality among the women interviewed was the employment of avoidance, withdrawal and silence as their preferred way of dealing with shame. These were presented as protective activities to prevent exposure of their shameful self. Instead of taking their accounts as neutral statements or representations of their personality, I concentrated on their function and on how shame is constructed and negotiated in speech. I thus bypassed the dichotomy between shame as existing in a vacuum or 'out there', as it is argued by some social psychologists (Goss et al., 1994; Hoglund and Nicholas, 1995; Okano, 1994), or as an exclusively intrapsychic affect, as it is mainly held by psychoanalytic theories (Campbell, 1984; Hibbard, 1994; Morrison, 1984) and clinical psychology (Jones and Zalewski, 1994; Nathanson, 1994; Tangney et al., 1996).

Mainly following the Wetherell and Potter tradition (Potter et al., 1990; Potter and Wetherell, 1987, 1989; Wetherell and Potter, 1992), the discursive analyses carried out on these extracts explore the subject position of shameful when functioning as practical ideology (Gill, 1993; Wetherell and Potter, 1992); that is how versions of facts are constructed in speech to accomplish social actions (Edwards and Potter, 1992) and to exclude possible competing versions (Madill, 1995). This strategy allowed me to identify the constraints placed on meaning by particular theoretical schemes and by everyday, personal and cultural frames of reference, thus opening up alternative readings of the dynamic play of subject positions in discourse and relations of power.

I start by making some orienting remarks that establish basic theoretical perspectives within psychoanalysis and feminism, and use an extract from an interview with one woman, Sarah, to deconstruct the essentialist assumptions in these theories. I then deploy a feminist reading of a special oral identity for women, and the possibility of resistance through silence, and express a concern for their practical consequences at a personal and social level. The need to grapple with wider cultural issues and conflicts around the use and abuse of power for women features strongly here. The chapter concludes with a more meta-theoretical reflection upon the special mix of theoretical sensitivities involved in the presented analysis, and conveys the unerring conviction that emotional suffering cannot be avoided merely by passively accepting oppression.

Some basics of psychoanalytic theory and the problem of essentialism

Shame is a disempowering and acutely painful experience about the self, in which the subject feels they 'could die' or 'crawl through a hole' (Lewis, 1971). The Germanic root *skam/skem* of the word 'shame' can be traced back to the Indo-European *kam/kem*: 'to cover, to veil, to hide'; the prefixed 's' (*skam*) adds the reflexive meaning: 'to cover oneself' (Wumser, 1981). These meanings suggest that shame experiences embody a sense of deep exposure (Lynd, 1958), of bodily or psychological nakedness (Yorke, 1990). Therefore the 'purpose' of shame has been repeatedly connected to hiding and disappearing in order to isolate the person from the danger of exposure (Lewis, 1992; Wumser, 1981). Biblically, this is graphically expressed by Adam's fall and the attempt to hide, which represented the exposure before God (Lewis, 1992). Observations of the phenomenological expression of shame (head bowed, avoidance of gaze, shrinking of the body) also support the idea that shame engenders a wish for concealment and avoidance. Thus shame anxiety is believed to be evoked by the imminent danger of unexpected exposure, humiliation and rejection (Lewis, 1971; Wumser, 1981). Shame anxiety can be seen as a response to the overwhelming trauma of helplessness previously experienced. Alternatively, it may function as a signal, triggered by a milder type of rejection and warning that a more intense one could reach traumatic proportions (Wumser, 1981).

People use various strategies to shelter themselves from the occurrence of shame, that is in psychoanalytic terms, they employ defences. Intrapsychic defences, although sometimes discussed as being employed in aid of resistance (Sandler et al., 1992), are considered protective measures with the aim of maintaining an intrapsychic homeostatic balance. They are adaptive and psychologically valuable (Kohut, 1977).

Shame is in a complex relation to defences: shame can have itself the function of defence (for example in the case of reaction-formation,[1] where shame prevents unacceptable drives and wishes from becoming conscious) at the same time that other defences are called upon to protect the self from shame (Nathanson, 1992). Rage, contempt, envy and depression, for example, can all have the function of defending against shame.

Strikingly, despite this complex situation and the wide variety of defensive measures attributed specifically to coping with shame – turning passive into active, grandiosity and idealization, lying, masochistic flaunting of degradation and externalization by the humiliation of others (Wumser, 1981), the women interviewed repeatedly referred to silence and withdrawal as their way of dealing with shame. This was described by different women in different ways: some referred to instances in which they literally walked away from the situation, others talked of avoiding exposure by staying silent. The situations described involved being humiliated, or shown as inadequate or helpless. Often the situations involved conflict about power.

These accounts are consistent with feminist claims that women seem to find it more difficult than men to be assertive about their capacities in a social situation (Bartky, 1990; Walkerdine, 1990). Walkerdine has observed that, in education, although women tended on average to be better students than men, they displayed far less confidence in their ability to master the material (Walkerdine, 1990). This is in agreement with Bartky's (1990) observation that women use what linguists call 'women's language', that is their speech is marked by hesitations and false starts. They tend to introduce their comments with self-denigrating expressions like, 'You may think this is a stupid question, but . . .'. They often use a questioning intonation which in effect turns a simple declarative sentence into a request for help or affirmation. Also, there is often the excessive use of qualifiers, for example 'Isn't it true that [x] might be . . .'.

In the two studies mentioned above, the behaviour of the female students was interpreted by the researchers to be indicative of a desire to take up as little space as possible, to be inconspicuous or even invisible. This is explained in turn as the result of oppression in patriarchal society. The problem with these feminist readings is that they may be preventing alternative readings emerging. For example, the women interviewed accounted for withdrawal as a defence to hide from shame, which implicitly proposed the existence of a shameful self as a given fact. This is a strategy identified by discourse analysts as 'everyday empiricist accounting' (Edwards and Potter, 1992: 162), where the facts force themselves on the human actors who have an entirely secondary role (see also Gilbert and Mulkay, 1984; McKinley and Potter, 1987; Mulkay 1985). We need to pursue the possibility of suspending the reading of avoidance as connected to an inadequate, shameful self and explore alternative and contradictory subject positions. In the following extract, for example, I suggest that by taking the position of inadequate and shameful, Sarah is positioning herself as unthreatening and free of blame.

1	*Bruna*:	Was it [shame] about not being good enough?
2	*Sarah*:	Or too good (.) so being the last one to be chosen, but also if
3		I was chosen, or being special in some ways, I mean, I must
4		have been quite bright and I started school early and I have
5		a brother two years older than myself and I went through
6		the infant classes quicker than he did, so I was actually in
7		the same classes with him at about seven and I would feel
8		quite embarrassed when the teacher would ask me to do
9		things (.) obviously I also felt proud of the capacity side (.) if
10		I was chosen to do things, I remember being chosen to
11		present the headmaster a bunch of flowers on [inaudible]
12		day, so being the one, the goody who was chosen to (.)

This account constructs the shameful self in two opposite ways: there is shame for being the last to be chosen (shame for failing), but also shameful for being chosen (for being special). This is accompanied by another contradiction – her expression of the embarrassment of being singled out as special and, in the following line, the pride at her capacity. This is in total contrast with the polarized outlook offered by the literature on shame which states that shame is the opposite of pride and that, while shame is the accompaniment to failure and lowered self-esteem, pride comes with success and increased self-esteem (Nathanson, 1987; Pines, 1987, 1995). Yet here there is attribution of shame to success.

Within the theory that shame and pride are determined by social norms, certain actions are deemed to provoke shame whereas others provoke pride. What, on the contrary, transpires from this account is that the same position of being successful is constructed both as shameful and proud at the same time. This, I would suggest, has some dependence on the actors involved in negotiating the attribution of meaning. There is no indication that the shame is constructed between Sarah and her teacher; the teacher, it seems, was the one most likely to recognize the capacity she felt proud of. Sarah clearly locates the belief in her capacities not in herself, but implies that someone else must have thought that she was capable. This she accomplishes by phrasing it in terms of disbelief '*I must have been quite bright*' (lines 3–4) and positioning herself not as the agent of the judgement but as a passive object of someone else's judgement.

Later Sarah explains that her peer group had greatly influenced her feelings, as it was against her peer-group culture to show interest in school matters. This is hinted at in the last line when being the one chosen is described as the 'goody', implying that being studious or the 'teacher's pet' constituted a betrayal of adolescent, anti-conformist rebellion against the adult world.

Alongside these already contrasting and coexisting scenarios, a third can be identified at the beginning of the extract, on which Sarah focuses immediately. This involves the introduction of Sarah's brother, who is two years older than her. The account implies that her brother is less bright and less academically successful than Sarah, to the point that she not only caught up with him, but despite the age gap was still the one chosen as special in the class. This situation presents a moral dilemma: if Sarah positions herself as proud and successful, that automatically positions her brother as inadequate and shameful. This is why I think Sarah takes both subject positions at the same time – of being proud and ashamed of her success. This allows her to do well at school and, at the same time, to get on with her peers and not shame her brother. It also allows her to avoid challenging the 'obvious' expectation that her older and male brother should do better than she does.

A moral identity for women: a closure of readings

It has been pointed out how competition and achievement are rarely straightforward for women and how even if women manage to achieve their objectives, they sometimes subvert themselves, denigrating any praise and attention they may receive. There seems to be an awareness or fear that their ambitious urges are 'improper', or even destructive (Coward, 1992). These observations, along with others on the same lines (Bartky, 1990; Walkerdine, 1990), raise the question of why being weak, ignorant or invisible seem to be 'easier options' for some women.

According to Anthony, despite his adoption of a psychodynamic framework, shame syndromes in women are 'constitutional, physical and psychocultural' (Anthony, 1981: 208), due to the vulnerability of women's still emergent identity. He describes how, in order to negotiate the historical submerging of their identity in the service of the male ego, women have taken on a 'pseudo-identity' characterized by negative attributions of self-denial, general inferiority and shame. This is very consistent with the general identity transpiring through the interviews and would also explain how powerfulness and success would be experienced as unfamiliar and dissonant to a sense of identity built around inferiority.

In this context, Welldon (1988) talks in terms of 'success anxiety' in women which, she argues, could become the equivalent of castration anxiety ascribed by certain earlier writers. This sense of danger has also been identified by Gilligan (1982).

> . . . men and women may perceive danger in different social situations
> and construe danger in different ways – men seeing danger more often in
> close personal affiliation than in achievement and construing danger to
> arise from intimacy, women perceiving danger in impersonal achievement
> situations and construing danger to result from competitive success. . . .
> the danger women portray in their tales of achievement is a danger of
> isolation, a fear that in standing out or being set apart by success, they
> will be left alone. (Gilligan, 1982: 42)

Thus representations of women are vested with positive and negative connotations which carry implications in terms of well-being and self-esteem, but also of denial of responsibility and evasion. However, very problematically, Gilligan takes it a step further and frames this conflict in moral terms. In addressing the meaning of morality for women, Gilligan looks at the attributions that success and ambition have for many women. She argues that because women are often caught in the opposition between selfishness and responsibility, and because women's lives are lived in response, guided by the perception of others' needs, they can see no way of exercising control without risking an assertion that seems selfish and hence morally dangerous (Gilligan, 1982: 71).

There is thus a suggestion that the attribution of women's distaste for power should be attributed to women's 'intrinsically better nature'. This attribution, which is now part of the prevalent cultural fantasies about women, has been widely criticized (Coward, 1992; Segal, 1991; Stanley and Wise, 1993). This is certainly one of the implications of Gilligan's claim, for which she has been criticized (Faludi, 1991; Segal, 1991).

The popularity of Gilligan's thesis, is due to the fact that it provides apparent confirmation of the wistful belief that women are less individualistic and selfish than men, that they are better attuned than men and more empathic than them to emotional and relational issues. (Sayers, 1986: 19)

What concerns me here is how this is an example of feminist readings falling into essentialism and constructing a 'too neat' picture of women's conflicts about power. In this picture there is no space, for example, for the psychoanalytic view that shame might function as a protection against envy through a technique called 'masochistic flaunting of degradation': 'If I am suffering and low it proves that I can't be a threat to anybody and I can't take the power away from anybody' (Wumser, 1981: 41). It is further suggested that masochistic submission is often better than the guilt of envy and rivalry. This kind of strategy is exemplified as an attack on the 'horrid self' that wants to take away from others what they own.

It is understandable, considering that one of the tasks Gilligan had set herself was to argue against a male-centred view of morality which penalized women, that Gilligan attempted to counteract the situation by shedding a positive light on women's choices. However, she fails to see that this 'positive' outlook might legitimize women's inertia and glorify their passivity. Besides, by looking at avoidance and withdrawal as a personal, moral choice rather than as an ideologically meaningful subject position, we cannot investigate the complexities of the negotiation involved, the implications and the possibility for resistance which the position allows. These tensions will be the focus of the discourse analysis to follow, based on two extracts, both from an interview with Molly.[2]

Molly's account: extract one

1	*Molly:*	When I was a child, I was seven and the teacher asked
2		another child how much it is four times eight (.) I knew it,
3		but she had asked the other child who didn't know, and as
4		probably she knew that I knew the answer she asked me
5		and I said thirty-two, but I felt very embarrassed because
6		the other girl didn't know the answer and the teacher
7		asked me to stand up and go to the blackboard and she
8		gave me a stick and she asked me to beat the other child
9		(.) I didn't want to (.) so she held my hand and forced me
10		to beat her (.) this gives me a sense of shame, very strong
11		and I remember this as a very bad thing
12	*Bruna:*	Why do you think you felt ashamed?

13	*M*:	Because I had no authority to beat the girl and the teacher

13 *M*:   Because I had no authority to beat the girl and the teacher
14   I felt she was forcing me to do the thing that I didn't want
15   to do, and she put me in front of the whole class to do a
16   bad thing and because I knew the answer I had to beat
17   another child, and it is a very strong confrontation
18   because you have to beat the other one and I felt all these
19   things even if I was only seven and it was very strong [. . .]
20 *B*:   [And] after that you didn't want to say? [. . .]
21 *M*:   No, never (.) I didn't want to because I didn't enjoy that
22   the other ones knew that I knew something, I wanted to
23   keep quiet, perhaps it had some effect until now because it
24   was very strong [. . .]
25 *B*:   But you felt ashamed
26 *M*:   Yes because I felt that I didn't want to do this, and I was
27   forced to do it because she held my hand against my will
28   and she forced me to, I couldn't escape from the situation
29 *B*:   And also do you think the fact that it was in front of the
30   other children made it (.) it was important?
31 *M*:   No, what made me feel strongly was what I did [it] against
32   my will, because I remember that I wasn't looking at the
33   class but I was looking at the girl, but I don't remember
34   the girl I remember the stick and my hand doing a thing
35   that I wouldn't like to do, this is what I remember, and the
36   teacher behind me [. . .] I don't want to have the power to
37   beat another one and the fact that I knew the answer gave
38   me the power to beat another one who didn't know, it
39   would have been easier to be on the other side, to be in the
40   weak position

If we look at this extract from the point of view of psycho-dynamic defences, both formulations (shame functioning as defence and the employment of defences against shame), can be identified. Shame can be read as a defence against an unacceptable drive, whereby Molly's shame is a defensive reaction to her sadistic pleasure in hitting the other girl. Her sadistic impulses have been repressed through the 'damming' action of shame (Freud, 1905) which has transformed pleasure into its opposite: a painful feeling. The splitting-off of the conflict is also highlighted by her dissociation from her own hand: it was the hand that did the bad thing, outside of her control.

At the same time this extract could be read from another point of view, which is what Molly herself suggests. Shame and the memory of it, which has persisted for many years, becomes the focus of the story. Molly is not in control; she is forced to do something unacceptable and experiences intense shame and embarrassment. This experience, a trauma, is at the basis of the shame anxiety. She then associates traumatic shame to situations of 'knowing

something' (lines 16; 22) and of 'speaking up' (lines 20–3). Therefore in order to avoid shame, she avoids situations which, through
this association, would cause shame.

In a psychodynamic reading of the text, Molly is isolated from
the context. The events and the other actors in the external world
are only functional, if not totally irrelevant, to the conflict which is
viewed intrapsychically. On the contrary, a discursive analysis
moves away from the analysis of intentions and hypotheses about
the internal world and looks instead at the 'social' interaction. In
the above extract, this involves three actors (Molly, the teacher and
the other pupil); the 'shameful self' is a joint construction resulting
from their interaction. These three actors occupy three positions in
the account *vis-à-vis* their different relations to power and to each
other.

One of the actors, the female teacher, is in a powerful position
due to her being adult in relation to children and being a teacher in
relation to the pupils. She also holds power within a power/
knowledge discourse. However, this power is not represented as
positive or desirable, but as cruel and sadistic. The teacher's position stands in contrast to that of the girl who does not know the
answer: she is a child, a pupil and she does not know.

Molly's position, however, is at the centre of the action and is the
focus of my analysis. She is in the middle: she is a child and a pupil,
but she has knowledge. It is the knowledge that gives her the power,
identified in the extract as a negative power: '*the fact that I knew the
answer gave me the power to beat another one who did not know*'
(lines 37–8).

From the account, one would assume that the shame was connected to having beaten the other child. To avoid this, one might
expect that the lesson learned would be to refrain from physically
beating others. But when Molly talks about how this affected her
life, what she withdrew from was having knowledge, and the power
associated with it: '*I didn't want to [speak] because I didn't enjoy
that the other ones knew that I knew something, I wanted to keep
quiet*' (lines 21–3). This suggests that the position of shameful is
here constructed as being the one who knows. Hence, 'strong and
knowledgeable' is shameful and has to be avoided, 'weak, ignorant,
victim' is preferable: '*it would have been easier to be on the other side,
to be in the weak position*' (lines 39–40).

However, there is a further subtlety in the text. The issue is not
simply about who knows and who does not, but moreover by
someone knowing that somebody else knows. This is first stated in
lines 4–7 and reiterated in lines 27–8. In line 2 ('*I knew it*') there is
no indication that the knowing is problematic. The situation

becomes conflictual when the teacher knew that she knew (line 4), that is when the private 'I' that knows becomes public and is engaged in a social interaction. It is at this point that Molly becomes silent. What interests me is how the subject moves from being silent to shameful.

There are various avenues open to us in attempting to make sense of this representation; I will first consider the issue of conformity. In the light of the existence of cultural expectations *vis-à-vis* women's relationship to success and power in a patriarchal society, Molly's shame can be read as conformity to these implicit cultural norms. By positioning herself as shameful Molly does not disrupt the cultural expectations of her. In fact she does more than that, because the shameful position in this case (particularly in the light of Gilligan's work), is construed as morally superior. This position could be taken to represent an application of what Wetherell, Stiven and Potter (1987) have called 'practical ideologies', which allow the speaker to justify under a positive light her submission in a power confrontation.

Therefore her withdrawal from conflict and lack of rebelliousness is presented under the positive light of 'non-violence' and refusal to be implicated in the abuse. This presentation of oppression as 'free choice' can be seen in terms of the Foucauldian idea of the 'docile subject', where physical or overt coercion becomes unnecessary as the subject 'chooses' to comply (Foucault, 1977). Ideology, it must be remembered, disguises real relations of power as something more acceptable, more benign, thus assuring the preservation of the power relation (Althusser, 1971; Thompson, 1975). In this instance, the shift from openly physical and psychological coercion to self-oppression is graphically represented. However, what is also stated very clearly in the text is that Molly does not really have a choice whether to be implicated or not.

Crucial to the analysis of this extract from a feminist standpoint is the assumption that the account is located within a patriarchal society and that the interactions have significance (i.e. describe/construct) within it.[3] The patriarchal ideology, however, is hidden by the fact that the dynamic is totally negotiated between women. I find it very significant that what is represented here is the absence of a positive representation of empowerment for women, which, however, is overshadowed by the presentation of the dilemma as a moral choice.

I have already expressed my reservations with the employment of moral discourse to justify women's 'free refusal' of power, and the consequent construction of women as 'better human beings'. One of the most serious consequences of these arguments is that power is taken out of its historical context and becomes a thing *per se*, rather than something that women could use to better their lives. In this instance, for example, Molly could have taken on the teacher's power and become a different kind of teacher or found some way to 'speak up' for the other girl. But by positioning herself as shameful, Molly construes herself as totally powerless, but nevertheless as a moral being. This positions her as a 'nice' girl, who would rather sacrifice herself than hurt other people. This obviously does not exclude the shame for not having resisted.

Resistance, the silent (but docile) subject, and practical ideologies

Molly's reaction can also be read as a resistance to power which is oppressive; she can see what comes with having power and wants no part of it. In order to explore this reading further I want to go back to the conflict between the private, knowing 'I' and the silent, public 'I'. If we take the silencing as the action of power, it is still in the silence that we can find the resistance to the same power. This I identify in the discrepancy described above. The silencing is restricted to the public 'I', because Molly remembers that she knew; she says that she has stopped saying, not stopped knowing. The shame belongs to the public self. In this way I am reading Molly's silence as a way of distancing herself from an oppressive regulatory action she disapproves of (Bhavnani, 1990; Marks, 1993), as a strategy of opposition.

This is a very seductive reading of the text as it allows some space for defiance, but it also has serious repercussions for organized resistance. First, I think that it is very problematic to analyse silence as a language, whether as communication or as strategy. Secondly, silence as a strategy has very isolating and limiting consequences; in terms of organized struggle it isolates women from each other, prevents the sharing of experience and contributes to the view that women's struggles are personal, individual.

And yet, from a merely rhetorical point of view, positioning herself as shameful allows Molly to hold both contradictory positions, at least for the time being. In the second extract, however, the two readings I have suggested so far are represented again and the position of silence is taken to its consequences.

Molly's account: extract two

```
1   M:   [. . .] put down, yes, put down and humiliation and that you
2        are not so strong and you don't know anything about
```

3		something, you are not important, you are something,
4		someone (.) I am thinking of another example, I must have
5		been 6 and I was in the classroom and everything felt very
6		strange, I had just began school and in the break we went to
7		the playground (.) the teacher said something very strange but
8		I believed her. She said to put a sheet of paper on your desk
9		and think of something to be drawn on it and you ask Jesus to
10		come and draw it for you (laughs) and I put my best pencil
11		and I went to play and when I came back there was nothing, I
12		felt so (.) oh God [. . .] how could have I believed her? it was a
13		mixture of feelings (.) humiliated because I trusted her and
14		nothing happened, without power to go there and ask her
15		'where is my drawing, you are a liar, you are not correct' and
16		because I didn't talk I felt ashamed because probably to talk
17		is important, to free the feeling, but I didn't
18	*B*:	And what did you do?
19	*M*:	Nothing, I looked for the paper and I felt that Jesus didn't
20		love me, I am not so good to be loved, because the teacher
21		had said if your behaviour is good in the playground . . . (.)
22		so I thought I had behaved very bad and it was my fault
23		(laughs)

At first glance, this extract seems to describe a very similar situation to the first account as it takes place in the classroom, I assume with the same teacher and at around the same time. There is, however, a crucial difference: this time there are only two people involved: Molly and her teacher and Molly is at the receiving end of the abuse. This takes away Molly's choice whether to be implicated or not.

There is a lot to say about this extract: the difference in connotation attributed to 'knowing', the repeated references to humiliation, weakness, being unimportant and how these feelings are rhetorically used, the depersonalizing implications of referring to herself as 'something, someone', and the description of the classroom, possibly as a site of power, as strange and unfamiliar.

It is, however, what happens between lines 12 and 23 that interests me most, as Molly is forced by the events to abandon the position of observer. She presents two alternative and opposite subject positions: the angry or the shameful position. In lines 16–20 there is the position of anger: Molly hangs on to the knowledge and rebels against the teacher. This position is construed around finding power in one's knowledge. By positioning herself as the knowledgeable, she positions the teacher as the liar. In this context speaking up is clearly presented as empowering and liberating.

The other position follows this in lines 19–23. This is the silent, shameful Molly who turns the anger against herself, denies her knowledge and power and submits to the teacher's representation of events. This is warranted by her positioning herself as unlovable, which reinstates the teacher's authority. It could be argued that this was never fully accomplished, as the position of shame allows Molly to remember the abuse and that she knew she had been wronged.

One could question what benefit challenging the teacher could have brought her, in a situation where there was no real alternative to the establishment. But I am also aware of the fact that subject positions have implications for one's sense of self and self-esteem. Molly's example illustrates how the absence of alternative positions may favour the employment of individual measures with high costs for one's sense of reality.

Finally, if we reconnect the participants' construction of themselves to wider political issues, their silence and withdrawal has serious implications in terms of women's complicity with reproducing what has always been an 'acceptable', but highly limiting and self-destructive view of women. Women's positions in these extracts seem to be in line with an investment in seeing themselves as altruistic and selfless, rather than competitive and needy. This, it has been argued, is due to the fact that 'traditional womanly values' still grant women some power (Coward, 1992). Women might try to access at an individual level some of the power they are excluded from at a social level in a patriarchal society, but in this way leaving social power structures unchallenged.

Conclusions

In this chapter I have explored, through the detailed analysis of two women's accounts, the function of 'practical ideology' (Wetherell and Potter, 1992) of women's positioning themselves as shameful. I have claimed that by doing that, the women interviewed are not just describing but constructing a version of reality that allows them to avoid wider cultural issues and conflict about their access to power. I now want briefly to connect these analyses to the wider concerns of this chapter and the methods of investigation employed. As I stated at the beginning, one of my aims was to address the question of whether poststructuralism is compatible with feminist struggles.

In this chapter I have illustrated how the application of a discursive approach to some feminist theories can reveal how these theories might be instrumental in ideologically re-producing stereotypes of female identity. However, to invoke the need to deconstruct the category 'woman' as unitary and cohesive does not automatically imply having to relinquish the need to gather together around a common cause. More to the point it implies renouncing the illusion of women's shared experience or having privileged access to it simply based on being women. To put it simply, to introduce the idea of difference does not automatically imply giving up common struggle. What it does imply, however, is having to clarify and reflect on one's feminist standpoint. Poststructuralist discursive approaches can be an invaluable tool to do precisely that. In this chapter, for example, I have suspended the automatic self-attribution of women as shameful which has allowed me to then investigate some of the potential investment for women in defining themselves in terms of victimhood.

In terms of shame what I have tried to illustrate in this chapter is how, from a classical psychoanalytic perspective, shame is mainly an intrapsychic phenomenon and accounts of it are expressions of the externalization of internal conflicts. There are two fundamental problems with this rendition from a feminist and poststructuralist point of view. The first is that the conflicts are situated within the individual who in turn is taken out of context, thus inhibiting the awareness of pressures which pertain to women's position in a patriarchal society. This approach has the ideological effect of making a socially constructed issue into an individual problem. The second is that language, in classical psychodynamic practice, is viewed as a means to access a dynamic which takes place in the individual psyche, rather than ideologically constructing it. I have therefore used a poststructuralist discursive approach and feminist concerns to counteract psychoanalytic perspectives on shame. Again, in this way I have demonstrated how analyses of discourse can be used with feminist concerns in mind.

So, does this mean that there is no space left for an extra-discursive dimension in the analysis of subjectivity? Some discourse analysts have answered this question with an emphatic 'no' and argue that experience, and thus subjective psychological reality, is constituted through language and the process of representation. The feeling, therefore:

> . . . is always inevitably identified, labelled and constructed through narrative, language and stories. It is the narrative which packages and thus, in some sense, creates and produces the identity and the desire, and, indeed, it is the narrative we adopt which defines the experience as one of those sorts of experiences and not some other kind of experience. (Wetherell, 1995: 134)

This is very much in line with my argument: I have looked at how the narrative constructs the shameful subject, but also how the account constructs the experience of the feeling of shame. Being able to suspend the belief in the existence of a feeling of shame which exists independently from the context, has allowed me to explore the ideological function of the accounts in question.

However, some authors have lamented the avoidance of the extra-discursive in discursive approaches in social science, for resulting in the false reduction to the premise that the world can be understood as discursive and in the reduction of subjectivity to the sum of positions in discourses (Hollway, 1983, 1995). This, in my view, becomes particularly problematic when 'understanding' is not sufficient and the situation requires action of some kind, as, for example, in clinical settings or with political action. Once we have ascertained that taking one subject position instead of another has real implications for people's well-being and sense of self (Burman and Parker, 1993), what do we do with it?

I would argue against answering the question in terms of forced choices and dichotomies. We need not choose between a psycho-analytic reading when we are in the consulting room, a social constructionist one when in academia and a feminist one when talking politics. Instead, I suggest reciprocally interrogating our discourses and how they inform/construct our practice. Because ultimately, as far as I am concerned, it is the practice which is going to make a difference. I am indeed in agreement with S. Hall when he argues that 'The purpose of theorising is . . . to enable us to grasp, understand, and explain – to produce a more adequate knowledge of – the historical world and its processes; and thereby to inform our practice so that we may transform it' (Hall, 1988: 36).

Thus I have used a psychoanalytic framework to investigate shame, but I have also looked at psychoanalysis as discourse and how it constructs subjectivity. On the other hand, I have also connected the interviewees' accounts to wider feminist discussions on women's relation and access to power in a patriarchal society. Again, in this case too, I have looked at these theories as constructive of a particular female subjectivity. For me it is not a question of having to decide whether all these points of view are compatible; we do not have a choice. We need them all to be able to understand, counteract and prevent people's suffering and oppression. This is, in my view, the point of mutual interrogation: a thorough exploration of the implications of the discursive practices we adopt in our clinical practice, in our writing and in our political activity is the only way forward to recognize our 'blind spots'.

Notes

I would like to thank Karen Henwood and Colleen Heenan for their insightful comments and suggestions on earlier drafts of this chapter.

1 Freud first introduced the idea of shame as a reaction-formation as part of the so-called 'topographical' model (Sandler et al., 1972–75). The topographical model of the mind derives its name from the idea that the mind is divided into systems: the Unconscious, Preconscious and the Conscious which are spatially organized from the depth to the surface (Freud, 1915). Instinctual drives coming from the Unconscious press for gratification or discharge by attempting to become conscious. When the drives are unacceptable they are repressed. Shame, according to Freud, is one of the measures employed to repress unacceptable drives and functions, together with guilt, as a 'dam' which prevents their access into the Conscious (Freud, 1905). In particular, shame is employed to counteract sexual and exhibitionistic drives (Freud, 1905).
2 Many relevant issues will have to be left out for the sake of brevity. An important issue, left undiscussed, is that in both the following extracts we are dealing with women's adult reconstructions of early childhood, educational contexts where issues of power and resistance are specifically framed.
3 This does not exclude other power dynamics, the most important being the real power imbalance between teacher/pupil, adult/child.

References

Althusser, L. (1971) *Lenin and Philosophy and Other Essays*. London: New Left Books.
Anthony, E.J. (1981) 'Shame, guilt and the feminine self in psychoanalysis', in Kaye C. Tuttman and M. Zimmerman (eds), *Object and Self: A Developmental Approach*. New York: International Universities Press.
Bartky, S.L. (1990) 'Shame and gender', in S.L. Bartky's *Femininity and Domination*. London: Routledge.
Bhavnani, K.-K. (1990) 'What's power got to do with it? Empowerment and social research', in I. Parker and J. Shotter (eds), *Deconstructing Social Psychology*. London: Routledge.
Burman, E. and Parker, I. (eds) (1993) *Discourse Analytic Research: Repertoires and Readings of Text in Action*. London: Routledge.
Campbell, F.A. (1984) 'The concept of shame', *Perspectives in Psychiatric Care* 22 (2).
Coward, R. (1992) *Our Treacherous Hearts*. London: Faber & Faber.
Edwards, D. and Potter, J. (1992) *Discursive Psychology*. London: Sage.
Faludi, S. (1991) *Backlash. The Undeclared War against Women*. London: Vintage.
Flax, J. (1990) *Thinking Fragments: Psychoanalysis, Feminism and Postmodernism in the Contemporary West*. Berkeley: University of California Press.
Foucault, M. (1977) *Discipline and Punish: The Birth of the Prison*. London: Allen Lane, Penguin Press.

Freud, S. (1905) *Three Essays on the Theory of Sexuality*. The Standard Edition of the Complete Psychological Works of Sigmund Freud, Vol. VII. London: The Hogarth Press and the Institute of Psychoanalysis.

Freud, S. (1915) *The Unconscious*. The Standard Edition of the Complete Psychological Works of Sigmund Freud, Vol. XIV. London: The Hogarth Press and the Institute of Psychoanalysis.

Gilbert, G.N. and Mulkay, M. (1984) *Opening Pandora's Box: A Sociological Analysis of Scientists' Discourse*. Cambridge: Cambridge University Press.

Gill, R. (1993) 'Justifying injustice: broadcasters' accounts of inequality in radio', in E. Burman and I. Parker (eds), *Discourse Analytic Research: Repertoires and Readings of Texts in Action*. London: Routledge.

Gilligan, C. (1982) *In a Different Voice*. Cambridge, MA: Harvard University Press.

Goss, K., Gilbert, P. and Allan, S. (1994) 'An exploration of shame measures: 1. The other as shamer scale', *Personality and Individual Differences* 17 (5).

Hall, S. (1988) 'The toad in the garden: Thatcherism among the theorists', in C. Nelson and L. Grossberg (eds), *Marxism and the Interpretation of Culture*. Urbana: University of Illinois.

Hibbard, S. (1994) 'An empirical study of the differential roles of libidinous and aggressive shame components in normality and pathology', *Psychoanalytic Psychology* 4.

Hoglund, C.L. and Nicholas, K.B. (1995) 'Shame, guilt and anger in college-students exposed to abusive family environments', *Journal of Family Violence* 10 (2).

Hollway, W. (1983) *Subjectivity and Method in Psychology: Gender, Meaning and Science*. London: Sage.

Hollway, W. (1995) 'Feminist discourses and women's heterosexual desire', in S. Wilkinson and C. Kitzinger (eds) *Feminism and Discourse – Psychological Perspectives*. London: Sage.

Jones, D.J. and Zalewski, C. (1994) 'Shame and depression proneness among female adult children of alcoholics', *International Journal of the Addictions* 29 (12).

Kohut, H. (1977) *The Restoration of the Self*. New York: International Universities Press.

Lewis, H.B. (1971) *Shame and Guilt in Neurosis*. New York: International Universities Press.

Lewis, M. (1992) *Shame, the Exposed Self*. Hillsdale, NJ and London: Lawrence Erlbaum.

Lynd, H.M. (1958) *On Shame and the Search for Identity*. New York: Harcourt, Brace.

McKinlay, A. and Potter, J. (1987) 'Model discourse: interpretative repertoires in scientists' conference talk', *Social Studies of Science* 17: 443–63.

Madill, A. (1995) 'Subject position and discursive process of change in one successful case of psychodynamic-interpersonal psychotherapy', in A. Madill, A Discourse Analytic Approach to Change Processes in Psychodynamic-Interpersonal Psychotherapy. Unpublished PhD thesis, University of Sheffield, Department of Psychology.

Marks, D. (1993) 'Case-conference analysis and action research', in E. Burman and I. Parker (eds), *Discourse Analytic Research: Repertoires and Readings of Text in Action*. London: Routledge.

Morrison, A.P. (1984) 'Working with shame in psychoanalytic treatment', *Journal of the American Psychoanalytic Association* 32 (3).

Morrison, A.P. (1989) *Shame: The Underside of Narcissism*. London: The Analytic Press.

Mulkay, M. (1985) *The Word and the World: Explorations in the Form of Sociological Analysis*. London: Allen and Unwin.

Nathanson, D.L. (1987) 'A timetable for shame', in D.L. Nathanson (ed.), *The Many Faces of Shame*. New York: Guilford Press.

Nathanson, D.L. (1992) *Affect, Sex, and the Birth of the Self*. London: W.W. Norton & Company.

Nathanson, D.L. (1994) 'Shame, compassion and the borderline personality', *Psychiatric Clinics of North America* 17 (4).

Okano, K.I. (1994) 'Shame and social phobia – a transcultural viewpoint', *Bulletin of the Menninger Clinic* 58 (3).

Pines, M. (1987) 'Shame – what psychoanalysis does and does not say', *Group Analysis* 20: 16–31.

Pines, M. (1995) 'The universality of shame: a psychoanalytic approach', *British Journal of Psychotherapy* 11 (3): 346–58.

Potter, J. and Wetherell, M. (1987) *Discourse and Social Psychology*. London: Sage.

Potter, J. and Wetherell, M. (1989) 'Fragmented ideologies: accounts of educational failure and positive discrimination', *Text* 9 (2): 175–90.

Potter, J., Wetherell, M., Gill, R. and Edwards, D. (1990) 'Discourse – noun, verb or social practice', *Psychological Philosophy* 3 (2): 205–17.

Sandler, J., Dare, C. and Holder, A. (1992) *The Patient and the Analyst*. London: Karnac Books.

Sandler, J., Dare, C. and Holder, A. (1972–75) 'Frames of reference in psychoanalytic psychology I–VII', *British Journal of Medical Psychology* 44.

Sayers, J. (1986) *Sexual Contradictions. Psychology, Psychoanalysis and Feminism*. London: Tavistock.

Segal, L. (1991) *Is the Future Female? Troubled Thoughts on Contemporary Feminism*. London: Virago.

Soper, K. (1990) 'Feminism, humanism and postmodernism', *Radical Philosophy* 55: 11–17.

Stanley, L. and Wise, S. (1993) *Breaking Out Again: Feminist Ontology and Epistemology*. London: Routledge.

Tangney, J.P., Wagner, P.E., Hillbarlow, D., Marschall, D.E. and Gramzow, R. (1996) 'Relation of shame and guilt to constructive versus destructive responses to anger across the life-span', *Journal of Personality and Social Psychology* 70 (4).

Thompson, J. (1975) *Studies in the Theory of Ideology*. Cambridge: Polity Press.

Walkerdine, V. (1990) *Schoolgirl Fictions*. London: Verso.

Welldon, E.V. (1988) *Mother, Madonna, Whore: The Idealisation and Denigration of Motherhood*. London: Free Association Books.

Wetherell, M. (1995) 'Romantic discourse and feminist analysis: interrogating investment, power and desire', in S. Wilkinson and C. Kitzinger (eds), *Feminism and Discourse: Psychological Perspectives*. London: Sage.

Wetherell, M. and Potter, J. (1992) *Mapping the Language of Racism: Discourses and Legitimation of Exploitation*. London: Harvester Wheatsheaf.

Wetherell, M., Stiven, H. and Potter, J. (1987) 'Unequal egalitarianism: a preliminary study of discourse concerning gender and employment opportunities', *British Journal of Social Psychology* 26: 59–71.

Wumser, L. (1981) *The Mask of Shame*. Baltimore, MD: Johns Hopkins University Press.

Yorke, C. (1990) 'The development and functioning of the sense of shame', *The Psychoanalytic Study of the Child* 45: 377–409.

8

Gender Practices: Steps in the Analysis of Men and Masculinities

Margaret Wetherell and Nigel Edley

In this chapter we want to focus on men and forms of masculinity. Our aim is to explore some of the approaches and concepts which we think should form the basis for an adequate *feminist social psychology* of masculine identities. We will argue that such a social psychology can draw from recent developments in poststructuralist theory (broadly defined) but must also take as its topic the everyday practical activities of men, and thus must find ways of productively researching masculinities *in situ*, in context.

The term 'feminist' signals, of course, a particular standpoint or orientation to research on men and forms of masculinity. In common with other feminist writers we see our work as having a strongly 'deconstructive' flavour. One of the most important achievements of feminist research and politics has been to *problematize* men's privileged position as knowers and social actors (see Edley and Wetherell, 1995: Chapter 6 this volume; Griffin and Wetherell, 1992; Segal, 1990; Wetherell and Griffin, 1991, for reviews of feminist research). Indeed, feminism succeeds to the extent that men become questionable and gendered, no longer normal and unremarkable or 'foundational'. In a profound sense, the aim of feminism has been to *relativize* masculinity and men's claims to authority in all domains. These goals and achievements recently have been reinforced and strengthened through post-structuralist and postmodern feminist explorations (Butler, 1990; Haraway, 1991; Nicholson, 1990).

The development of an appropriate and useful feminist social psychology of masculine identities is a huge task. Our intention in this chapter is simply to take one step along that road. We want to focus on some selected notions of *gender practice* and then move on to a few, more limited, reflections on the articulation of identities. Our guiding questions are these: how can we make sense of what men do in social life? What theoretical approaches might be most productive? And, how can we instantiate global analyses of this practice on the ground, specifically, in the texture and substance of men's talk and in the discourses which produce masculinity?

In this chapter we begin by taking up two of the more interesting notions of social practice which are available. In both cases we see some clear connections with the theoretical moves characteristic of poststructuralism, even if these connections are not necessarily endorsed by their authors. The first section takes up the notion of practice found in the highly influential feminist sociology of masculinities developed by Connell (1987, 1995a) and his colleagues (Carrigan et al., 1985). The second section examines notions of the practical found in ethnomethodological studies (Boden and Zimmerman, 1991; Garfinkel, 1967; Heritage, 1984). We then go on to consider notions of practice found in discursive psychology (e.g. Edwards, 1997; Edwards and Potter, 1992; Potter, 1996; Potter and Wetherell, 1987; Wetherell and Potter, 1992) and in wider discourse theory before, finally, in the last two sections, developing some thoughts on subjectivity and the process of identification.

Social practices and social structures

Connell's work in recent years has become a central reference point for many, if not most, writers on men and masculinity. The attraction derives from his unusually consistent and articulate pro-feminist stance and his lucid analyses of the social practices and social structures of gender relations. In terms of the debates which inform this volume, however, Connell stands in a rather anomalous position. On the one hand, as will become clear, aspects of his theoretical commitments are commensurate with feminist post-structuralist analyses. Yet, on the other, he has been sharply critical of new emphases on gender as performance (e.g. Butler, 1990), the stress on shifting sexual identities and queer theory, and what he sees as a focus on signification and discourse at the expense of material and structural forms of organization. The danger, for Connell, is that discursive 'play' comes to replace 'serious politics' (e.g. Connell, 1995b: 385).

Connell's interests lie in the nature of the social processes which organize man's lives and from which forms of masculinity emerge. He stresses two themes in his account of these processes and much of his writing consists of puzzling over the relationship between them. On the one hand, he wants to analyse gender as practice; as a process of negotiation, choice and human production. Gender relations, he argues, emerge from people's practical activities and within a social field which is always, one could say, heaving and boiling. Connell stresses the historical and transformative nature of social action, the restless flow of human activity which makes up social life. From this perspective, gender is always *accomplished*, it is something produced by people in their daily activities at work, at home, in schools, through the consumption of goods and services, and so on. Connell wants to focus on what people *do* to actively constitute social relations.

So there is practice, but in Connell's scheme there is also structure. He argues that structures (defined as order, pattern, organization, constraint) emerge from practice (understood in broad terms as human activity). It is not the case that anything goes – people cannot do just as they wish – there is order and pattern to people's productions. Connell wants to convey:

> . . . a strong sense of the constraining power of gender relations (and other structures like class and race), a sense of something that people fetch up against. Yet this 'something' is neither abstract nor simple, being real in other people and their actions, with all their complexities, ambiguities and contradictions. And this reality is constantly being worked on and – in ways pleasant and unpleasant – transformed. (Connell, 1987: 61–2)

This problem of how to relate human action with social order is, of course, not a new one and has been central to much sociological discussion. In the way in which he tries to put both together, Connell (1987) aligns himself with social theorists such as Sartre, Kosik, Bourdieu and Giddens (although he is also critical of trends in this work). Following Kosik, Connell describes practice as 'ontoformative'. In other words, people's decisions and actions are seen as creating realities which then condition, constrain or set the scene for their future practice. 'Practice never occurs in a vacuum. It always responds to a situation, and situations are structured in ways that admit certain possibilities and not others' (Connell, 1995a: 65).

Connell illustrates these points in more concrete terms in the life histories developed in his book *Masculinities* (1995a) and in the case study of the teenage girl he calls Delia Prince in *Gender and Power* (1987). He argues that Delia's life, her decision to leave school early, her desire to emulate her mother and become a bank clerk and even her self-perception as someone who is fond of animals are strongly patterned and yet open-ended. These decisions and attributes are a clear product of personal choices and preferences which, at the same time, are socially organized. The specific arrangement of Delia's family relationships and experiences, the allocation of work along gendered lines, the intersection of class, 'race' and gender produce a set of constraints and limits to the play of practice which can also be experienced, at times, as exciting possibilities and opportunities.

In particular in these analyses, Connell wants to avoid a number of features he associates with conventional structuralist-functionalist sociology and with the structuralism of Levi-Strauss and Althusser, for example. These present an analysis of social life which, in Connell's view, is not sufficiently weighted towards the transformative power of practice. There is too much emphasis on social life as a system which could be modelled or analysed as a set of rules, containing a fixed internal logic, or set of originary determining causes. Connell (1987: Chapter 5) argues that it is more appropriate for the analysts to see their task as taking a 'structural inventory' of the constraining features in a particular social situation but regarding these features as continually being constituted and transformed in 'real time'.

In common with a number of feminist writers (see Walby, 1990), Connell argues that there is not just one gender structure (such as an overarching, singular, patriarchal system) but a number of different sites and regimes which, while constantly transforming, work to maintain gender inequality. Some of these structures may conflict with each other such as, for instance, the assignment of domestic work to women and the requirements placed on women in professional workplaces. Similarly, the lives of many gay men in the military are organized by their implicit or explicit challenge to the regulatory structures of heterosexuality, but also by the privileged forms of masculinity encouraged in such institutional sites.

Connell's emphasis on practice leads him to stress (in a move reminiscent of poststructuralist and postmodern theorizing) the multiple, local, fragmented and highly contextual nature of gendered identities. Power is also central to his analysis and the ways in which power relations produce subjectivities. Invoking Gramsci's analysis of the development of hegemony in class relations, Connell argues that the social field of gender is riven with struggles for ascendancy. Dominance is achieved culturally and ideologically as much as (or as well as) through other forms of control, force and authority. It is also (usually) relative – a balance of forces and alignments rather than a once-and-for-all victory.

As a consequence of these emphases on the continual production of dominance in the form of hegemonic masculinity and the plural rather than unitary character of men's experiences, a more complicated picture of sexual politics emerges. As Carrigan, Connell and Lee (1985) note, most men benefit from patriarchal practices and most women do not. There is certainly a considerable 'patriarchal dividend' most men accrue which produces masculine characters. But it is also possible to identify 'subordinated masculinities' and 'complicit masculinities' where the alignment with hegemonic forms of masculinity is more complex (see Connell, 1995a, for further details).

Broadly speaking, then, Connell's sociology of gender relations develops one possible 'take' on what it might mean to say that masculinity is a *practical* accomplishment. There is a theory here of the interweaving of the personal and the social and a sketch of the nature of the male subject or social actor as a practitioner in a structured social field. Yet, as mentioned earlier, in terms of debates about poststructuralism, postmodernism and discourse theory, Connell stands in a rather ambiguous position. His is a theory which has not been overtly informed by recent accounts of the decentred subject or developments in discourse theory. Indeed, Connell often explicitly rejects such developments. Nevertheless, his work hits on a number of themes and makes a number of theoretical commitments which are not incommensurate with a feminist social psychology of men and masculinities informed by poststructuralism. What remains mysterious, however, is what practice looks like 'on the ground'. What kind of activities are these? And, how do masculinities emerge 'in practice'? How is this sense of something external, constraining and superordinate which is also productive, active, changing and flowing to be managed analytically? Difficult as it might be in theoretical and analytical terms to put these things together (see Boden and Zimmerman, 1991), some answers to these questions can be found within ethnomethodology.

Masculinities as participants' methods

What sense of practice and the practical is found in ethnomethodology? Here the pattern of emphasis changes from the more or less organized to the more or less self-organizing. Practice in the most general sense becomes more clearly defined as practical *accomplishment* in the here and now. Ethnomethodologists examine the ways in which ordinary people put together activities in everyday life (see Heritage, 1984). They look at how people make sense of these activities and, most importantly, make them *accountable*. The topic is 'participants' methods' or people's common-sense understandings of how to be in different social contexts.

To take an example – a shop-keeper going about her business produces a stream of relatively orderly and predictable activity. In Connell's terms one might say she is engaging in a social practice which helps to constitute the social and economic structures of capitalism. From an ethnomethodological perspective, however, the point would be to examine *being* a 'shop-keeper' – as a practical achievement. The person is engaged in a wide range of relevant activities which relate to tasks and which may 'invoke' more than one identity. The focus would be on studying the standard sequences which make up service encounters and the ways in which they arise from and may depart from the more basic business of social interaction.

The claim is that social order is not a 'top-down' process, the regulation of practice by past practice solidified into social structures, but instead orderliness is created out of participants' artful methods. Furthermore, activities depend on collaboration with others. The 'solidity' of social relationships thus depends on an ongoing process of accountability. 'Shop-keeperness' is a joint production with all participants (positioned as customers, suppliers, bankers, delivery boys and girls) drawing on their common-sense understandings to produce this activity. People are accountable to each other in interaction and thus departures from 'what everybody knows to be appropriate' require explanation and create 'trouble' in the interaction which will need repair.

One of the most persuasive examples of the application of this type of analysis to gender remains Garfinkel's (1967) study of Agnes, a person whose sexual status was in doubt (see also Kessler and McKenna, 1978; West and Zimmerman, 1991). Anatomically male, Agnes claimed to be 'naturally female'. Garfinkel's interest was in how Agnes produced herself as such, how she passed as feminine in her daily life, and made herself accountable to others as feminine. Garfinkel insisted that this study was relevant, not just to the community of those with gender and sexual identities deemed problematic, but also to those regarded as 'just normal'. Agnes could reveal many aspects of 'ordinary' participants' methods for being gendered. For Agnes, what seems to come mostly 'naturally' had to be an object of careful study. In constructing herself as just an ordinary female, Agnes revealed the details of a process of production usually hidden in the taken for granted.

As John Heritage points out:

> . . . it is surprising to realise the extent to which gender differentiation consists of a filigree of small-scale, socially organised behaviours which are unceasingly iterated. Together these – individually insignificant – behaviours interlock to constitute the great public institution of gender as a morally-organised-as-natural fact of life. This institution is comparatively resistant to change. To adapt Wittgenstein's famous analogy, the social construction of gender from a mass of individual social practices resembles the spinning of a thread in which fibre is spun on fibre. And, as Wittgenstein points out, 'the strength of the thread does not reside in the

fact that some one fibre runs through its whole length, but in the overlapping of many fibres' (Wittgenstein, 1958: para. 67e). But if gender manifests itself as a density of minutiae, the latter are nonetheless stabilised both individually and collectively by the apparatus of moral accountability which we have repeatedly seen in action. (Heritage, 1984: 197)

It is our contention that Connell's conception of gender practice and Garfinkel's focus on participants' methods can be made to fit together even though there are also some points of conflict. For instance, Connell, like the ethnomethodologist, rejects any simple sense of people as rule-following or as socially determined. Connell (1987) argues cogently, for example, against the determinist stance of role theories and wants to celebrate instead people's creativity, inventiveness and the *constitutive* nature of their activity. Now ethnomethodologists could be said to have actually instantiated these claims. They have demonstrated very effectively that people cannot be said to follow rules in the way a pen, for instance, follows a template. On the contrary, social rules (such as they are) have to be invoked, worked up, made relevant and managed as a local scheme of accountability. The main force of rules, indeed, is often rhetorical. In Connell's perspective we are left with a sense of people as not determined but nonetheless constrained by social structure or past social practice where what 'constraint' might look like is left rather vague. The enormous advantage of ethnomethodology, and the study of participants' methods and procedures of accountability, is that it begins to explicate how 'constraint' might operate and what 'constraint' is in terms of procedural consequentiality.

Where Connell's notion of social practice and ethnomethod-ology's stance on the 'practical' part company, however, is in terms of analysis and in the drawing of conclusions from examples and case studies. On the one hand, sociologists of social practice are usually happy to describe a practice as imbued with power, as ideological in its effects or clearly relevant to the maintenance of gender inequalities. They are satisfied that power, ideology and inequality can be 'discovered' or identified by the analyst, and may be in no sense an obvious participants' concern or even necessarily evident in the immediate interactional procedures. On the other hand, however, advocates of forms of analysis based on ethno-methodological principles such as conversation analysis advocate a kind of analytic scepticism (see Schegloff, 1991). Put crudely, the challenge might be: well, show me how gender structures (in whatever sense) are relevant to understanding the organization of this particular interaction? In what sense are these displayed as participants' concerns? Show me the procedural consequences for the organization of the interaction? Where *exactly* is this gender business happening?

Clearly it is not easy to reconcile these two positions. For example, how can we begin to look for the workings of ideology when, in principle, we are restricted by the limits of participants' concerns? Must we really have to wait until they start talking about power and patriarchy before we, as analysts, can invoke such concepts? In our view we do not. However, in order to do an adequate discourse analysis of gender practice we need to move away from the kinds of analyses which involve very short sequences of interaction transcribed using a full conversation analytic scheme. Instead, what we need are more extended bodies of data, involving larger samples of interaction, such that it becomes possible to identify discursive patterns or regularities across a wide variety of social and institutional contexts. Only then can we begin to see the ways in which gender operates in practice. Only then will we be able to appreciate its dual nature as both constituted and constitutive (see Wetherell and Potter (1992) for an analysis of this kind on racist discourse).

To sum up the argument so far – from Connell we take the focus on social practice as the prime site where gender happens. In addition, we take the point that this is a site of power and privilege where, from a feminist perspective, inequality and exploitation are generated. But, to reiterate, what is missing in Connell's analysis is any immediately useful form of social psychological analysis of practice in context. In comparison, the advantage of ethnomethodology is that in this (and related) disciplines, practice is fleshed out in much more detail as a phenomenon and, we would argue, as a psychological event and process. Neither of the two approaches considered so far could be described as obviously feminist poststructuralist in their orientation. Their concerns become more commensurate, however, when placed within the orbit of a third sense or conception of the practical; that found within discourse theory and discursive psychology.

Discursive practice

As Garfinkel points out, for Agnes, a key issue was learning to 'talk like a woman'. Equally, 'talking like a man' is central to the production of masculinity. One of the most important developments typically linked to poststructuralist (and to a lesser extent) postmodern currents of thought has been this emphasis on discourse and discursive practice, encouraging the proliferation of discourse theories across the field of gender studies. There is much that divides these discourse theories. But what they share in common is a decisive break with a view of language as a transparent or reflective medium – epi-phenomenal and after the fact. As Edwards succinctly puts it, this is a move away from a view of 'discourse as representation, expression, communication, best sense, best efforts, decontextualised, doing-nothing pictures of mind and world: reflection on activities rather than activity itself' (1997: 270).

In terms of the social psychological perspective we wish to develop, there are several different (and more or less contentious) ways in which this notion of discourse as social action modifies notions of practice. These concern both the 'global' (the broad understanding of social life) and the 'local' (our understanding of the relevant psychological field). We will take the broad re-conceptualization first. Here, of course, the various readings of Foucault's work have been most decisive.

Foucault's emphasis on the constitutive power of language understood as discourses, or as discursive or epistemic regimes, has made it more difficult to rely on any simple division of social practices into the symbolic versus the material (see also Laclau and Mouffe, 1987). Our sense of the nature of the social field has changed. Any distinction between what is 'just words', 'just signification' or 'just talk' versus what is 'really real', 'really effective' or 'real politic' becomes harder and harder to sustain in any coherent way. Certainly, we agree with Connell that the kinds of gender politics generated by discourse perspectives need to be scrutinized for their effectiveness. But Connell's critiques (1995a: 51) of what he sees as 'wholly semiotic' (and thus automatically ineffective) accounts of gender are, in our view, a misunderstanding of the force of these new developments.

All things are brought into being for humans, and have their nature defined, through systems of meaning. In studying the social practices relevant to masculinity from this general perspective, it is a case of asking the kinds of questions established so persuasively by Foucault and those influenced by his work. What, for example, is the history (genealogy) of a particular form of knowledge practice? How have the objects and categories central to the practice been formulated? What kinds of subjects have been produced? What are the power relations which are operating in this constitution? Famously, Foucault demonstrated how the conditions of transformation and possibility associated with medicine and other 'caring professions' could be analysed in this way (Foucault, 1977, 1979).

These were useful questions to ask in our own empirical work on middle-class male school students (Edley and Wetherell, 1997;

Wetherell and Edley, 1994). Questions, for instance, about the history of the practices of the institution, the particular school in which the boys were embedded, such as practices around sport (rugby) and the honours system based on sporting prowess. Various commentators have noted the importance of the public school sporting ethos in the emergence of bourgeois notions of 'manliness' in the nineteenth century (e.g. Park, 1987). It also seemed important to ask about the kinds of subjectivities which became constructed and valorized in this practice, and, to develop an argument about the power relations between groups of young men constituted through these accepted forms of 'self-discipline'. All in all, this Foucauldian-influenced stance on practice leads to a better understanding of notions of hegemonic masculinity introduced by Carrigan, Connell and Lee (1985).

While this is informative about the broad conditions and constitution of practice, the development of discursive psychology (Edwards and Potter, 1992; Potter and Wetherell, 1987), cultural psychology (Bruner, 1990), studies of rhetoric (Billig, 1987), social constructionism (Gergen, 1985), and action theory in developmental psychology (Wertsch, 1991) has re-worked the relevance of immediate, interactional, culturally and socially informed practices for understanding people's psychology. At this point, the focus changes from 'discourse as a noun' to 'discourse as a verb' (Potter et al., 1990). The claim is that one prime site for the social psychologist is mundane everyday talk – conversation and chat. From this angle, radically different understandings of processes typically understood as cognitive, private and internal (memory, emotion, categorization, attitudes, and so on) emerge. In general, the effect of these kinds of interventions on notions of the practical and practice have been to re-focus attention on language, discourse and the semiotic and to produce a thorough examination of the dependence of social and psychological life on the discursive.

Studying masculinity as a discursive practice in these combined senses has meant, among other things, examining how the meaning of masculinity (the kind of thing it is for participants) flows across texts and contexts (such as the transcript of a conversation or interaction among boys about the nature of their sixth-form common room). Examining the texts which make up our research project, for instance, it is possible to see a constant process of stabilizing and destabilizing around what masculinity represents. Meanings are established, reflectively and unreflectively, for numbers of turns, only to be opened up, re-worked, made provisional, destabilized and re-stabilized. It is this kind of variation which led Billig, Condor, Edwards, Gane, Middleton and Radley

(1988) to argue for a view of the ideological field as 'dilemmatic', inconsistent, fragmented; a patchwork or kaleidoscope which people reproduce as they puzzle over the fragments. Yet this is also an ordered or patterned fragmentation, full of repetition, continuity across conversations and predictable positionings of self and others.

Discourse theory, therefore, irretrievably alters notions of practice. But what is happening here to our understanding of the practitioner? To see where we have got to in this discussion we want to come back now to male subjectivities.

Contrasting analyses of subjectivity

In fact, the notions of gender practice we have been exploring tread an uneasy path between the person as practitioner and the person as 'practised upon'. Take Connell, for example (Wetherell, 1996). He argues in *Gender and Power* (1987) for a view of subjectivity which has a lot in common with the positions on 'human nature' found in existential psychoanalysis and versions of humanistic marxism. For Connell, personality, like social life, is best understood as a stream of practice (activity). He notes that social practice and personal practice amount to one and the same thing – these are just different angles or perspectives on what humans do. The sociologist is interested in how these activities constitute social life, while for the individual, these choices and actions, the working over of available social materials, come over time to constitute a personal history, a distinctive life, character and personality.

Furthermore, following Sartre, Connell argues that people can be known by their 'identity projects'. These projects are sets of choices or attempts at the reconciliation and unification of diverse and often contradictory social 'logics'. People are caught at the cross-roads of various social structures such as those associated with gender, class and race. However, they do not passively act out or reproduce social conflicts but work these into a set of personal choices, into a personality, and sometimes what could be called a 'psychopathology'. Sartre's (1988) biography of Jean Genet represents the best attempt at this style of analysis. He shows how Genet's choices to be 'saint' and 'thief' make sense as an active working through of a complex set of social constraints. The result is a life history which is unique, stylized, chosen but also patterned and socially constituted, one which reproduces social structures through personal practice.

This outline of the formation of individual subjectivity and character is very appealing. Yet, again, as a social psychology it is lacking in detail, 'floating above' the level of materials we want to analyse. It is more developed, however, than the notion of subject found in ethnomethodology. There all that has seemed necessary is a sketch of some general characteristics. The 'members' analysed by Garfinkel and others are productive, active, reflexive and performative. It is these largely unexplicated qualities which make accountability effective, and allow for the recognizing and repair of 'trouble'.

In contrast, the subject of Foucault's discourse theory is strongly 'positioned'. Foucault argues that Western notions of the autonomous and independent social actor and our notions of character, personality, the inward life and, indeed, the 'life project' itself are an effect of discursive practices. Discourses produce subject positions, and in speaking and being constructed by them, the person becomes 'subjected'. Life history thus becomes a form of 'genealogy'. Rose describes this change in emphasis as follows:

> A genealogy of subjectification takes this individualized, interiorized, totalized and psychologized understanding of what it is to be human as delineating the site of a historical problem, not providing the grounds for an historical narrative. Such a genealogy works towards an account of the ways in which this modern 'regime of the self' emerges, not as the outcome of any gradual process of enlightenment, in which humans, aided by the endeavours of science, come at last to recognize their true nature, but out of a number of contingent and altogether less refined and dignified practices and processes. To write such a genealogy is to seek to unpick the ways in which 'the self' that functions as a regulatory ideal in so many aspects of our contemporary forms of life . . . is a kind of 'irreal' plan of projection, put together somewhat contingently and haphazardly at the intersection of a range of distinct histories – of forms of thought, techniques of regulation, problems of organization, and so forth. (Rose, 1996: 129)

Although the study of the various techniques of self-production Rose identifies must be a central part of a social psychology of gender, this is also too broad brush an account to deal with the moment-to-moment display of gender business in everyday life.

As its critics (Bowers, 1988; Madill and Doherty, 1994) have noted, discursive psychology has moved rather unevenly between the Foucauldian sense of discourse as constitutive of the self (see also Burman and Parker, 1993; Parker, 1992) and the notion of the self found in ethnomethodology and conversation analysis as an active and reflexive performer. In studies of areas such as memory, one strategy has been to focus on the formulation of memory in discourse, the discursive activities topicalized as remembering, while remaining 'agnostic' about cognitive theories of memory processes (Edwards and Potter, 1992). A similar strategy could be applied to notions of agency, personality or individual difference – how do individual differences become topicalized in discourse, under what circumstances and to what end (e.g. Marshall and Wetherell, 1989)?

These two notions of self as positioned and as active creator need to be constantly juggled, and come in and out of focus depending on the analytic frame. As Billig (1991) has noted, both these senses need to be carried forward in social psychological research. A similar point has been made recently by Hall (1996) in a brilliant introduction to some of the difficulties around the term 'identity'. The questions Hall raises concern the process of 'identification'. He notes that, on the one hand, identifications are moments of interpellation, moments of successful incorporation as the speaking subjects of discourses. To identify is to be persuasively addressed and overcome by the available 'subject slots' in the relevant discursive regimes. However, to go too far with this emphasis, is to make the mistake Hall associates with Foucault, particularly in his early work. Where is the space for resistance, for social change and transformation? What is required, in Hall's view, is some analysis of *articulation* (how the speaking subject becomes stitched into discourse) and *investment* (the eagerness, emotion and desire the act of identification assumes).

> The question which remains is whether we also require to, as it were, close the gap between the two: that is to say, a theory of what the mechanisms are by which individuals identify (or do not identify) with the 'positions' to which they are summoned; as well as how they fashion, stylize, produce and 'perform' these positions, and why they never do so completely, for once and all time, and some never do, or are in a constant, agonistic process of struggling with, resisting, negotiating and accommodating the normative or regulative rules with which they confront and regulate themselves. In short, what remains is the requirement to think this relation of subject to discursive formations *as an articulation.* (Hall, 1996: 13–14, emphasis in original)

This is a useful manifesto for a social psychology of gender practice. The task becomes one of developing analytic concepts which capture this sense of articulation and the double sense of 'practitioner' and 'practised upon' discussed earlier (Hall's second specification of 'investment' remains a story for another day).

Identification in practice

It is not our intention in this theoretical chapter to engage in detailed analysis of discursive material but, to conclude, we want now to look at one piece of such material as a way of recapitulating on some of our main points. This fragment of data concerns 'identification' in Hall's sense and consists of a conversation between three young men (given the pseudonyms of Carl, Adrian and Philip) and their interviewer (Nigel Edley). This material was part of our research into the production of middle-class masculinity in the school we studied.

Nigel:	(. . .) are there any people in the media, in maybe in film, or anything to do with music who you would identify with in any particularly strong way?
Carl:	I don't think there's any particular person.
Adrian:	There are people who I would like to identify with but not unless they were . . .
Nigel:	Who are they?
Adrian:	Erm . . .
Philip:	Do you mean their pose, the way they look or the way they think?
Nigel:	No, I'm just interested in any sort of media image as I say it could be film, magazines, it could be the musical realm or sport for that matter, who you would identify yourself with or find attractive? I mean who were you going to say about liking to identify with? (to Adrian)
Adrian:	Well it's just like the kind of thing, the way he is like erm, I like Harrison Ford, I think, like the Indiana Jones kind of image, it's quite an appealing image I think.
Nigel:	Right do you . . .
Adrian:	Because of the explorations . . . what he does. I think that's a kind of appealing image to me.
Nigel:	So, very sort of active and exciting sort of thing?
Adrian:	Yeah
Nigel:	Is he very . . . is he macho or not?
Philip:	In the film he's portrayed as both . . .
Adrian:	He's humorously macho.
Nigel:	Ah hmm
Carl:	He's not sort of like erm like Rambo?
Adrian:	No . . . but there's a hint of humour in what he does.
Nigel:	Right, do you like the Harrison Ford figure? (to Philip)
Philip:	He appeals to everybody, I suppose, I mean that adventure type thing, it would appeal to everybody.
Carl:	I think his character has got a certain amount of affection to it as well, not just being macho but he's also er, he's affectionate, he's
Philip:	Vulnerable.
Nigel:	Vulnerable?
Philip:	I suppose.
Adrian:	Like um, did you watch that King Solomon's Mines the other night with Richard Chamberlain in?
Nigel	No
Adrian:	That was a kind of . . .
Philip:	That was *amazing*!

> *Nigel*:   Was it an old film?
> *Adrian*: No, it was relatively . . .
> *Carl*:   1989 (inaudible)
> *Philip*: But it's just that it was *so* terrible.
> *Adrian*: It was a really good film, bizarre, I thought, it was like . . .
> *Philip*: It was so bad that it sort of . . .
> *Adrian*: It was the kind of thing that's quite appealing, I mean going out into Africa, into the outback if you call it that in Africa, into the jungle, I think that's quite appealing.
> *Nigel*:   Yeah, yeah, I think there's some connection there with a past description or a type of masculinity, if you like . . . erm . . . sort of lone ranger, off he goes into the sunset, to discover what the world is like.

In this sequence, which is part of a much longer and frequently recurring conversation about media images in our materials, the interviewer (Nigel) presents various possible hegemonic masculinities for discussion. He develops an intertext of masculine positions which are also, of course, racialized and classed positions (e.g. Indiana Jones, Rambo). The conversation can be seen in effect as one (small) moment of gender practice. But, crucially, it is a conversation not just about masculinity; it is also a conversation which *does* masculinity, in the ethnomethodological sense. The participants, as they talk, are continually constituting themselves as gendered speakers and as characters with stories to tell, people with beliefs, views and standpoints. This is a conversation, like all interaction, which is intensely located, where the relevant contexts are multiple and related in complex ways. At one level, for instance, this is a conversation for an audience (in this case an audience of social scientists). It is a set of formulations defined as part of research and is permeated with participants' understandings of such events and the genre of the 'interview'. However, this is also a conversation among friends which resonates with and carries forward voices, positions and identities from other contexts and other conversations (see Maybin's (1997) analysis of voice and identity).

Usefully, it also displays and illustrates the tensions around identification Hall discusses. On the one hand, it is possible to see Adrian, Carl and Philip (particularly Carl and Philip) as resisting any easy sense of identification with cultural heros. Indeed, in the first part of the extract, any such identification is hedged. The performance of heroes is only 'quite appealing' or 'quite enjoyable' and any appeal is justified and distanced through noting that 'everybody would feel this way'. There is something troubled here about assenting to Nigel's suggestions and requests for examples of identification (see Widdicombe and Wooffitt, 1995). One could argue that the interpellations suggested by Nigel are resisted because a more powerful subject position is at stake here: the rational or thoughtful and above all independent individual, one who is the judge of what is presented rather than the one who is (childishly) engaged and swept away by fantasy. Any movement from one category to the other needs repair and careful management.

In a sense, therefore, this short extract serves to demonstrate how the theoretical exploration of the notion of practice, the double sense of positioning and being positioned, and Hall's notions of articulation are necessary territory and background. We have drawn in this chapter on a number of sources which exemplify some of the issues at stake in the development of a feminist, broadly post-structuralist, social psychology of gender. Despite the paradoxes and points of tension, the orientation to practice provided by Connell's work, ethnomethodology and discourse theories provides a frame for making partial sense of the events, subjectivities, interactions and personal histories we wish to describe and which were evident in the extract above. These understandings don't solve the problem of how to talk about the patterns in discursive material, or how to frame the local analytic concepts which would make up a social psychology of gender, but we have tried to argue that they do set the scene for those concepts in useful ways.

Note

The empirical research described in this chapter was funded by an ESRC Grant No. R000233129. Margaret Wetherell would like to thank Jonathan Potter (Loughborough University) for many useful discussions of ethnomethodology and conversation analysis and Paul du Gay and Liz McFall (Open University) for focusing her mind on the problems with simple accounts of social practice.

References

Billig, M. (1987) *Arguing and Thinking: A Rhetorical Approach to Social Psychology.* Cambridge: Cambridge University Press.

Billig, M. (1991) *Ideology, Rhetoric and Opinion.* London: Sage.

Billig, M., Condor, S., Edwards, D., Gane, M., Middleton, D. and Radley, A. (1988) *Ideological Dilemmas.* London: Sage.

Boden, D. and Zimmerman, D. (1991) *Talk and Social Structure.* Cambridge: Polity Press.

Bowers, J. (1988) 'Review essay: discourse analysis and social psychology', *British Journal of Social Psychology* 27: 185–92.

Bruner, J. (1990) *Acts of Meaning.* Cambridge, MA: Harvard University Press.

Burman, E. and Parker, I. (eds) (1993) *Discourse Analytic Research. Repertoires and Readings of Texts in Action.* London: Routledge.

Butler, J. (1990) *Gender Trouble.* New York: Routledge.

Carrigan, T., Connell, R.W. and Lee, J. (1985) 'Towards a new sociology of masculinity', *Theory and Society* 14: 551–604.

Connell, R.W. (1987) *Gender and Power.* Cambridge: Polity Press.

Connell, R.W. (1995a) *Masculinities.* Cambridge: Polity Press.

Connell, R.W. (1995b) 'Democracies of pleasure: thoughts on the goals of radical sexual politics', in L. Nicholson and S. Seidman (eds), *Social Postmodernism: Beyond Identity Politics.* Cambridge: Cambridge University Press.

Edley, N. and Wetherell, M. (1995) *Men in Perspective: Practice, Power and Identity.* London: Harvester Wheatsheaf.

Edley, N. and Wetherell, M. (1997) 'Jockeying for position: the construction of masculine identities', *Discourse & Society* 8 (2): 203–17.

Edwards, D. (1997) *Discourse and Cognition.* London: Sage.

Edwards, D. and Potter, J. (1992) *Discursive Psychology.* London: Sage.

Foucault, M. (1977) *Discipline and Punish: The Birth of the Prison.* London: Allen Lane, Penguin Press.

Foucault, M. (1979) *The History of Sexuality. Vol. 1: An Introduction.* London: Allen Lane.

Garfinkel, H. (1967) *Studies in Ethnomethodology.* Englewood Cliffs, NJ: Prentice-Hall.

Gergen, K. (1985) 'The social constructionist movement in modern psychology', *American Psychologist* 40: 266–75.

Griffin, C. and Wetherell, M. (1992) 'Feminist psychology and the study of men and masculinity. Part 2: Politics and practices', *Feminism and Psychology* 2: 133–68.

Hall, S. (1996) 'Introduction: who needs "identity"?', in S. Hall and P. du Gay (eds), *Questions of Cultural Identity.* London: Sage.

Haraway, D. (1991) *Simians, Cyborgs, and Women: The Reinvention of Nature.* London: Routledge.

Heritage, J. (1984) *Garfinkel and Ethnomethodology.* Cambridge: Polity Press.

Kessler, S. and McKenna, W. (1978) *Gender: An Ethnomethodological Approach.* New York: Wiley.

Laclau, E. and Mouffe, C. (1987) 'Post-Marxism without apologies', *New Left Review* 166: 79–106.

Madill, A. and Doherty, K. (1994) '"So you did what you wanted then?": discourse analysis, personal agency and psychotherapy', *Journal of Community and Applied Psychology* 4: 261–73.

Marshall, H. and Wetherell, M. (1989) 'Talking about career and gender identities: a discourse analysis perspective', in S. Skevington and D. Baker (eds), *The Social Identity of Women.* London: Sage.

Maybin, J. (1997) 'Children's voices: the contribution of informal language practices to the negotiation of knowledge and identity amongst 10–12 year-old school pupils'. Unpublished thesis, The Open University.

Nicholson, L. (ed.) (1990) *Feminism/Postmodernism.* New York: Routledge.

Park, R.J. (1987) 'Biological thought, athletics and the formation of a "man of character": 1830–1900', in J.A. Mangan and J. Walvin (eds), *Manliness and Morality: Middle-class Masculinity in Britain and America, 1800–1940.* Manchester: Manchester University Press.

Parker, I. (1992) *Discourse Dynamics.* London: Routledge.

Potter, J. (1996) *Representing Reality: Discourse, Rhetoric and Social Constructionism.* London: Sage.

Potter, J. and Wetherell, M. (1987) *Discourse and Social Psychology*. London: Sage.

Potter, J., Wetherell, M., Gill, R. and Edwards, D. (1990) 'Discourse: noun, verb or social practice?', *Philosophical Psychology* 3: 205–17.

Rose, N. (1996) 'Identity, genealogy, history', in S. Hall and P. du Gay (eds), *Questions of Cultural Identity*. London: Sage.

Sartre, J.P. (1988) *Saint Genet: Actor and Martyr* (Bernard Frectman, trans.). London: Heinemann.

Schegloff, E.A. (1991) 'Reflections on talk and social structure', in D. Boden and D. Zimmerman (eds), *Talk and Social Structure*. Cambridge: Polity Press.

Segal, L. (1990) *Slow Motion: Changing Men, Changing Masculinities*. London: Virago.

Walby, S. (1990) *Theorising Patriarchy*. Oxford: Blackwell.

Wertsch, J. (1991) *Voices of the Mind*. London: Harvester Wheatsheaf.

West, C. and Zimmerman, D. (1991) 'Doing gender', in J. Lorber and S.A. Farrell (eds), *The Social Construction of Gender*. Newbury Park, CA: Sage.

Wetherell, M. (1996) 'Life histories/social histories', in M. Wetherell (ed.), *Identities, Groups and Social Issues*. London: Sage.

Wetherell, M. and Edley, N. (1994) A socio-psychological analysis of discourse. End of Award Report, London: Economic and Social Research Council.

Wetherell, M. and Griffin, C. (1991) 'Feminist psychology and the study of men and masculinity. Part One: Assumptions and perspectives', *Feminism and Psychology* 3 (1): 361–93.

Wetherell, M. and Potter, J. (1992) *Mapping the Language of Racism: Discourse and the Legitimation of Exploitation*. London and New York: Harvester Wheatsheaf and Columbia University Press.

Widdicombe, S. and Wooffitt, R. (1995) *The Language of Youth Subcultures: Social Identity in Action*. London: Harvester Wheatsheaf.

Wittgenstein, L. (1958) *Philosophical Investigations* (Second Edition). Oxford: Basil Blackwell.

9

An Outsider Within: A Feminist Doing Research with Men

Sara Willott

The power dynamics between the researcher and the researched are complex and sometimes contradictory. This is especially so when, as in my case, the researcher is a feminist exploring the construction of masculine identities, and is a woman interviewing men. Over the course of the last few years I have been involved in two research projects exploring the relationships between unemployment, crime and male identity. This has involved both discussions with groups of men and constructing life stories with individual men. My research has centred around the assumption that unemployment and, therefore, the inability to earn a wage in the public sphere poses a structural challenge to traditional versions of masculinity. Rather than re-construct their masculine identities along pro-feminist lines, the working-class unemployed men who participated in the first study tended to re-nogotiate an identity based on traditional talk and activity. This allowed them to continue representing themselves as, for example, the family breadwinner (Willott and Griffin, 1997). In this chapter I will not, however, discuss the findings of our research. My focus will instead be on my experiences as a feminist woman researching men. I will discuss these with reference to several illustrative vignettes drawn from my research diary. I kept this diary particularly during group-work discussions and the individual life-story interviews carried out at open prisons in the middle and south of England and probation centres and bail hostels in the West Midlands, UK. During this fieldwork, I experienced a growing awareness of the conflicts and contradictions around power in my relationship with the men I talked to as a woman and as a feminist researcher.

If power relationships are considered at all in the research situation, there is a common assumption that the researcher is more powerful than the participant (e.g. Mishler, 1986; Plummer, 1983. For exceptions see Laws, 1990; Smart 1984). In the majority of cases this assumption is representative of research relationships, given that the researcher is often male, white, middle-class, heterosexual, educated and able-bodied. In choosing the questions to be asked, carrying out analyses and reporting the research, the researcher's voice typically has centre stage (Bhavnani, 1990). Oakley (1981), being aware that this power differential was inappropriate when she interviewed other women, developed feminist interview techniques which challenged the traditional androcentric representation of the disengaged, expert researcher. However, as Smart (1984) has pointed out, Oakley's feminist research ethos is based on the assumption that the interviewees are not powerful. There are many contexts in which the dynamics of this power relationship between researcher and researched become more complex and contradictory. For example, Smart (1984) discusses the political and practical dilemmas of interviewing 'locally powerful' men in the judiciary and Bhavnani (1990) discusses the complex and contradictory issues of participant empowerment in relation to the wider social, political and economic nexus.

In conducting my research, both researcher and participant were situated in multiple different positions with respect particularly to class, education, race, age and gender.[1] The specific and unique power relations associated with each of these can be seen as placing the researcher or the researched either outside or inside of what is normative and powerful in contemporary British society. For example, as a woman I am always located as an outsider within the male-dominated arenas in which I carry out my fieldwork and as a feminist I have a 'view from below' (see Mies, 1991). Therefore, from this critical perspective, I am in a position to challenge the universal male gaze and redirect our vision towards the powerful (see Burman, 1995; Smart, 1984). However, I want to avoid becoming a voyeur. If I simply analyse male discourse in terms of a unitary patriarchy, I will merely be using the flip side of the same coin and pathologize men. By doing so, I risk failing to see the big picture in terms of other systems of oppression. This in turn may make me blind to ways in which I might oppress the men I interview. I am middle-class, educated, white and was represented as 'from the University' (read 'is an expert') by the probation or prison officers when they introduced me to the participants. Therefore, I am an insider with respect to many societal norms and therefore to some extent blinded to barriers which cloud a mutual under-standing. Assuming that those located in less powerful positions and therefore outside the normative definitions can more easily develop a critical perspective on those definitions, I was both an insider and an outsider in my relationships with the different men participating in the research. In the course of talking to the men, analysis and subsequent dissemination, my intention was to avoid privileging any one voice over another, be it mine or theirs. Unfortunately, all too often I was unaware of the myriad and subtle ways in which we were positioned in relation to the knowledge power structure nexus.

In the first section of the chapter I will outline the case for feminist research with men. Next, I will discuss four vignettes from my research diary which illustrate both the distance and the unequal power relationships between myself and the men I talked to and draw out problematic aspects of dealing with these power relations for me personally, socio-politically and for the research project as a whole. Then I will explore ways in which a version of feminist poststructuralism can deal with these problems and briefly mention relativism, as a source of tension between feminism and post-structuralism. Finally, in working through this tension, I look to feminist praxis and suggest that a dialogic version of feminist poststructuralism provides a way in which the problems arising from unequal power relations in the research context can be tackled productively.

Feminist research with men

For me, a feminist standpoint means, among other things, that I have an explicitly political agenda in what I choose to research, in the research relationships I develop with participants, and in my critique of what I 'find'. Exceptions apart (e.g. Chesler, 1978), feminist research has typically chosen to explore the talk and experience of women, previously silenced by an androcentric academy (e.g. Squire, 1989; Warren, 1988). In the last decade or so, however, feminists have begun to study men (e.g. Griffin and Wetherell, 1992; Layland, 1990; Scott, 1985). Feminist research into the construction of masculine identities is important partly because femininities are constructed in relation to masculinities and it makes sense that as feminists, we understand this relationship. Mies puts it this way: 'a new perspective on the totality of society means, however, that we bring relationships to light which previously remained in darkness. That is to say, when we speak of women, we must speak of men' (Mies, 1991: 78). Exploring the construction and re-negotiation of different masculine identities in relation to each other is another way to understand the relationship between femininities and masculinities (Cornwall and Lindisfarne, 1994). The implicit norm in traditional psychological research has been based on an almost fictional white, middle-class, Oxford or Cambridge-educated, heterosexual, able-bodied man in possession of 'received' pronunciation. We must, however, take account of all systems of oppression in any analysis of gender and study the lives and talk of men who perpetuate and are subordinated by this norm, thereby throwing light on dominant versions which oppress women and different men.

Being a feminist *and* doing research with men can, however, be problematic. Given the inseparable and complex connection between power and all systems of oppression such as gender, class and race, when people divided by such systems interact, there is a necessity both to reflect on how each is positioned and to seek ways to redress inequality. A re-reading of my research diary suggests that I had filtered out some of the ways in which I was structurally distanced from the men I interviewed and therefore ignored the ways in which each of us made rhetorical use of the discursive resources available. I would argue that these complex and often contradictory power dynamics (a) impact upon an individual's feeling of empowerment or disempowerment, (b) have social and political implications for the possible reinforcement or contesting of dominant and oppressive patterns of discourse and structures, and (c) have implications for the particular piece of research engaged in. The following four vignettes provide material with which to explore some of the issues around age, class, sexuality and gender, and the impact of these upon power relationships between myself and the male research participants with whom I worked. The vignettes are ordered chronologically and all the participant names are pseudonyms.

In a 'them and us' situation, who are the 'good guys' and whose side am I on?

I had been regularly attending a probation centre in the West Midlands once a week for about a month, when one of the probation officers began to talk to me about the importance of masculinity as a 'mediating' factor in crime. The following week, this officer invited me to facilitate the weekly group-work session on the subject of masculinity. I declined for a variety of reasons and took part in the session as one of the participants. He launched into what he beforehand described as a 'suck it and see' experiment in an attempt to challenge the clients' masculinity. There were about a dozen men in the group, many of them new to the centre, and half-way through the session, half a dozen of the men started to dominate the discussion and talked in a way that appeared to me to be misogynistic and homophobic. At one point someone said that if he caught his son playing with dolls or putting on perfume he would hit him, and that if his missus let his son do it, he would hit her as well. Then there followed a dispute between a few clients as to whether they would literally throw their son out of the house if he came out as gay. One man turned to me and asked me if I had let my son play with dolls. I said that I had given him a doll when he was a toddler, after which I was ignored for the remainder of the session.

I had been reticent to lead the group-work session partly because I did not know most of the men. Moreover, the didactic approach adopted by the probation officer facilitating the session gave the impression that unlike the clients, who needed to discard their aberrant (criminal) masculinity, he had no need to reflect on gender issues personally. Apart from disliking this approach generally, as a researcher I did not want to endanger my relationships with future participants by creating a 'them and us' situation and therefore risk losing the opportunity of glimpsing the insider's perspective. However, I felt increasingly disempowered as the majority of men in the group-work session discussed their low opinion of women and gay men. I was also aware that keeping silent can be interpreted as agreement (see also Smart, 1984). So, in addition to the personal and research repercussions, what I said and how I said it mattered socio-politically.

A fly on the wall?
At about the same time, I became conscious of the dress code I had adopted. Nothing too outrageous and nothing that I thought could even remotely be interpreted as sexually provocative. I chose clothes which best mirrored the clothes the men tended to wear. I nearly always wore what became known at home as my uniform: trainers, a pair of black loose Levi jeans and a checked shirt over a black T-shirt. This strategy worked relatively well at first, in as much as I experienced very little to make me feel uncomfortable. The lack of discomfort mirrored my lack of awareness of the potentially problematic nature of the research scenario as well as the superficiality of research relationships.

My attempt to appear almost gender neutral was an effort not to attract attention to myself as a woman, but it involved a failure to reflect on ways in which my being a woman would impact upon the research process. In research settings, women are traditionally seen as harmless (e.g. Warren, 1988), as less threatening (Smart, 1984), as listeners, as powerless (Easterday et al., 1977) and as more emotional than men (Williams and Heikes, 1993). Furthermore, textbook advice on establishing rapport with research participants mirror these traditional representations (e.g. Bogdewic, 1992). This presents the female researcher with a dilemma. To gain acceptance in a male-dominated research context and win the trust of potential participants, we are advised to act in a 'stereotypically' feminine manner (see Gurney, 1985). To not do so risks non-participation or even active rejection of the researcher. In other words, because the interviewer is typically represented as feminine (Burman, 1995), to fulfil these textbook suggestions may build trust and simultaneously reinforce oppressive patterns of discourse. To muddy the waters further, another textbook suggestion is that the researcher makes a gradual transition to 'competent expert' which, as Gurney also points out, is difficult if a woman interviewer has adopted the 'feminine' style of interaction in the early stages. Overall, then, there is a textbook assumption that in order to gain access to insider knowledge, the researcher should adopt a stereotypically feminine (read as powerless) position, but then, as trust is established and knowledge gleaned, the expert should reveal her 'true' (read as male) colours. Both assumptions are problematic with respect to developing equal power relations with research participants.

I daresay that as a woman, I benefited from these 'stereotypes' in building initial trust with research participants within the probation centre and prisons; settings which tended to engender mistrust and suspicion. The researcher is often seen as a spy (Warren, 1988), but such feelings would be paramount for participants who experienced a high degree of state surveillance through techniques such as benefit investigations and probation orders. However, although women may be seen as less threatening, the relationship between gender and the suspicion of spying is not straightforward (again, see Warren, 1988). Traditionally, men are seen as politically dangerous but straightforward and women are sometimes linked to the Mata Hari snake-woman image of sexual hypnotism, enticing men towards death and destruction. Women are traditionally seen as more devious because they are less powerful. Warren concludes that women tend to be seen as more suspicious if they do not conform to gender stereotypes. So in an unconscious effort to avoid flouting these expectations and a more conscious effort to avoid conforming to them, I attempted to appear almost 'without gender', a fly on the wall. But of course I am a woman and that would not have gone completely unnoticed in a room full of men. Who was I kidding? The men must have talked so easily to me partly because I was a woman, and I probably used traditional gender expectations in order to gain trust. Therefore my inattention may well have reinforced rather than resisted traditional and oppressive patterns of gender discourse for the men in the group.

If I put my head in the sand, you can't see me
I had been regularly attending the probation centre for about six months before I was subjected to a barrage of unwanted sexual

innuendoes and open invitations. The first incident developed as I poured myself a cup of tea before a group-work session. Liam sidled up and whispered 'I had an amazing dream about you last night' to which I rather lamely replied 'oh'. Alarm bells started to ring but I ignored these feelings, dismissing them with what might be seen as a typically gendered reaction, telling myself not to be so arrogant. Later that morning he invited me to the pub for a drink at lunch-time. In retrospect I should have responded with a firm 'no', but I wanted to retain his goodwill, knowing how heavily his mood could affect the group dynamics. So instead I squirmed a bit and said that drinking between group-work sessions was frowned upon and that I would risk the facilitators' displeasure if they found out. When he realized that I was less than keen to go for a drink but had not firmly declined, he tried a more explicit line:

Liam: Why don't you and I get together sometime, just you and me.
Sara: No, I don't think so.
Liam: Why not?
Sara: I'm married.
Liam: So am I and it doesn't worry me.
Sara: Well it does worry me.

I felt disempowered by this interaction and frustrated when I reflected on how Liam had physically and rhetorically cornered me. Denise Riley describes how 'becoming or avoiding being named as a sexed creature is a restless business' (1988: 3). I also felt angry with myself for compromising my feminist principles when I resorted to the 'hands off, I'm someone else's property' strategy at the close of our interaction. However, as a researcher I was aware that reciprocity helps to maintain research relationships and was grateful to the participants for even talking to me. Given that there were very few favours that I could perform for the clients at the probation centres, refusing to even go out for a drink seemed churlish. The longer I remained in a particular research setting, the more I experienced situations in which I was uncomfortable despite, or maybe because I was building closer relationships. The irony was that although I had attempted to down-play my status as a woman using tactics such as the neutral dress code, my reason for being in the setting was to explore gender construction. However, when gender was foregrounded in the probation centre group-work, I became overtly talked about and to as a heterosexual woman. Immediately prior to this first uncomfortable incident, a couple of male actors were invited to do a series of sessions on gender roles. As a consequence, issues of sex and gender become more salient and I therefore experienced a degree of suspicion and attraction not apparent to me before. Unlike the experiences of some female researchers (e.g. Easterday et al., 1977; Warren and Rasmussen, 1977), my presence in the setting had not demanded that I face the dilemma of whether to flirt or act the coquette, therefore what seemed to me to be an explosion of sex-talk caught me off-guard.

Why fish don't usually theorize about water

Towards the end of the data collection phase of the project, I interviewed half a dozen upper-middle-class 'economic fraudsters' at an open prison. There were many comments, by prison officers especially, about my age, gender and presumed heterosexuality. They had no doubt about the ease with which I would find willing participants for the research. Comments such as 'a nice young girl like you . . .' and 'old dinosaurs don't need incentives . . .' came thick and fast. Interviewing middle-aged, upper-middle-class men at the prison was quite a contrast to the men at the probation centres. In many ways I felt less powerful in this arena, partly because I was the only woman among 400 men as I walked about the prison, but also because these men were powerfully positioned in terms of age and class. On one particular occasion, I remember walking back through the prison grounds after a rather abstract interview with Stephen, a man whose confident manner and appearance reflected his military schooling. As we passed fellow inmate and research participant Sandie, Stephen shot out a barbed comment, aiming to put Sandie in his place (evidently well below Stephen's in his opinion). Sandie replied with something equally snide, though less articulate, and Stephen delivered the final death-blow by correcting his grammar. I assumed that the only reason why Stephen abstained from correcting my grammar, was that I happened to be a young woman whom he was trying to impress.

Negotiating a place among the upper-middle-class men serving custodial sentences for white-collar fraud made me reflect on issues of age and class, in addition to sex and gender. On a physical level, I felt less threatened than in the probation centres. This was partly because the men were both incarcerated and a long way from my home turf. In addition, they were more gentle and the few sexual invitations offered were so covert that they could easily be side-stepped during conversational banter. Although this difference may have amounted to a smoother way for me to compromise my feminist principles, it did matter that I felt physically safer. When I talked to the men in the probation centres and bail hostels I was aware on reflection that I accentuated my regional accent and emphasized certain aspects of my previous experience, such as having lived on social security benefits as a single parent and being sent to an academically poor secondary modern school at the age of eleven. Why is it, then, that I did not explicitly reflect on class or race as a 'problem' in my research relationships until I interviewed the upper-middle-class men described in the last vignette? To be honest, the probability is that because I was educated and middle-class, I down-played the importance of these structural divisions until I felt disempowered by the divisions (see Horn, 1995). In the same way that fish seem oblivious to water,[2] class was not salient to me until I felt less powerful (see also Laws, 1990). Although I cannot second guess the feelings of the men I talked to, any blindness to feelings of disempowerment must surely have affected our research relationship for the worse. In the course of our interactions we could also have inadvertently reinforced oppressive patterns of discourse around race, class and what counts as valid (expert) knowledge.

Feminism and poststructuralism

In the first section of the chapter I concluded that although a feminist analysis of the construction of masculine identities is crucial to the emancipatory project, feminist research with men can be problematic. I then recounted four vignettes from my research diary which illustrated these problems and their individual, social-political and research implications for the feminist researcher. These can be summarized as follows. First, on a personal level, my research resulted in unequal power relations between myself as researcher and the research participants I interviewed, which in everyday life I try to avoid or redress. Individual feelings of power are a problem if either the researcher or the participant feels disempowered by any talk in the research process if this talk draws on a system of oppression in which the disempowered is already disadvantaged. Second, the research process itself encouraged the use of discourse which I see as reinforcing oppressive social structures. Reflecting critically on how interactions with participants made me feel personally, prompted me to reflect on how these interpersonal scenarios are both a microcosm of wider social and political issues as well as a site of daily reinforcement or resistance. Third, the inequality in my relationship with the participants is likely to affect the data that I collect. For example, in the group-work outlined in the first vignette, I said little due to the nature of the discussion among the men and therefore failed to build any kind of relationship or suggest further one-to-one interviews with anyone from that particular group.

So there is a tension between being a researcher and being a feminist. As a feminist I want to see a change in the patriarchal relations between men and women. I would like this change to extend to my relationships with the research participants, but found it difficult to challenge directly. As a researcher I was careful to nurture relationships, to avoid stepping over invisible lines in which these relationships might be jeopardized, and to 'enter sympathetically into the alien and possibly repugnant perspectives of rival thinkers' (Harding, 1992: 572). Laws (1990) describes two kinds of understanding involved in her interviews with men. First, an understanding as a woman (and presumably a feminist woman), which often led to feelings of anger or despair, and secondly, an understanding with the men, in order to map out their construction of meanings. Again, this reflects the uneasy relationship between outsiders and insiders. We need a language with which to discuss these dilemmas and a standpoint from which tension and contradiction is seen as productive rather than a nuisance.

I will now argue that a version of feminist poststructuralism can move us forward in relation to some of the problems faced by the feminist researcher by providing such a theoretical standpoint. Feminism and poststructuralism are two diverse frameworks which on one level are natural allies (see Flax, 1987) and yet in other ways are uneasy bed-fellows (see Nicholson, 1990), particularly when post-structuralism is associated with political relativism. First, I will outline a version of poststructuralism (drawing mainly on poststructuralist French feminists and Foucault) which is helpful to feminist standpoints. After this I will look at extreme relativism, which is less than helpful. Finally, I will conclude by suggesting that feminist praxis and dialogics would not only help feminist poststructuralism avoid some of the problems that extreme relativism poses, but helps tackle the unhelpful distance between researcher and participant.

How poststructuralism can work for feminism
What I find most helpful in poststructuralism is, first of all (a) an emphasis on discursive language, and (b) a relationship between discourse and power. For poststructuralist research, language is a focus of study in its own right, not a window on to an underlying cognitive substrate such as an attitude (Potter and Wetherell, 1987). This emphasis on language draws attention away from particular individuals and looks instead at meanings within discourse. The main dynamic upon which these constructions and re-negotiations

revolve is power (e.g. Foucault, 1980). So for example, the inter-action with Liam can be read as 'shared' meanings over how men and women should feel and behave. These meanings can be identified and critically evaluated as patterns of discourse which reflect and reinforce unequal gender relations. It is in language that subjectivity is constructed and reconstructed (e.g. Burman, 1995) and macro structures reinforced or contested, all played out within the minutiae of daily interactions. The rhetorical devices employed by Liam drew upon patterns of discourse around gender and sexuality which served to disempower me in the course of our interaction concerning the invitation for a 'drink'. Nevertheless, there was potential for resistance and re-negotiation, however understandable my dilemma. Politically, therefore, this approach offers potential for emancipatory change.

Poststructuralism also provides (c) a deconstructive critique of assumed truths. If meaning is constructed in language and language is dynamic, it follows that the truth claims of dominant groups can be interrogated and taken apart. There is no automatic recourse, for example, to biological givens or scientific assumptions set in stone. For example, we can challenge notions such as women being natural interviewers or that the men participating in the research described here had criminal personalities or an aberrant masculine identity. This approach allows us to reject such essentialist notions and look instead to discourse and power and change.

(d) Poststructuralism provides an understanding of identity as both contradictory and dynamic. Wetherell (1995) has pointed out that because the cultural narratives upon which we draw are not coherent, our self knowledge is also incoherent. Although feminist poststructuralism has deconstructed the idea of a rational unitary self (e.g. Gavey, 1989), this model continues to underpin most social-psychological theorizing. The unitary self can be replaced with a feminist, poststructuralist theory of subjectivity which borrows, for example, from psychoanalytic theory (see Hollway, 1984), the 'new French feminists' (e.g. Kristeva, 1981), and theorists such as Butler (1990) and Riley (1988). This alternative picture is one of multiple identities and social positions, of fragmentary and contradictory layers in one's sense of self and of every category as historically constructed and continually contested in daily life. This way of looking at identity construction provides a framework for theorizing the interdependence of gender, class and sexual desire in my interaction with Liam, and with the inevitable contradictions in power dynamics.

(e) Poststructuralists tend to analyse current social and political contexts in the light of socially and historically constructed discursive patterns (e.g. Foucault, 1978; Parker, 1990). This serves to increase our understanding not only of meaning at any socio-historical moment, but to highlight pathways for future resistance (Tierney, 1993). For example, some features of modern constructions of masculinity can be traced to the development of capitalism, individualism and the growth of a consumer society (e.g. Mies, 1986; Willott and Griffin, 1997).

(f) Poststructuralist discourse analysis also reflects upon itself (Parker, 1990). The researcher is not a neutral tool objectively collecting data. Rather, the researcher enters the scene laden with subjective baggage. It follows from this that the researcher should be explicit about her standpoint (Harding, 1992) and contribution to the meanings constructed. In this way it is possible to develop a critical reflexivity which is politically accountable.

Finally, one important feature of research that focuses on discourse in social context is the potential impact on the reader. When presented with analysis of discourse, the reader finds it less easy to place her or himself outside the narrative and distance her or himself from the research context. The reader is asked to acknowledge her or his own position in relation to these patterns of discourse and power. In the same way that feminist researchers have critiqued the 'distant-expert' (Oakley, 1981) or the 'spectator-knowledge' (Mies, 1993) approach of the researcher, we can also challenge the representation of reader as voyeur. Although the writer cannot create discursive positions for the reader, if the narrative is expressed on a large canvas upon which the reader recognizes snatches of her or his own discourse, then the author's conclusions will have a resonance for the reader that is unlikely to be present when reading more traditional social-psychological research.

Avoiding the pitfalls: feminist praxis and dialogics

It may well be sufficient to use poststructuralism merely as a methodological tool rather than wrestle with epistemology and ontology (see Sampson, 1993). However, relativism has become a theoretical and political thorn in the poststructuralist flesh (Nicholson, 1990). According to Parker (1992), 'high' poststructuralism is equivalent to Nietzschean perspectivism in which there are no truths but only competing stories. Feminism is a practical social movement and a central tenet of feminist standpoint research is the demand for theories which are interwoven with emancipatory politics. Extreme relativism, however, works against this; if there is no basis for deciding which story is best, then there can be no grounds for critique or political action. Feminist poststructuralists do not, however, have to embrace either a Derridean apoliticality or a value-free epistemology (Gill, 1995; Soper, 1991). Rejecting foundationalism does not necessarily lead to relativism (Stanley and Wise, 1990). In other words, having rejected the argument that there are a priori sources of truth, I do not have to accept that there are no truths. However, the way of accomplishing, say, equality is not universal or unchanging, and in any one socio-historical context various discourses could be employed to accomplish this aim.

Practically, there are various strategies which can be employed in order to avoid political paralysis in the research process, including (a) the development of an accountable reflexivity, (b) a focus on marginal groups and (c) political action as part of the research process. These strategies are rooted in theoretical frameworks such as dialogics (e.g. Sampson, 1993), action research (e.g. Freire, 1996) and feminist praxis (e.g. Stanley, 1990). Sampson draws on theorists such as Bakhtin, Mead and Vygotsky as well as a range of feminist accounts and recent developments in the turn to language in order to put forward the case for celebrating the other. The dominant group are the constructors of a monologue, in which the servicing others are necessarily left without a voice. Given that our subjectivities are constructed and re-negotiated socially in talk, a dialogic approach invites us to explore any scenario in which a dominant group is constructed and thus provides a framework which gives equal salience to all voices in the research situation. Accomplishing this celebration of the other in the research process requires, from a feminist praxis perspective, a rejection of traditional separations between ontology and epistemology and between theory and practice. A feminist praxis position therefore recognizes that the researcher's standpoint, ways of knowing and the doing of research, are inseparable and sees political action as a necessary part of the research process (e.g. Mies, 1986; Stanley, 1990).

In the development of an accountable reflexivity, Gill (1995) suggests a combination of a poststructuralist-based epistemological scepticism alongside a 'passionate inquiry' (see Raymond, 1986). Having accepted that research cannot be value-free, Gill argues that we should not only be explicit about our political agenda but write in such a way as to encourage discussion of the political implications of the research. Such a passionate inquiry would include an accountable reflexivity rather than the pseudo-pluralism of extreme relativists. According to Gill, the pseudo-pluralist form of reflexivity serves to rebut criticism before it happens by anticipating possible critical responses. Rather than being open to criticism, this form of reflexivity deflects criticism in advance. Pseudo-pluralism mimics dialogue by presenting multiple voices in the text, but every voice belongs to the author. Therefore, rather than encouraging dialogue, the text amounts to a sealed monologue.

Another way in which research can overturn the traditional self-celebrating monologue of androcentrism and expertise in a research project is to focus on marginal groups. This focus should include a critical deconstruction of the multiple ways in which those in powerful positions can silence marginal voices. However, what constitutes a marginal group or how best to draw attention to the invisible privileged is not necessarily obvious. In this chapter I have explored some tensions and dilemmas that result from the multiple and contradictory power relationships between the researcher and the researched. How, for example, can the men who participate in the research dialogue with me when I am unaware of the important ways in which I am positioned in relation to the participant, and how can I dialogue with men determined to pursue a monologue? First of all, I can develop an accountable reflexivity which answers not only to feminism, but also to the emancipation of any oppressed group. This is necessary because men are not a homogenous group and therefore patriarchy is not a single unified discursive structure. So in order to understand the different and complex ways in which men oppress women, I must also understand the subordination of certain men by other men. Furthermore, I wish to be accountable to other emancipatory projects because the oppression of any group is wrong. It is important to also accept and analyse the complex power relations that arise in the course of doing social research and to employ strategies to reduce inequality and distance between the researcher and the researched. This will involve empowerment of the participants through a reworking of the traditionally hierarchic structure of the interviewer–interviewee relationship (Mies, 1993; Mishler, 1986) by, for example, allowing the research collaborators to tell their story in context using their own narrative style or the researcher allowing herself to be interviewed by the participants. In situations where I am silenced as a researcher, I should also develop ways of speaking and being heard in the research process without silencing others.

In conclusion, I have argued first of all that poststructuralism provides (a) a theoretical framework which incorporates the inevitable messiness in power relations and (b) a tool for political change. Second, that the use of discourse analysis from a poststructuralist perspective can draw the reader into the research report and thereby reduce the voyeur–other dualism in research dissemination. However, emancipatory change is not an inevitable outcome of using poststructuralist discourse analysis. If every voice is given free reign, then the powerful will dominate. This pitfall can be avoided by mapping out the complex and contradictory nature of power relations in any given situation and a refusal to privilege one voice over another

Notes

The vignettes discussed in this chapter were drawn from research carried out with Chris Griffin and funded by the UK Economic and Social Research Council (Grant no. R000236020). I would also like to thank Ros Gill, Chris Griffin, Karen Henwood, Ann Phoenix and Mark Torrance for helpful feedback on earlier drafts of this chapter.

1 As such, we do not carry around a fixed amount of power, dependent solely on our socio-economic class or gender. Rather, power relationships are context specific. They are determined by the discourses constructed by those conversing, which are, of course, intertwined with systems of oppression such as class and gender.
2 'Since they are accustomed to move about in such relations, they find nothing strange therein. A complete contradiction offers not the least mystery to them. They feel as much at home as a fish in water' (Marx, 1974: 779, also cited in Martin, 1987: 11).

References

Bhavnani, K. (1990) 'What's power got to do with it? Empowerment and social research', in I. Parker and J. Shotter (eds), *Deconstructing Social Psychology*. London: Routledge.

Bogdewic, S. (1992) 'Participant observation', in B. Crabtree and W. Miller (eds), *Doing Qualitative Research*. Newbury Park, CA: Sage.

Burman, E. (1995) '"What is it?" masculinity and femininity in cultural representations of childhood', in S. Wilkinson and C. Kitzinger (eds), *Feminism and Discourse: Psychological Perspectives*. London: Sage.

Butler, J. (1990) *Gender Trouble: Feminism and the Subversion of Identity*. New York: Routledge.

Chesler, P. (1978) *About Men*. London: The Women's Press.

Cornwall, A. and Lindisfarne, N. (eds) (1994) *Dislocating Masculinity: Comparative Ethnographies*. London: Routledge.

Easterday, L., Papaemas, D., Schorr, L. and Valentine, C. (1977) 'The Making of a female researcher: role problems in field work', *Urban Life* 6 (3): 333–48.

Flax, J. (1987) 'Postmodernism and gender relations in feminist theory', *Signs: Journal of Women in Culture and Society* 12 (4): 621–43.

Foucault, M. (1978) *The History of Sexuality. Vol. 1: An Introduction*. (R. Hurley. trans.). Harmondsworth: Penguin.

Foucault, M. (1980) *Power/Knowledge: Selected Interviews and Other Writings, 1972–1977* (C. Gordon, ed., C. Gordon, L. Marshall, J. Mepham and K. Soper, trans.). New York: Pantheon.

Freire, P. (1996) *Pedagogy of Hope: Reliving the Pedagogy of the Oppressed*. New York: Continuum.

Gavey, N. (1989) 'Feminist post-structuralism and discourse analysis', *Psychology of Women Quarterly* 13: 459–75.

Gill, R. (1995) 'Relativism, reflexivity and politics: interrogating discourse analysis from a feminist perspective', in S. Wilkinson and C. Kitzinger (eds), *Feminism and Discourse: Psychological Perspectives*. London: Sage.

Griffin, C. and Wetherell, M. (1992) 'Feminist psychology and the study of men and masculinity. Part 2: Politics and practices', *Feminism and Psychology* 1 (3): 133–68.

Gurney, J. (1985) 'Not one of the guys: the female researcher in a male-dominated setting', *Qualitative Sociology* 8 (1): 42–62.

Harding, S. (1992) 'After the Neutrality Ideal: Science, Politics, and "Strong Objectivity"', *Social Research* 59 (3): 567–87.

Hollway, W. (1984) 'Gender difference and the production of subjectivity', in J. Henriques, W. Hollway, C. Urwin, C. Venn and V. Walkerdine, *Changing the Subject: Psychology, Social Relations and Subjectivity*. London: Methuen.

Horn, R. (1995) 'Reflexivity in placement: women interviewing women', *Feminism and Psychology* 5 (1): 94–8.

Kristeva, J. (1981) 'Woman can never be defined', in E. Marks and I. de Courtivron (eds), *New French Feminisms*. Brighton: Harvester.

Layland, J. (1990) 'On the conflicts of doing feminist research into masculinity', in L. Stanley (ed.), *Feminist Praxis: Research, Theory and Epistemology in Feminist Sociology*. London: Routledge.

Laws, S. (1990) *Issues of Blood: The Politics of Menstruation*. Basingstoke: Macmillan.

Martin, E. (1987) *The Woman In the Body*. Milton Keynes: Open University Press.

Marx, K. (1974) *Capital: A Critique of Political Economy*. Vol. 3. London: Lawrence and Wishart.

Mies, M. (1986) *Patriarchy and Accumulation on a World Scale: Women in the International Division of Labour*. London: Zed.

Mies, M. (1991) 'Women's research or feminist research? The debate surrounding feminist science and methodology', in M.M. Fonow and J. Cook (eds), *Beyond Methodology: Feminist Scholarship as Lived Experience*. Bloomington: Indiana University Press.

Mies, M. (1993) 'Towards a methodology for feminist research', in M. Hammersley (ed.), *Social Research: Philosophy, Politics and Practice*. London: Sage.

Mishler, E. (1986) *Research Interviewing: Context and Narrative*. Cambridge, MA: Harvard University Press.

Nicholson, L. (ed.) (1990) *Feminism/Postmodernism*. New York: Routledge.

Oakley, A. (1981) 'Interviewing women: a contradiction in terms', in H. Roberts (ed.), *Doing Feminist Research*. London: Routledge.

Parker, I. (1990) 'Discourse: definitions and contradictions', *Philosophical Psychology* 3 (2): 189–203.

Parker, I. (1992) *Discourse Dynamics: Critical Analysis for Social and Individual Psychology*. London: Routledge.

Potter, J. and Wetherell, M. (1987) *Discourse and Social Psychology: Beyond Attitudes and Behaviour*. London: Sage.

Plummer, K. (1983) *Documents of Life: An Introduction to the Problems and Literature of a Humanistic Method*. London: Unwin Hyman.

Raymond, J. (1986) *A Passion for Friends: Toward a Philosophy of Female Affection*. London: Routledge.

Riley, D. (1988) *Am I that Name? Feminism and the Category of 'Women' in History*. London: Macmillan.

Sampson, E. (1993) *Celebrating the Other: A Dialogic Account of Human Nature*. London: Harvester Wheatsheaf.

Scott, S. (1985) 'Feminist research and qualitative methods: a discussion of some of the issues', in R.G. Burgess (ed.), *Issues in Educational Research: Qualitative Methods*. Brighton: Falmer Press.

Soper, K. (1991) 'Postmodernism, subjectivity and the question of value', *New Left Review* 186: 120–8.

Squire, C. (1989) *Significant Differences: Feminism in Psychology*. London: Routledge.

Smart, C. (1984) *The Ties that Bind: Law, Marriage and the Reproduction of Patriarchal Relations*. London: Routledge and Kegan.

Stanley, L. and Wise, S. (1990) 'Method, methodology and epistemology in feminist research process', in L. Stanley (ed.), *Feminist Praxis: Research, Theory and Epistemology in Feminist Sociology*. London: Routledge.

Stanley, L. (1990) (ed.) *Feminist Praxis: Research, Theory and Epistemology in Feminist Sociology*. London: Routledge.

Tierney, W. (1993) 'Self and identity in a postmodern world: a life story', in D. McLaughlin and W. Tierney, *Naming Silenced Lives: Personal Narratives and Processes of Educational Change*. New York: Routledge.

Warren, C. (1988) *Gender Issues in Field Research*. Newbury Park, CA: Sage.

Warren, C. and Rasmussen, P. (1977) 'Sex and gender in field research', *Urban Life* 6 (3): 349–68.

Wetherell, M. (1995) 'Romantic discourse and feminist analysis: interrogating investment, power and desire', in S. Wilkinson and C. Kitzinger (eds), *Feminism and Discourse: Psychological Perspectives*. London: Sage.

Williams, C. and Heikes, E.J. (1993) 'The importance of researcher's gender in the in-depth interview: evidence from two case studies of male nurses', *Gender and Society* 7 (2): 280–91.

Willott, S. and Griffin, C. (1997) 'Wham bam, am I a man? Unemployed men talk about masculinities', *Feminism and Psychology* 7 (1): 107–28.

10

Beyond Innocence: Feminist Mental Health Care and the Postmodernist Perspective

Janneke van Mens-Verhulst

Among the various areas of feminist practice, feminist mental health care (FMHC) is in many ways one of the most interesting. The field is now almost 30 years old and many professionally educated women (psychologists) have participated in its development. FMHC is an important domain in which women (psychologists) have tried to 'live' feminism. In doing so, they have learned a lot about its limits and potential. This learning process has included, for example, exploring the opportunities and dangers raised for feminism by postmodernist and poststructuralist theories.

The present exploration will begin with a brief history of FMHC and its main characteristics. The results of the virtual 'encounter' between FMHC and postmodernist and poststructuralist thought will then be presented. This encounter is structured around a consideration of six concepts relevant in both spheres: autonomy, equality, oppression (as an absence of freedom), subjectivity, knowledge and the sex/gender distinction. My conclusion is that both postisms are of limited use for women's sociogenesis through FMHC as they themselves both suffer from an irresponsible innocence.

My description of FMHC alludes to the international context, but is primarily based on the Dutch situation where the behavioural and cognitive therapy paradigm prevails. The influence of the psycho-analytic paradigm is slight but it does have an impact on the therapists' professional education and reflection. Within this context the FMHC operates eclectically.

History of FMHC: from protest to professionalism

In the early 1970s Dutch FMHC began to criticize traditional mainstream mental health care for its misrepresentation, unequal treatment and unjustified pathologizing of women which resulted in oppressive and disciplining/punitive effects. As such, it combined the movements for democratization and deprofessionalization in health care along with a switch from a predominantly illness-oriented form of health care to one which placed greater emphasis on clients' well-being. Alternative (mental) health practices were developed by both professional and lay volunteers. Initially these were self-help groups varying from 'Women in the Menopause' and 'Feminist Radical Therapy Training Groups' to 'Homes for Battered Women'. Gradually, FMHC also emerged inside the regular channels of assistance. For reasons of equal distribution, quality enhancement and innovation within the health services, the Dutch government decided to subsidize FMHC in 1983. (It was then re-labelled Women's Mental Health Care to avoid controversy.) A prerequisite of this financial support was its integration into the established channels of mental health care. Today 'regular' FMHC has outgrown its alternative roots. It is represented at some level in all 58 regional institutions for ambulatory mental health care (RIAGG's) and in two-thirds of the 43 general psychiatric hospitals, although in other institutions for mental health care the percentage of FMHC is still low (Plemper et al., 1996).

Obviously, FMHC has altered over the years. There have been changes, not only in the problems it addresses but also in the methods it uses, the theories it relies upon, and the visions to which it refers. This is a result of its relatively independent professionalization, of its integration into a variety of institutional contexts, and of changes in society in general. Even so, FMHC practices still share at least three characteristics, although not always to the same degree.

Characteristics of feminist mental health care

FMHC is characterized by its sex-specific, politicizing and client-centred approach (van Mens-Verhulst, 1985, 1988; van Mens-Verhulst and Schilder, 1994; Nicolai, 1992; for a useful summary see Watson and Williams, 1992). The sex-specific approach counters the abhorred sex neutrality of most traditional mental health care practices. It asks for an acknowledgement that while problems may look the same (addiction, low assertiveness, marital problems), the reality of their experience differs between women and men. They may result from different processes, and consequently they may require different treatments. Differences between sexes are not predominantly localized in biology, but in society. As they grow up, women have to deal with values, norms, roles and opportunities which are very different from those of men, but their mental state is judged by male standards (Broverman et al., 1970).

The politicizing approach of FMHC counters the individualistic assumptions that are so common in traditional practices. It focuses on the influence of societal and cultural contexts on the problems of women and their therapeutic relationships. In this vision inequality of power is the central theme. At its most extreme these inequalities are manifest in cases of sexual abuse where a woman's physical integrity is violated. But in effect, all women are confronted with forms of oppression which can give rise to health complaints. Some of the fundamental contentions of this approach are: (a) social autonomy is denied to women and causes personal distress; (b) society places the responsibilities for caring upon women as a category, causing feelings of guilt and shame when they cannot meet those expectations; (c) the social division of labour marginalizes them from the labour market, deprives them of the full rewards of labour, and denies them their entitlement to personal care; (d) women are subjected to unequal treatment and discrimination on a daily basis which undermines their self-confidence, and results in repressed anger; (e) mental health care rehearses socio-cultural oppression within the hierarchical set-up of the therapeutic relationship.

A politicized approach implies an attitude of anti-domination and concern with methods of empowerment (Brown, 1994). Empowerment refers to a comprehensive personal as well as collective strengthening. It is defined by McWhirter as:

> the process by which people, organisations, or groups who are powerless (a) become aware of the power dynamics at work in their life context, (b) develop the skills and capacity for gaining some reasonable control over their lives, (c) exercise this control without infringing upon the rights of others, and (d) support the empowerment of others in their community. (McWhirter, 1991: 224)

In other words, empowerment produces consciously social, moral and political subjects.

This client-centred approach strikes back at the self-closure of traditional therapists and institutions; it counters their inclination to let institutional procedures and schedules and professional prescriptions, methods and language prevail over clients' needs. In contrast, it considers clients as active and competent participants whose subjectivity should be respected and nourished – when they are female just as much as when they are male. In the words of one slogan: women know for themselves what is good for them. Thus, client-centredness advocates a caring attitude towards clients, and undermines the 'patriarchal' vision of women.

Feminist mental health care: beyond innocence

Gradually, the naivety of the early FMHC enterprise has become apparent. Its weaknesses have been shown directly by protests from, or the indifference of, groups who felt excluded, and by the analyses of critical feminist theorists. Its failings have also been indicated by postmodern and poststructuralist insights into the complexities involved in FMHC. The following paragraphs describe the evolution of the first three humanist FMHC principles: autonomy, equality and oppression.

Autonomy

In the earliest stages of FMHC the ideal of autonomy was taken for granted. Its liberating force lay in the representation of women as potentially autonomous beings; a sovereign position they had historically been denied. However, the therapeutic quest for the autonomy of women came to be understood as less value-free and universal than the early second-wave feminists had thought. The condition of being one's own authority – independent from any one else – was recognized as a narrative of the patriarchal order and as an oppressive dogma. First, the ideal of autonomy tended to marginalize dependent women. The procedures of FMHC did not attend to those clients who were unable to show the minimum of self-determination which was assumed to be present from the start (Mens-Verhulst 1987, 1991).[1] Dependency could be tolerated only where there was an expectation of 'improvement'. As a consequence, permanently care-dependent women (for example, with chronic illness or serious psychiatric disorders) felt excluded. So too did women from cultures where collectivism is prized (Babel and Hitipeuw, 1992). Secondly, the consequences of achieving autonomy stimulated doubts. Women at times seemed to be punished for their newly acquired assertiveness (Fodor, 1985). Moreover, their pursuit of independence could be at the immediate expense of such vulnerable others as children. Thirdly, the emphasis on autonomy stressed human independence rather than interdependence, and denied the value of connection. These issues became more pronounced after the Stone Centre therapists published their work on connection and mutuality (Jordan et al., 1991). For example, as autonomy promotes separation as healthy and disavows connection as immature or pathological, it biases the understanding of mother–daughter relationships (Mens-Verhulst, 1995).

The postmodern project of contextualization and deconstruction has given further impetus to the unravelling of autonomy as an ideal. Feminist therapists and political theorists have participated in this process. Thus, the therapeutic goal of autonomy was recognized to reflect the predominantly upper-middle-class position and orientation of therapists themselves (Hare-Mustin and Marecek, 1986). The opposition between autonomy and 'being-in-relation' was dismissed, for 'autonomy without being in relation can easily degenerate into mastery', but 'forms of being in relation can be claustrophobic without autonomy' (Flax, 1990: 181). Instead, autonomy and connection can be thought of as two independent dimensions coexisting simultaneously. Moreover, autonomy has been revealed to be a myth by which the varying degrees of dependence and independence that we all experience in the course of our lives are masked. The myth turns dependency into a weakness, and in this way contributes to the production of 'otherness'. But the autonomy myth can be maintained only as long as the political order (and the citizens it privileges) succeeds in hiding the dependent and vulnerable part of human experience, for example by rigidly separating the spheres of public and private life, and the domains of health and illness (Sontag, 1991; Tronto, 1993).

Today, the function of autonomy as an identifying characteristic of (Dutch) FMHC is being increasingly criticized as being too static and individually oriented. A more dynamic and contextual conceptualization has been suggested (Mens-Verhulst, 1992; N. Nicolai, 1994a) in order that a greater responsiveness to less western and (upper) middle class oriented groups of women, and to more (care)dependent people may be created.

Equality
The original FMHC narrative leaned heavily on the 'modern' narrative of equality for its legitimation. Equality, it was thought, would counteract the oppression of women. In hindsight, reformist as well as radical narratives can be reconstructed. The reformist ones focus on women's adaptation to the established social system and culture; the radical ones on the necessity of changing the women oppressing dominant (patriarchal) assumptions, norms and institutions (Brown, 1994). Neither of these presents a simple delivery on the promise to counter oppression through empowerment.

One narrative concentrates on equal treatment within counselling. It promises women the same respect and attention as that expected and received by men. For example, their problems would no longer be denied or trivialized – as has happened with experiences of violence and the menopause. Their 'non-feminine' behaviour would no longer be pathologized – as has happened with women who attempted to gain financial independence, preferred a lesbian lifestyle, refrained from motherhood, and so on. They would no longer be blamed for being raped (APA 1978; Broverman et al., 1970; Chesler, 1972). A related narrative tells about the symmetrical relationship between client and therapist. It does not mean that power is absent from the therapeutic interaction. On the contrary, power is acknowledged to be an inevitable part of the relationship, but it is regarded as an aspect that has to be carefully monitored in order to prevent its exploitative use (Brown, 1994).[2]

An additional narrative concerns the production of equality in the outcomes of therapy. It presents the mission of FMHC as contributing to the advancement of a better social and political position for women; a better balance between the sexes. Therefore, the criteria for healthy functioning are similar for both sexes (autonomy, for instance) but the therapeutic process must serve as a school that provides for the elements women are lacking: skills, self-reliance, political consciousness, social action.

Quite another narrative concentrates on the specificity of women's psychological and moral make-up and proposes that it has to be valued similarly to the mentality specific to men. Typically, this narrative stands outside contemporary discussions of problems of essentialism to argue that women's greater orientation to connection and care is no less respectable than men's greater orientation to separation and justice. Accordingly, it makes FMHC's endeavour one of respecting and protecting the female orientation in and by the counselling process.

The most radical narrative speaks about FMHC as inspiring a socio-cultural revolution, in support of gender equality in a fundamentally differently organized society. In that society care labour is valued as much as other types of labour, and both sexes take their fair share. FMHC is one of the paths to achieve that future.

In the course of time, important disruptions of the FMHC's equality narratives have emerged. Many women have discovered the idea of sex-based oppression to be a reductive simplification of their troubles. Among them are women who are chronically ill, childless (involuntarily and voluntarily), working-class and black, who often have never been given a choice between housekeeping and productive labour (Brown, 1990; McLeod, 1994). Some feminist counsellors reported their experience with clients who were sufficiently power-conscious to use the egalitarian therapeutic relationship for their own ends, and nothing more. They were not concerned with equality or the need to become equally valued, but with acquiring a shelter or residence permit, or procuring financial assistance. Thus a more nuanced application of the equality principle seemed necessary (Schilder and Kaaijk, 1994).

Ideas about connection have also led to questions about the nature of social and cultural equality FMHC would want. What is its use if it does not challenge the valorization of autonomy and the division of labour in the family and marketplace? Would it not be better to promote feminine relatedness and in this way proclaim women's moral equality or even superiority? Simultaneously, 'diversity' has been introduced as a better principle for FMHC which allows it to promote recognition of multiculturalism and of work towards anti-racism (Brown and Root, 1990). Diversity in feminist therapy means incorporating, appreciating, and building on the differences among women (Barrett, 1990). It requires respect for what is different and abstains from the inclination to suppress or trivialize 'otherness'.

In the meantime, a deconstruction of equality versus difference undertaken within women's studies has undermined the opposition on three grounds: its undifferentiated view of the nature of the debate; its inappropriate mixing of descriptive and normative connotations; and the way it falsely structures an impossible choice. Its undifferentiated view leads to disregard of the different areas of equality and difference which can vary from 'natural', biological, psychological, social, economic, cultural and moral to legal. Debates on equality and difference easily lead to confusion as they switch from one area to another, pretending that social differences can be directly transposed into biological ones, or biological differences into psychological ones (Komter, 1990). It inappropriately mixes descriptive and normative connotations by associating equality with equivalence, normality, fairness and justice, and difference with non-equivalence, deviance, unfairness and oppression.[3] As a consequence, difference or otherness can hardly be positively valued. The false structuring of an impossible choice arises since equality cannot exist without difference. Ultimately, 'equality might well be defined as deliberate indifference to specified differences' (Scott, 1990: 142). Consequently, one cannot speak naively about equality, but must always inquire into the qualities or aspects that are being compared. The answers will vary with the particular context and purposes that are involved. So equality is by no means simply good and difference simply bad or vice versa. Both options may give rise to oppressive relationships as an equality perspective may ignore relevant dissimilarities and a difference perspective may obscure relevant commonalities.

Following Scott (1990), we can conclude that as feminists we can neither give up equality as long as we want to speak to the principles and values of our political system – which celebrates equality. Nor can we give up 'difference' as it is one of our most creative analytic tools. A comparable dilemma occurs in Dutch FMHC because those involved also have to relate to the principles and values of the wider mental health care system. In general, this system claims to make purely 'techno-professional' distinctions and guarantees an individually tailored treatment while assuming the irrelevance of social differences – sex included.[4]

The practical aftermath of these analyses is that the equality narratives of FMHC no longer need to be dealt with as absolutes, and can be handled better as strategic questions to be answered in a specific context, for a specific period. Moreover, postmodern analysis of the equality principle provides new insights into *diversity*. Its strategic value will be worthwhile if it is not mechanically inscribed in the 'difference cluster', as the opposite of unity. It should be reserved for categories of differences compiled on the basis of distinctions that are consciously and carefully made because of the problem(s) to be solved and the context involved. Diversity thus refers to a strategic articulation of differences and commonalities in those physical, mental, social, political, economic and cultural realms judged to be relevant in that place and time. It is not a principle to be written in stone. However, we must continue to be vigilant about those who are placed in the position to judge: what is their position in the landscape of oppressing and privileging forces?

Oppression

At one stage oppression was considered a marker of FMHC. In radical therapy and its problem-solving groups it has functioned as a core concept in the analysis of (women's) mental problems (Steiner, 1975). It referred to the position of female clients as being oppressed by society's and the professions' lies and myths, and was complemented by the notion of internalized oppression. This latter concept points to the process by which people may mentally absorb the prejudices of the dominant culture and, as a consequence, lose their self-worth, self-confidence and connection with their own feelings, becoming uncertain and self-alienated. They may accept social inequality but with a huge amount of suppressed anger. Women were recognized to be caught in patriarchal norms and institutions and to have internalized that oppression.

Consciousness-raising groups and problem-solving groups were formed in which the lies were revealed in order to give way to anger. It was assumed that, by sharing experiences and analyses in groups, the social and economic meaning of those myths could be unravelled and opposed. This approach has not only been applied to women in general (Wyckoff, 1977) but also to sub-categories of women and men (Pheterson, 1986).

In many of the 'alternative' Dutch FMHC practices this narrative of universal patriarchal oppression remains alive. Mostly, their counsellors construct a tally of separate systems of oppression for each group: along the lines of sexism, classism, racism, hetero-sexism, disablism, ageism, and so on (see Adleman and Spencer Faunce, 1990; Green, 1987). Groups such as black or immigrant women, lesbian psychiatric patients, and women over 60 years old are considered to be doubly or triply oppressed. This may result in discussions about who are more oppressed and by whom. In general, it prompts the need for a more specified and integrated concept of oppression (see Kanuha, 1990).

As the integration of FMHC within traditional therapeutic schools and within regular mental health care progressed, its concepts become less radical and 'oppression' lost something of its utility. It was too confrontational for non-feminists, therapists and clients. From then on it became fashionable to speak of the 'social position' and 'socialization' of women as important factors in the generation and perpetuation of their mental health problems. Since the 1980s, other theoretical sensitivities have been stimulated too, by the Foucauldian relational perspective on power. The suggestion here is that any fixing of positions of domination/subordination occurs within complex webs of relationships involving mutual attempts at influence and resistance.

Postmodern insights into oppression, as surveyed by Iris Young (1990), are useful in helping us to recognize the distinctions and commonalities that qualify and complicate the social positions of, and power relations among, women, although, as yet, her work is not widely known in Dutch FMHC. For instance, Young rejects the assumption that the state of 'being oppressed' is tied to an act of tyranny or a particular actor. Instead, 'being privileged' is advanced as a counterpart. By paying attention to difference in privileges between women, their differences in oppression can be more adequately contextualized. So, the difference in appraisal of rape and robbery by black working-class victims and their white middle-class therapists becomes better understood (Boyd, 1990) as well as the difference in needs for and trust of feminist therapy felt by white and black women (Hurtado, 1989). This pair of related concepts (oppressed/privileged) also makes it possible to imagine the simul-taneity of being oppressed and privileged;[5] for example, of being lesbian and white, or black, middle-class and able-bodied, or of being biracial. These dynamics can further clarify the contradictions implicated in the development of identity when it involves a combined status, and of its share in the physical and mental malaise of people as they try to balance being dominant and complicit on the one hand and being victimized or tokenized on the other. Biracial individuals, for example, cannot simply identify with one of their parents. They have to find their way amidst the varying prejudices of family, community and peers, and they cannot escape from internalized oppression by rejecting either part of their racial heritage (Root, 1990).

This approach may also help to untangle the web of oppression and domination that can afflict those who hold a dominant-group membership but feel terror about the possible fragility of that privileged position because they have internalized an oppressive attitude afflicting them as well as the 'other'. Brown (1994: 86–8) gives the example of a single, heterosexual, youthful, able-bodied and quite affluent male attorney who suffered from non-specific unhappiness until he learned to see how he was captured by his disconnection from vulnerability and his adherence to the strategy of 'being more dominant than thou', in a continued pursuit of privilege.

Moreover, Young offers an additional differentiation of oppression by uncovering a family of concepts and conditions. She distinguishes five 'faces' of oppression that may reinforce each other: imperialism in the cultural realm (disregarding or trivializing aside from stereotyping of differences); exploitation and marginalization in the socio-economic realm; disempowerment by professionals and holders of information; and systemic violence (dehumanizing others thus allowing for physical, sexual and mental brutality). These five categories can be very productive for understanding the commonalities and differences between women, between women and men, and between clients and therapists. They will enable counsellors to comprehend gender-based oppression or privileging, as it is interwoven with other types of oppression. As such, they may extend the possibilities of openness offered by feminist counselling to a diversity of people who could benefit from its dual commitments of opposing domination and emphasizing empowerment.

Postmodernism: beyond innocence

The encounter between FMHC and postmodernism and post-structuralism has done more than expose unsustainable areas of innocence in FMHC. In respect of human agency, knowledge claims and sexual differences, similar reservations must be expressed about the post-isms themselves.

Female subjectivity

From the start, FMHC has paid considerable attention to the subjectivity of women clients. Initially, in radical and marxist approaches, the female self was thought to be alienated and false respectively (Chesler, 1972; Steiner, 1975; Wyckoff, 1977). Later, the psychoanalytic approach added the idea of an immature and vulnerable female self which was the result of unaccomplished separation and ensuing weakness of ego boundaries (Chodorow, 1978). In all cases FMHC claimed to offer its clients the opportunity *and* power to find and define their real selves. For this redefinition, FMHC supplied a position of collective identity for women clients as sharing a common social location and socialization that influences – if not causes– their mental and physical problems and their alternatives for solution (if any). The final, real and healthy self was considered to be individual, autonomous, fixed and non-ambiguous.

In contrast with such a unified and separate self the connection-oriented therapists have promulgated the self-in-relation, especially for women (Jordan et al., 1991). This self is depicted as permanently connected and differentiating, instead of separating. Following this conceptualization, the ambiguity of the term 'being' (as noun and verb; structure and process) can be appreciated (Jordan, 1991). Within this narrative, soundness of mental health is associated with attaining and maintaining 'clarity in connection', on the grounds that this is the optimal expression of an intersubjective self that develops continuously.

The discussion about separated and connected selves has been transcended by the notions of a 'multiple self' and a 'becoming subject'. These concepts focus on a stream of identities – produced not only in cultural, social and psychological arenas but also in physical, sexual and genetic processes. They signal flexibility of outcomes and stress interaction with the political and historical context. Identity is conceived as an ongoing self-construction in interaction with continuous processes of collective identity-formation, as carried out by people of the same 'race', class, culture, sexual orientation, age, or disabilities, and their environments. In addition, the subject is understood as being retrospectively constructed. It is an emerging 'I' with the collective memory of a 'we' – but the 'we' is fluid too. (Flax, 1990; Mens-Verhulst, 1992, 1996; N. Nicolai, 1994b). Given these two interrelated formulations, the subject of self can be fragmented, but still be judged to be 'sound' as long as the person has a sensation of internal basic cohesion – or core self.[6] Accordingly, concepts such as the multiple self and the becoming subject have opened up the identity of women presupposed in the original (and later) FMHC narratives to greater diversity. Such diversity now includes the twin possibilities that not all women give priority to gender in their identities, and that the ranking of gender in one's life and problems may vary across the lifespan.

The above mentioned approach is clearly postmodern and poststructuralist in its inspiration, but without following these insights to their theoretical extremes. In particular, it does not end up with the so-called fictive self and a subjectivity emptied of any possible meaning or content, as a definitive parting from the Enlightenment tradition (Braidotti, 1991). Such avoidance is made possible by following those feminist philosophers, theorists and therapists who have rejected the 'post-ist' vision of the subject – for at least three reasons.

First, suspicion has been expressed about the timing of this funeral (Braidotti, 1989; Flax, 1990; Fox-Genovese, 1991; Stefano, 1988). As Fox-Genovese writes: 'the Western white male elite proclaimed the death of the subject at precisely the moment at which it was being forced to share that status with women and with the peoples of other races and classes' (1991: 189). The view being expressed here is that, historically, men already have a firm subject position in society, while women have been treated as objects and so still have to achieve solid subject positions as actors. Consequently, women cannot take the risk of the limitless game of positioning the self in language.

Secondly, Flax (1990) criticizes the foremen of postmodernism for confusing a unitary self with a core self and rejecting both. Apparently, their sense of continuity or 'going on being' is so much a part of their core self that it has become a taken-for-granted background for them. But, she continues, clinical experience demonstrates that people without a core self are prone to very painful mental health problems. Thirdly, Flax wonders why postmodernists do not juxtapose the individualist notion of self against a social and gendered self, instead of against a fictive or empty self. As a practising psychoanalyst, she supposes that behind this is a need to evade, deny or repress intimate social relations, and especially the primary relations between (usually) mother and child. So, the fictive subject is revealed to be another patriarchal narrative, but one with a postmodern signature.

Knowing women

First and foremost FMHC has been grounded in experiential knowledge, rather than professional knowledge and power. It has sought to distance itself from academic knowledge, given the

academy's objectification of women, and especially its medicaliza-
tion, psychologization and trivialization of their problems.
Consciousness-raising groups started as a vehicle for valuing
women's experiences, problem-solving groups in order to pool the
dissipated knowledge of (isolated) women, and truth-finding was
expected from the sharing and analysis of experiences. It was
assumed that listening to the body would bring to the surface much
latent wisdom about one's real self and one's own will (Bransen,
1994).

Growing out of this, came the concept of 'expertise through
experience', and this has had its own momentum. Officially defined
as distinct from lay knowledge, it is achieved by reflection on one's
own experiences and their meaning for others in other contexts.
Moreover, women (former or current clients) have been able to
derive prestige and sometimes payment from it – it may become
business. In medical health care the first experiments were run with
'experts through experience' having their consulting room next to
that of the gynaecologist (Boet and Tiems, 1996; Tiems, 1993). This
turn has been welcomed by some within Dutch FMHC as the
ultimate recognition of expertise through experience, although it has
also met with reluctance from others who see it as betraying the
original principles (L. Nicolai, 1994). Nowadays (women's) experiences are no longer indisputable, and the value of scholarly expertise
can also be acknowledged.

The development in FMHC is reminiscent of women's ways of
knowing as narrated by Belenky and co-authors (1986). They
describe women's epistemological, psychological and moral growth
as originating in a silenced voice position and moving towards a
position of constructing knowledge. In between they discern the
positions of received, subjective, connected and separated knowledge. *Silence* is the position in which women experience themselves
as mindless, voiceless and subject to the whims of external authority. *Received knowledge* refers to reproducing the (external) truths
presented by parents, friends, professionals and other authorities.
The position of *subjective knowledge* includes producing knowledge
by listening to 'the inner voice' possibly mixed with the first-hand
experiences of others most like oneself. It entails a piecemeal
articulation and differentiation of the self. *Connected and separated
knowing* are both forms of procedural knowledge, but the conventions that are followed differ in character. In the connected
mode the prevailing (inter)actions are understanding, empathy and
the sharing of experience, discoveries and interpretations. In the
separate mode, analysing, judging and controlling are the ruling
activities. Finally, *constructed knowledge* involves the integration of

several types of knowledge. It is characterized by a high tolerance for internal contradiction and ambiguity and recognizes truth as a matter of the context in which it is embedded.

The launch of the FMHC movement can be understood as women leaving the positions of silenced voice and of received knowledge behind. Only subjective and connected knowledge was to be trusted. Later on, received and separate knowledge were also allowed, but mainly where they could support the collective knowledge construction and identity-seeking. Step-by-step, the tolerance of internal contradiction and the inclination towards contextualization has increased. Today, we see discussion developing around the question of what knowledge mix is adequate at what time for which group with what problems.

However, according to the poststructuralist premise, language precedes the subject. This premise renders suspect the authenticity and reliability of women's experiences as a source of knowledge. Postmodernism also denies the possibility of a knowing (woman) subject, and of anything 'deep inside' us that is not a product of discourse. Although nobody in the FMHC seems to agree with this poststructuralist and postmodernist radicalism, the debate on the (im)possibility of knowing women touches on important ambivalences. On the one side, the naming of experiences has proven to have a deeply subversive effect on the cultural hegemony. It is capable of mounting a strong challenge to the dominant narratives. Hence, marginal groups should not let themselves be deprived of this power.[7] Such considerations were brought forward by Alcoff and Gray (1993) in their analysis of transgression and recuperation in survivor discourse, and by the representatives of the black, migrant and refugee women who are working on empowerment (Boedjarath, 1994). On the other side, the mutual recognition of experiences is also acknowledged to have oppressive effects within the group they are derived from as well as on 'external' people that 'look' similar. In the past, women of the working class and black women have frequently protested against the attribution of experiences that were typically white and middle-class, such as the complicity of mothers in the silencing of their daughters. Nowadays this type of oppression also seems to occur between the generation of young feminists and the older ones who claim to have named women's problems and who also happened to more or less standardize the solutions. Anyhow, FMHC cannot deny its own claims for universal knowledge and the power ensuing from it. The limits of these claims must be admitted, but without totally rejecting the value of experience. It poses again the need to articulate sameness and otherness among categories of clients.

Sex/gender distinction

The distinction between sex and gender – which I will not further elaborate here – is made and ignored within the feminist (mental) health care movement. It is made in practice in so far as every feminist therapist emphasizes the socio-cultural influences women are subjected to, and makes the distinction between woman and femininity. However, linguistically the sex/gender distinction is not very popular in FMHC, chiefly because the term gender is judged to be unnecessarily alienating and is seen as complicating the conversation with clients and non-feminist colleagues.[8] Actually, for a long time, the biological side of sex has been a taboo in FMHC. Thus, an irresponsible reduction was induced in the understanding of eating disorders, menopausal problems, and so on. Obviously, FMHC cannot give up the sex distinction because that would imply abandoning its main legitimizing characteristics. But an interesting task division has emerged between the integrated and the 'alternative' parts of the movement. Within the integrated part, sex becomes nuanced more and more by adoption of the becoming subject against the background of permanent (re)articulation of sex relationships and sex representations. In the 'autonomous' parts, at least two strands can be discerned. One articulates the socio-political level of sex – mostly in a more reformist than radical version. The other highlights specific emotional and spiritual qualities of women to be honoured. However, no part of FMHC shares the mainstream postmodern thought that sex differences are just one of those articulations, and therefore women's liberation must be rejected as an illusion. All stick to the positive project of turning sexual differences into a strength, of affirming its positiveness – as Rosi Braidotti has postulated (1991). But the initial focus on the differences between women and men has been extended to a perspective that also encompasses differences among women, and within women – alongside their commonalities.

Conclusion: ongoing sociogenesis

In conclusion, women's liberation is an endless process, and the post-isms cannot be its guide. Postmodernism and poststructuralism seem to invite counsellors to refrain from any standpoint, feminist or otherwise. However, in feminist practices such an abstinence is not only technically impossible but also politically unthinkable and ethically unacceptable. Technically, it is simply impossible to live permanently in the deconstructive mode. It would drive people crazy, therapists as well as clients. In order to practice, counsellors must maintain some beliefs about what people need and why, and what they can do as professionals. The 'post-isms', however, have little to say about the practices and knowledge that could replace the current ones. Politically, the 'post-ism' games played with therapy can be unravelled from their own point of view. Then, the question arises who gains what and when by commitment to the rules. Following the 'post-ism' insights in power dynamics, the games finally will serve some elite audiences in the continuation of their privileged positions and irresponsibilities, and analogous collective memories. And this elite will not be as degendered as suggested. Ethically, the post-ism discourses suggest that liberating effects may be expected from the refusal of totalities and the embracing of difference, but they do not offer any positive vision of a good society, life or health care – and especially not in relationship to women.

Simultaneously, FMHC cannot escape from recognizing its activities as initially North European and Anglo, middle-class and white-oriented. Thus, it risks reproducing the very forms it struggles to break down. To avoid such 'innocence', a permanent critical feminist epistemological stance is required by which the collective and individual sociogenesis of women is creatively furthered. It promises a feminist posture that manifests itself by a gender-, power- and care-conscious perspective, which should also be applied to its own position and function: continually vigilant for oppressive tendencies in the prevailing constructions and imperatives, and always willing to rethink them.

Notes

1   A client's decision voluntarily to enter therapy was appraised as a sign of strength; or even as 'a hidden form of power and resistance to patriarchal norms' (Brown, 1994: 114–15).

2   Early FMHC focused intensively on guidelines and arrangements that may further symmetry between therapists and clients. Clients were challenged to make their own choices about the therapy they would follow. This was made possible by offering them a trial session, and an open therapy group of six sessions in which they could 'taste' the characteristics of FMHC, such as the sex-homogeneous setting; the combination of verbal and non-verbal, individual and group methods; self-formulation of goals and their regular evaluation (Mens-Verhulst, 1987, 1991).

3   Descriptively, equality refers to concepts such as sameness, similarity, resemblance or commonalities while difference is associated with otherness, dissimilarity, contrast and distinction (Komter, 1990).

4   This is somewhat different from preventive health care in the United States of America and the United Kingdom.

5   An interesting and important contextualization is offered by Hurtado (1989). White women, she says, have been oppressed but also privileged in their

relationship with white men. But these privileges were dependent on complete and constant submission. Moreover, these privileges resulted in frequent interactions with white men thus reinforcing docility, passivity and allegiance. Therefore, white women are at a greater disadvantage than women of colour in reclaiming their identity. And she concludes with: 'As a result, the white feminist movement is the only political movement to develop its own clinical approach – feminist therapy – to overcoming oppression at the interpersonal level' (Hurtado, 1989: 145).

6   It is this sensation that could provide the basis for the distinction between patients who, according to the *Diagnostic and Statistic Manual for Mental Disorders*, are categorized as having a 'borderline syndrome' (in which the self is thought to be painful and disablingly fragmented) or having a 'multiple personality syndrome'.

7   As Flax warns us: 'without a location and participation in collective memory and its retelling or reconstruction, a sense of "we" cannot emerge or be sustained' (1990: 221).

8   The reservation reminds me of Susan Condor's commentary (1993) that ordinary people are much more sophisticated and differentiated in their use of the terms 'sex', 'femininity' and 'masculinity' than (psychological) theorists usually suppose. She suggests that the assumed non-reflexive certitude in daily language is a construction of psychologists themselves, eager as they are for consistency and coherence.

References

Adleman, J. and Spencer Faunce, P. (eds) (1990) 'Ethics in practice: considerations of some specific oppressions', in H. Lerman and N. Porter (eds), *Feminist Ethics in Psychotherapy*. New York: Springer Verlag.

Alcoff, A. and Gray, I. (1993) 'Survivor discourse: transgression or recuperation?', *Signs* 18 (2): 260–90.

American Psychological Association (1978) 'Report of the Task Force on sex bias and sex role stereotyping in the psychotherapeutic practice. Guidelines for therapy with women', *American Psychologist* 33: 1122–23.

Babel, M. and Hitipeuw, D. (1992) *Langzaam gaan deuren open*. Vrouwenhulpverlening in relatie tot zwarte vrouwen. Amsterdam: De Maan.

Barrett, S.E. (1990) 'Paths towards diversity: an intrapsychic perspective', in L.S. Brown and M.P.P. Root (eds), *Diversity and Complexity in Feminist Therapy*. New York: Haworth Press.

Belenky, M.F., Clinchy, B.M., Goldberger, N.R., Tarule, J.M. (1986) *Women's Ways of Knowing*. New York: Basic Books.

Boedjarath, I. (1994) 'Vrouwengroepen: over oude principes en nieuwe doelgroepen', in J. van Mens-Verhulst and L. Schilder (eds), *Debatten in de vrouwenhulpverlening*. Amsterdam: Babylon/de Geus.

Boet, A. and Tiems, A. (1996) 'Cliënten aan het woord', in A. Tiems (ed.), *Werkprogramma Vrouwenhulpverlening*. Rijswijk: VWS.

Boyd, J.A. (1990) 'Ethnic and cultural diversity: keys to power', in L.S. Brown and M.P.P. Root (eds), *Diversity and Complexity in Feminist Therapy*. New York: Haworth Press.

Braidotti, R. (1989) 'The politics of ontological difference', in T. Brennan (ed.), *Between Feminism & Psychoanalysis*. London: Routledge.

Braidotti, R. (1991) *Patterns of Dissonance.* Cambridge: Polity Press.

Bransen, E. (1994) 'De holistische benadering: heel de vrouw?', in J. van Mens-Verhulst and L. Schilder (eds), *Debatten in de vrouwenhulpverlening.* Amsterdam: Babylon/de Geus.

Broverman, I., Broverman, D.M., Clarkson, F.E., Rosenkrantz, P. and Vogel, S.R. (1970) 'Sex role stereotypes and clinical judgements of mental health', *Journal of Consulting and Clinical Psychology* 34: 1–7.

Brown, L.S. (1990) 'The meaning of a multi-cultural perspective for theory-building in feminist therapy', *Women and Therapy* 9: 1–21.

Brown, L.S. (1994) *Subversive Dialogues: Theory in Feminist Therapy.* New York: Basic Books.

Brown, L.S. and Root, M.P.P. (1990) *Diversity and Complexity in Feminist Therapy.* New York: Haworth Press.

Chesler, P. (1972) *Women and Madness.* New York: Doubleday.

Chodorow, N. (1978) *The Reproduction of Mothering: Psychoanalysis and the Sociology of Gender.* Berkeley: University of California Press.

Condor, S. (1993) 'Denken over sekse als sociale categorie', *Tijdschrift voor vrouwenstudies* 55 (14–3): 280–94.

Flax, J. (1990) *Thinking Fragments: Psychoanalysis, Feminism, and Postmodernism in the Contemporary West.* Berkeley: University of California Press.

Fodor, I.G. (1985) 'Assertiveness training in the eighties: moving beyond the personal', in L.B. Rosewater and L.E.A. Walker (eds), *Handbook of Feminist Therapy: Women's Issues in Psychotherapy.* New York: Springer.

Fox-Genovese, E. (1991) *Feminism without Illusions: A Critique of Individualism.* Chapel Hill and London: University of North Carolina Press.

Green, M. (1987) 'Women in the oppressor role: white racism', in S. Ernst and M. Maguire (eds), *Living with the Sphinx: Papers from the Women's Therapy Centre.* London: The Women's Press.

Hare-Mustin, R.T. and Maracek, J. (1986) 'Autonomy and gender: some questions for therapists', *Psychotherapy* 23: 205–12.

Hurtado, A. (1989) 'Relating to privilege: seduction and rejection in the subordination of white women and color', *Signs* 14 (4): 833–55.

Jordan, J. (1991) 'The relational self: a new perspective on women's development', in J. Strauss and G. Goethals (eds), *The Self: Interdisciplinary Approaches.* New York: Springer Verlag.

Jordan, J., Kaplan, A., Miller, J.B., Stiver, I and Surrey, J. (1991) *Women's Growth in Connection: Writings from the Stone Center.* New York: Guilford Press.

Kanuha, V. (1990) 'The need for an integrated analysis of oppression in feminist therapy ethics', in H. Lerman and N. Porter (eds), *Feminist Ethics in Psychotherapy.* New York: Springer Verlag.

Komter, A. (1990) *De macht van de dubbele moraal.* Amsterdam: Van Gennep.

McLeod, E. (1994) *Women's Experience of Feminist Therapy and Counselling.* Buckingham: Open University Press.

McWhirter, E.H. (1991) 'Empowerment in counseling', *Journal of Counseling & Development* 69: 222–30.

Mens-Verhulst, J. van (1985) Vrouwenhulpverlening van verzamelnaam naar therapie-soort. *Tijdschrift voor Agologie* 14 (3): 102–93.

Mens-Verhulst, J. van (1987) 'Female designed mental health care', in M. Renou and J. van Mens-Verhulst (eds), *Female Designing in Social Policies.* Dordrecht: Foris.

Mens-Verhulst, J. van (1988) *Modelontwikkeling voor vrouw-en-hulpverlening.* Utrecht: ISOR.

Mens-Verhulst, J. van (1991) 'Perspective of power in therapeutic relationships', *American Journal of Psychotherapy* 45 (2): 198–210.

Mens-Verhulst, J. van (1992) 'De autonomie voorbij: over conceptuele, praktische en morele verschuivingen in de vrouwenhulpverlening' ('Beyond Autonomy'), *Sociale Interventie* 1 (4): 188–96.

Mens-Verhulst, J. van (1995) 'Reinventing the mother–daughter relationship', *American Journal of Psychotherapy* 49 (4): 526–39.

Mens-Verhulst, J. van (1996) 'Vrouwenhulpverlening: diversiteit als bron van zorg. Inaugural speech, University for Humanist Studies, Utrecht.

Mens-Verhulst, J. van and Schilder, L. (eds) (1994) *Debatten in de vrouwenhulpverlening (Disputes in Women's Health Care)*. Amsterdam: Babylon/de Geus.

Nicolai, L. (1994) 'Professioneel omgaan met ervaringsdeskundigheid', in J. van Mens-Verhulst and L. Schilder (eds), *Debatten in de vrouwenhulpverlening.* Amsterdam: Babylon/de Geus.

Nicolai, N. (1992) *Vrouwenhulpverlening en psychiatrie.* Amsterdam: SUA.

Nicolai, N. (1994a) 'Autonomie en zorg', in J. van Mens-Verhulst and L. Schilder (eds), *Debatten in de vrouwenhulpverlening.* Amsterdam: Babylon/de Geus.

Nicolai, N.J. (1994b) 'Van sekse naar gender', in J. van Mens-Verhulst and L. Schilder (eds), *Debatten in de vrouwenhulpverlening.* Amsterdam: Babylon/de Geus.

Pheterson, G. (1986) 'Alliances between women: overcoming internalized oppression and internalized domination', *Signs: Journal of Women in Culture and Society* 12: 146–60.

Plemper, E.M.T., Rijkschroeff, R.A.L., Savornin Lohman, J. de and Steketee, M.J. (1996) *Vrouwenhulpverlening en cliënten (in) beweging* Utrecht: Verwey-Jonker Instituut.

Root, M.P.P. (1990) 'Resolving "other" status: identity development of biracial individuals', in L.S. Brown and M.P.P. Root (eds), *Diversity and Complexity in Feminist Therapy.* New York: Haworth Press.

Schilder, L. and Kaaijk, M. (1994) 'Gelijkwaardigheid in de hulpverleningsrelatie: je weet niet wat je ziet', in J. van Mens-Verhulst and L. Schilder (eds), *Debatten in vrouwenhulpverlening.* Amsterdam: Babylon/de Geus.

Scott, J.W. (1990) 'Deconstructing equality-versus-difference: or, the uses of poststructuralist theory for feminism', in M. Hirsch and E. Fox Keller (eds), *Conflicts in Feminism.* London: Routledge. 134–48.

Sontag, S. (1991) *Illness as a Metaphor: Aids and its Metaphors.* Harmondsworth: Penguin.

Stefano, C. Di (1988) 'Dilemmas of difference: feminism, modernity and postmodernism', *Women and Politics* 8 (3/4): 1–24.

Steiner, C. (1975) *Readings in Radical Psychiatry.* New York: Grove Press.

Tiems, A. (1993) *Over de integratie van vrouwenhulpverlening.* Zoetermeer: Hageman.

Tronto, J.C. (1993) *Moral Boundaries: A Political Argument for an Ethic of Care.* London: Routledge.

Watson, G. and Williams, J. (1992) 'Feminist practice in therapy', in J.M. Ussher and P. Nicolson (eds), *Gender Issues in Clinical Psychology.* London: Routledge.

Wyckoff, H. (1977) *Solving Women's Problems.* New York: Grove Press.

Young, I.M. (1990) *Justice and the Politics of Difference.* Princeton NJ: Princeton University Press.

11

The Child, the Woman and the Cyborg: (Im)possibilities of Feminist Developmental Psychology

Erica Burman

This chapter explores intersections between feminist readings of poststructuralist theory and psychological practices through reflections on my positions as a feminist teacher of developmental psychology and the contested domain this imports between women and children, and between women (as well as between women and men). While theoretical work has explored the consequences of connecting with the epistemological destabilizations of poststructuralist perspectives for both feminism (now feminism*s*) and psychology, I want here to situate my engagement with these ideas from my own embodied working history. I do this by way of illustrating how both a feminist standpoint and a commitment to a postmodern-style multiplicity and diversity can be exercised (and perhaps energized) by their juxtaposition with (developmental) psychology. While feminist and poststructuralist ideas offer useful critical vantage points from which to expose the oppressive commitments and practices of psychology, I will try to indicate in this chapter something of why their hold in developmental psychology is so tenuous. In particular, I will argue that this 'resistance' makes developmental psychology not only a key arena for feminist deconstructionist work, but, like any symptom, also affords a diagnostic reading of the broader complex of contemporary cultural and intellectual investments it expresses.

I direct this chapter towards the specific problematic of developmental psychology, by telling some stories. Some of these are 'mine' in the sense that they draw on the narrative genre of autobiography – indeed I would claim that they are 'true' in the sense that they form part of the fabric of the historical narrative of my experience. Others of the stories are more general, perhaps shared as cultural narratives, or even myths. Hence, while 'my stories' conjoin 'experience' and 'analysis', I tell them in the conviction that, owing to the cultural meanings exercised by concepts of childhood, these are more than 'mine'; that they have more general resonance for the politics of psychology, for the politics of feminist practice and for accounts of the so-called postmodern. Further, in doing this I should make clear that the autobiographical material presented here is as much a crafted account as is the (apparently) 'more theoretical' argument. That such oppositions (between theory and experience) are themselves collapsing under the weight of postmodernist critiques is made evident by this book and others. Hence even the writing 'I' as articulated here can itself be regarded an, albeit useful, fiction that is lived as 'true'.

I will leave further theoretical concerns to unfold with the rest of the chapter. What follows is an elaboration of seven key dilemmas or (sometime) oppositions that structure the engagement between feminism(s), poststructuralism(s) and developmental psychology.

So why focus on developmental psychology? Surely using such sub-disciplinary categories implies an acceptance of the existing structure of psychology? First, I want to 'play' up the importance of taking developmental psychology seriously as an object of feminist critique and intervention, as a branch of psychology that has material effects on women's lives. Secondly, I want to ward off the dominant reading of discourse, deconstructionist and poststructuralist ideas as relevant only to specific branches of psychology that are recognized to deal with gender and the social – in particular 'the psychology of women', or 'feminist psychology', and 'social psychology'. Thirdly, I want to propose that developmental psychology is a key stronghold of positivist and modernist thinking in psychology that makes it a particularly important arena for feminist and poststructuralist critique – but perhaps not of practice.

Developmental psychology and modernity

In what follows I make general critiques of developmental psychology in order to demonstrate how this is one of the last bastions of modernism in psychology. My account is presented in general terms because it is invidious to single out specific individuals as responsible for an entire problematic (but see Burman, 1994a, in press a, for more specific analyses). Developmentalism, the conviction that explanation or greater understanding lies in situating a phenomenon within its species as well as individual history, is one of the hallmarks of nineteenth-century European thinking (Morss, 1990, 1995). We are now only too familiar with the limits of such models, of the partialities that structured apparently natural and value-free models. The child, the 'primitive', women and the mentally ill were treated as immature versions of the adult, male, rational mind, as expressions of the binary oppositions between human and animal, European and non-European, male and female (e.g. Haraway, 1989). The popularity of the evolutionary notion that the individual in 'its' lifetime repeats the development of the species ('ontogeny recapitulates phylogeny') was one of the primary precipitators of what we would now recognize as developmental psychology (although it could also be seen as the founding moment of personality theory and 'individual differences' – since our current sub-disciplinary divisions belie common sources (Rose, 1985)).

Invested and performed within the study of the child, then, were all the key preoccupations of modernity. In particular, the faith in progress – that individuals, and societies, develop towards some 'better', more adaptive, more beneficial form of organization – is one vital conceptual connection that ties developmental psychology in with the colonial and imperialist themes of (equally current) models of economic development. Just as important and related to its imperialist themes are the commitments to science, truth and reason, to the objective impartiality of technologies of research and evaluation and the ways they structure positivism and empiricism so deeply within developmental psychology. If the child is the basic unit of study, the raw material for the work of social, physical and political development, then the means by which 'it' is studied are depicted as equally free from socio-political influence.

Two points follow from these connections between feminism and poststructuralism. First, while postmodernism and deconstruction have profoundly redefined the agenda for social psychological and methodological debates, theory and method have remained relatively untouched in developmental psychology by paradigm twists and turns elsewhere in psychology. As a teacher and researcher in developmental psychology I have become accustomed to hearing from students, conference commentators and journal reviewers, that my concerns relate to the domain of philosophy or politics, but not to developmental psychology. Secondly, critiques of developmentalist assumptions in psychology (e.g. Kessen, 1979; Morss, 1995) have remained largely disconnected from similar critiques directed towards economics (Cowen and Shenton, 1996; Crush, 1995; Mehta, 1995) and psychoanalysis (Mitchell, 1988). Developmental psychology seems to maintain its conceptual and political integrity in the face of the broader discrediting of developmental ideas throughout social theory and practice. Why is this? In what ways is this process similar or different from other disciplines of sub-disciplines of psychology? And what are the consequences of this resistance/endurance for the project of feminist intervention?

It would appear we have to look further. There is something about the rhetorical power of 'the child', of children, that renders claims and promises of developmental psychology seemingly incontestable. Even the most confirmed relativist would hesitate to deny that 'we' (children, adults, everyone?) have basic needs (but see Burman, 1996a; Woodhead, 1990, 1996), that children differ from adults in some crucial 'developmental' sense that is not mere social attribution, and that those who study, or pronounce upon or about, children do not indicate something about potent mysteries of nature and life. Age, the marking of time on bodies, seems to lie outside culture, within biology. Like gender, 'race', class and sexuality, age plays a key part in the organization of social relations, and, like these, differential treatment is typically justified by the appeal to 'nature'. But while assumptions about gender, 'race', class and sexuality are now being increasingly understood as social constructions that are historically and culturally contingent, age, and in particular 'the child', seems particularly intransigent to this contextual analysis.

One way of trying to shake off the power of the-child-as-exemplar is to recall that, like developmental theorizing, it too has a history. Carolyn Steedman (1995) points out that the power of the child not only arises from its nodal point in the modern narratives of mastery and improvement, it also personifies for the modern Western imaginary the sense of loss – of inner life forever separated from outer, of the irretrievability of the past, the transience of life and the inevitability of death – to which these narratives simultaneously gave rise as their necessary corollaries. If the child is the over-determined trace of all these complexes of the *modern* condition, of what relevance is it to feminist and postmodernist work?

First dilemma: women or children first?

If developmental psychology is a prime site for anti-feminist psychological practice, then this may offer some clue as to its continuity of themes. Feminist psychologists go elsewhere – to feminist psychology or women's studies, for example – to develop and voice their critiques. Thus the child-centred focus of developmental psychology remains Western liberal individualism writ large and also (as with liberal individualism) reinscribes women's subordinate positions within the private domain (Pateman, 1989). With the emergence of liberal democracy, the potential authoritarianism of the state was limited by measures assuring the privacy of the home except where family failed (see Middleton, 1971). This meant that the prototypical 'reasonable man' as the subject of rational law was indeed male, with women gaining little protection from such arrangements. The setting up of exceptions to the limits of privacy meant that the state could make an exceptionally visible entry into the home through its supposedly benign gaze upon the child. Modern industrialized states are characterized by a panoply of child-watching, child-saving, child-developing and educating professionals, with multinational varieties springing up to spread the good news worldwide. If, within the optimistic model of modernity, children are 'our future' (citizens and workers) then it is worthwhile to the state to ensure that they are appropriately prepared for such positions.

It is therefore no surprise that feminists have responded with some suspicion and hostility to child-focused interventions, drawing on Foucauldian accounts to characterize such practices as regulation, evaluation and control. Further, not only do they give rise to the abuse of women by childcare professionals (O'Hagan and Dillenberger, 1995), but also these regimes of truth are subjectively inhabited and experienced: we worry about whether our child is 'doing well enough', is developing at the right pace, is 'going through her milestones correctly', etc. As Urwin (1985) and Marshall, Woollett and Dosanjh (this volume) point out, this conceptual frame not only isolates each mother, and treats her as the originator or responsible agent for any 'problem', but it also thereby sets her in competition with other women.

As feminists have also pointed out, part of the power of developmental explanation lies in the slippage from the specific and singular to the general: from the child to children; from the way it is to the way it has to, or is supposed to, be (Lieven, 1980). The move from normal, in the sense of statistical, description to rhetorical prescription is the ideological bugbear beleaguering the truth claims of the modern social and human sciences, but rears its ugly head in psychology most acutely because of psychology's pretensions to scientific status. Further, if the normal becomes presumed, then it is the abnormal that excites attention or scrutiny. We thus have a double system of regulation of women: as invisible norms, or as oddities or problems. The norms (e.g. of heterosexuality, motherhood, marriage, whiteness) elude further analysis; they form the standard backcloth for the pathologization of all those who by virtue of their sexuality, their racialized or minoritized status, their economic need, do not 'fit' prevailing norms – giving rise to what Ann Phoenix calls their 'normalised absence/pathologised presence' (1987).

Developmental psychology makes specific contributions to this tendency to pathologize differences from supposed norms because of its desire to plot the regular, general course of development. Specific aberrations from that course are then treated, in a circular argument of self-confirmation, as offering useful clues about the general, rather than, say, showing its limits. Such a commitment to the general as instantiated in the particular has been vital in producing an account of development abstracted from social-political conditions. It individualizes and privatizes the manifold ways the care and containment of the young is profoundly structured according to culturally and historically specific models of 'what people are/should be like'. Not least among these is the way general notions of the 'environment' of the child have elided the social and the biological through such key terms as 'the natural'. This has allowed the structure of normalized absence/pathologized presence to exert its full weight of scrutiny upon mothers as the designated primary carers of children.

In addition, developmental psychological knowledge is not confined to academic tracts but insinuates itself into every crevice of policy and practice around children – with consequences for women as mothers. Even psychoanalysis, with its longstanding quarrel with empirical psychology (over the demonstrability of unconscious processes), turns with respect to the tradition of child observation. So, the Tavistock Clinic text *Closely Observed Infants* (Miller et al., 1989) (offering eight case studies as resources for social workers, therapists and doctors unable to conduct observations for themselves) might just as well have been entitled 'Closely Observed Mothers', since its records of early infant life, of everyday tasks of feeding, nappy changes, weaning and potty training comment as much on the mothers (and the culture of mothering) as on the babies. The inadmissability of the social in development returns, like the repressed, in covert form. In returning indirectly it performs a double misattribution: the interactive character of development gets located within the child, while the less facilitating or desirable features are re-allocated to the mother.

Second dilemma: essentialism or expertise?

An issue related to the regulation of women as mothers by developmental psychology is, of course, the matter of those women who are not mothers. The positioning of mother versus non-mother in the credibility and authority stakes between women has also played itself out within my own trajectory through developmental psychology (and into women's studies). It also illustrates another dimension that underlies the 'theory–practice' polarity structuring popular discourse on child development (and may also offer a resource for popular resistance to 'the experts' (Alldred, 1996)). Perhaps in a vain effort to shake off the feminine hue connoted by its gendered subject matter, or perhaps because of its implication within dominant social agendas, developmental psychologists have always been at pains to demonstrate their methodological rigour and commitment to 'high theory'. Thus I graduated from the heady heights of genetic epistemology to delivering lectures on what the baby does, and does next, to trainee health visitors, community psychiatric nurses, youth and community workers, as well as psychology students.

As I pronounced on (and often denounced) the theories, I found myself quizzed, particularly by the – usually much more mature – professionals in the groups about my own motherhood status. As (mainly) women together, we stood on opposed territory for the warranting of our (often similar) political positions. I had initially chosen to 'do' psychology because I had not wanted to specialize in any subject I had previously studied; and then took a degree in developmental psychology since it seemed to offer a way of studying all topics and issues within one discipline. I was a ripe subject for developmental modernism, and at a moment when cognitive science was going developmental, developmental theorizing knew no bounds – virtual or real. As a white, middle-class young woman, accustomed to academic success as the route to mastery (Walkerdine, 1985), it was the theoretical concerns that gripped me. It was also through the theory that I came to realize the limits of the models both conceptually and politically, and through a critical reading of the theory that I tried to counter the perniciousness of commonsense applications of developmental psychology.

By contrast, the professionals I taught – often older, working-class in origin – were steeped in the discourses of 'practice' and 'experience', that both served them well as a resource for suspicion of abstract and inappropriate psychological theory *and* was a means of dealing with the relatively disempowering position of returning to the classroom. So were we, a group of – largely women-centred – women, divided by discourses of 'expertise' and 'experience' that mapped precisely on to different strategies of feminists in relation to motherhood and professionalism (see also Downick and Grundberg, 1980; Gordon, 1990; Oakley, 1981; Ribbens, 1994). In my (experience-limited) biography, theory had (in the end) offered insight and critique, while for these (experience-enriched) students, theory threatened them and they challenged my rights to comment on what they knew and did on the grounds of insufficiency of my claims to know as a non-mother.

Authenticity and experience are current topics of discussion in feminist theory and research (Maynard and Purvis, 1994; Wilkinson and Kitzinger, 1996). Here I want to note how these different pedagogical and student positions between women are not simply complementary but are mutual constructions based on historical conjunctions and contradictions of gender, 'race' and class. My position as professional expert did not simply work to offset my lesser claim to experience as younger, child-less (or child-free); my youth and child-free/less status could be read by these more mature women, largely with children, as indices of the privilege (or the price?) of gaining and wielding such 'illegitimate' power. By such means and for these reasons, the political critique of developmental theory I offered could be obscured, ignored or even discounted.

Doubtless these stories are not unlike those of any beginning teacher, and I do not want to imply that I had an unusually difficult time, nor that I was a particularly unsuccessful teacher to these students. What I want to highlight is the contradictory positions mobilized for (feminist) teachers and students around claims to different kinds of knowledge, contradictions that mirror the tensions within the project of women's studies between women studying and the study of women's work (Coulson and Bhavnani, 1990). These express structural tensions and power relations involved in being a feminist teacher, as representing both what the students want, and what they want to resist. For women's studies this is often particularly difficult; we both challenge the academy and exemplify it. One lesson of poststructuralist ideas is that acknowledging these multiple positions can teach us to negotiate these political dilemmas better.

I present this tale because it highlights the complexities and investments set in play by the call to surrender special claims to voice or experience within the context of teaching critical psychology. Clearly it must be possible to be a non-mother/child-free and be considered qualified to teach or practise developmental psychology. To do otherwise would be to essentialize the experience of motherhood (and also gender) in ways that not only abstract and reify motherhood, but also render it open to even greater individual pathologization. While such an approach clearly runs counter to the contemporary climate of gender-bending and anti-essentialism, we also know when and why we want to maintain a strategic claim on the category 'woman' (Evans, 1990); we might need to reconsider speaking positions and rights in the feminist classroom in a similar light (see McNeil, 1992). Claims to specificity, diversity and historical positions of disadvantage are presented and contradicted when feminists teach developmental psychology. Even if 'deconstruction' is considered too 'difficult' or esoteric to teach, perhaps it offers some useful ideas for our teaching practice.

Third dilemma: relativism or the real?

My concerns about how developmental psychology peddles historically and culturally specific notions as universal truths, alongside its warrants for coercive scrutiny of disadvantaged and minoritized groups, led me to question how relevant Foucauldian critiques are to applications of developmental psychology outside its Anglo–US context of origin. My relativist leanings brought me into discussion with international child rights activists and child welfare agencies, yet it was my expertise in the 'realities' of child development that appeared to engage them most. I have struggled to avoid being positioned as 'knowing' what children 'need', and have pondered on the necessity and desirability of developing universal indicators of child development for use in monitoring the international legal instruments for child promotion and child protection such as the 1990 United Nations Convention on the Rights of the Child (e.g. Boyden, 1993). While measures to extend children's welfare, cultural and political rights are to be welcomed, procedures for their evaluation and implementation threaten to install highly normative and culturally specific notions of idealized child subjects and family forms (Burman, 1996a; Freeman and Veerman, 1992). If poststructuralism proclaims the death of the (Western Enlightenment) subject, should we not resist its reconstruction?

There are certainly residues of the child of the liberal Western imaginary structured within international child rights policies and legislation. The common slogans of 'stolen childhood', or the implicit opposition elaborated between children who 'develop' and those who (merely) 'survive' (Vittachi, 1989), privilege the model of childhood associated with the Western world. The active, spontaneous, playing, problem-solving, culturally-male child of Western developmental psychology sits as uneasily with the working boy or girl, with the street child, the child soldier or sex worker of the South, as it does within the various Souths within the North.[1] As records of the drafting process of the UN Convention indicate, notions of parental care structured into international legislation border perilously close to Western-defined notions of family and mothercare (Johnson, 1992). Similarly, programmes for the promotion of child development place ever greater emphasis on the role of home visits and parental training without much reflection on the cultural relevance of the theoretical resources informing their models.

However, the limits of relativism become apparent when we see respect for cultural diversity and traditions displace concerns about female circumcision within the UN Convention. Without a political framework that explicitly allows one position to be privileged, other agendas can be mobilized to win the day, and along with this 'culture' and 'tradition' become treated as essential, ahistorical categories:

> Without questioning the political uses of culture, without asking whose culture this is and who its primary beneficiaries are, without placing the very notion of culture in historical context and investigating the position of the interpreter, we cannot fully understand the ease with which women become instrumentalised in larger battles of political, economic, military and discursive competition in the international arena. (Rao, 1995: 174)

Nevertheless, professionals drawing on dominant discourses of childhood are not necessarily uncritical subscribers to it. Child rights and agency workers may well make use of the sentimentalizing feel-good factors of donor–recipient relations exemplified in charitable fund-raising for children (see Black, 1992). However, in other contexts their funding practices may depart dramatically from the exclusively child-centred orientation their publicity implies (e.g. giving money to community projects rather than specifically or solely for child-saving), and in their practice may challenge the historical and cultural abstraction of childhood by supporting community and community-defined development (although this can run the risk of simply replacing one romanticization – of the child – with another – the community – that itself is just as redolent of paternalistic legacies (Cowen and Shenton, 1996)). Moreover, the profoundly ideological discourse of child innocence, of the prior claim that children have in times of political conflict, can be deployed in surprising ways. Strategic essentialism of the child has been used (for the benefit of not only children) to negotiate temporary ceasefires for the delivery of immunization and essential food and medical supplies explicitly on the basis that children are 'peace zones' (Boyden, personal communication).

Fourth dilemma: reflexivity or rationalization?

Poststructuralist engagements with psychology – particularly as connected with feminist debates about research – have tended to highlight the importance of being reflexive. As a process of making clear the interpretive resources guiding one's questions and analysis, often in relation to audiences designated with particular powers of evaluation, reflexivity has been put forward as a key feature of accountability (e.g. Wilkinson, 1988). Yet notwithstanding its overt recognition of contradiction and complexity (e.g. Hollway, 1989), the model of subjectivity that underlies these proposals is one that resembles the rational unitary subject that poststructuralism claimed to have dispersed. Not only does a feminist reflexivity run the risk of departing from the tenets of poststructuralism (which may not be so heinous a sin), it also fuels the charge that accounts of research are not so much an honest sharing of motives and experience, but are (conscious or unconscious) manipulations.

Posed so baldly, this tension is revealed as a false opposition: if we accept that all accounts are textually mediated or crafted, then we cannot demarcate an absolute distinction between 'confession' and 'motivated justification'. Indeed, recalling Foucault's (1981) description of psychoanalysis as the secular confessional, we might see these practices as related. Our everyday understanding of confession (outside contexts of police interrogations) is the practice of making public one's innermost, private thoughts, but this tends to underestimate the structural importance to the account of the context in which it is made (see also Burman, 1992a). Inner revelation shades into (self-regulated) extortion, or at best selective recasting, to make acceptable either to oneself or another. Talk of confession seems particularly appropriate in the context of discussions about children, where theories of original innocence, or sin, are so prevalent – as respectively drawn upon within contemporary discussions about children who are abused, or are violent.

There are two other applications of this slippage between reflexivity and rationalization relevant to the concerns of this chapter. First, feminist (and other, e.g. discourse analytic) researchers who draw on the notion of reflexivity are clearly on shaky territory if they subscribe to claims of authentic, unmediated exhibitions of inner subjectivities (whether others' or their own). The claim that the author is dead was put forward precisely to undermine the readers' deference to authorial intentionality. This does not necessarily warrant an invitation to default on researcher or authorial responsibilities; rather, it implies the acknowledgement of the limits of what we can claim to know, and the different knowledges we bring to bear in different contexts. Similarly, the interpretation of reflexivity as an incitement to confess all, evident within some (especially novice student) readings (see Burman, in press b and c), should be recognized as a backdoor return to humanism and even positivism. Rather than aspiring for some 'total' account, autobiographical or otherwise, we should be looking for sufficient and convincing analyses of the structural relations involved in the research.

Secondly, the selective, and possibly distorted, character of recollection arises in an acute form in any dealings with children and childhood. Here we again encounter the vexed question of the textual structuring of 'experience', since one of the structural characteristics of childhood work is that it is almost always carried out by those who do not inhabit that social category (Mayall, 1996), but all of whom have been children. This arises for feminists as much as for any other commentators on, or researchers or workers with, children. How are we to make sense of the (dis)connections between our own memories and the (apparent) actualities of children's lives? How are we to, or can we, distinguish what we believe are our recollections of our early lives from their continuous reconstruction in the narratives we tell ourselves (and others) about our lives? It is hard to mention these issues without invoking the spectre of 'false memory syndrome' and its associated discourse of disbelief of survivors of sexual abuse and sexual assault (Scott, 1997). Yet the problem with this train of associations lies precisely in the ways dominant notions of childhood conflate our memories of the children we were with the children we study: our concepts of selfhood are so intertwined with those of childhood that it becomes hard to distinguish the longing for what we no longer have (and perhaps never had) from our convictions about (and desires for) what children are and should be now (Burman, 1996b, c). The task for us, as feminist psychologists, is to do the work of analytical reflection, of reflexivity – or rationalization – to help ward off the conflation of these different projects: the repair of one's own past and the study of children's present. A more informed knowledge of the socially structured irrationality of our life narratives may help feminist struggles against injustice.

Fifth dilemma: child-centred or woman-centred?

It would seem that feminists are well shot of developmental psychology, and much feminist effort has been devoted to disentangling the equation between women's interests and children's interests (New and David, 1985; Thorne, 1987). In economic development policy, women have long been addressed as sources of reproductive labour – whether as vessels for future labour or, in current formulations, in the relationship presumed between (higher) educational levels and (reduced) fertility. Women are also now recognized as a resource for production. Either way, it is important to challenge the presumed equivalence between measures introduced on behalf of children and those for women – in both directions. Women have not particularly benefited from childcare interventions, risking not only scrutiny, but also possible removal of their children, or semi-enforced sterilization. Women have also been targeted in developmental policy as the more effective means (than through male heads of household) of getting more aid to children: the assumption that financial aid to women 'trickles down' to children has been shown to be as erroneous (Peace and Hulme, 1995), as is the notion that raising the gross national product *per capita* will benefit disadvantaged members of a society (Mehta, 1993). It has been an important feminist strategy to identify women's entitlements separately and not in relation to children, and while the United Nations Commission on the Elimination of Discrimination Against Women was conducted alongside the Commission drafting the UN Convention on the Rights of the Child, it is significant that a major recent text, *Women's Rights, Human Rights* (Peters and Wolper, 1995), makes almost no mention of children, and fails to discuss any relationship between women's rights and children's rights.

It may be that child-saving always threatens to import the full structure of mother-blaming, and that child rights enthusiasts have often been anti-feminist. While the child of developmental psychology is prototypically male, the interplay of gender between child and parent in child-saving discourse works to tie responsibility firmly on to women. If the child is male, then the discourse of saving boys from bad mothers is mobilized, but more often the child in need of saving is portrayed as a girl (thus confirming the conflation of feminine gender and passivity with infantilization and victim-status). Nevertheless, it is a major conceptual and political mistake to treat women and children as absolutely separate categories. Girls (usually) grow up to be women, and we might interpret the awkward formulation circulating within contemporary (economic and psychological) development policy of 'the girl child' as (among other matters) indicating the anomaly of this position across and between these two categories (gender and age) of social discrimination (Burman, 1995b).

Further, we mistake strategy for principle if we accept the liberal rights discourse that treats rights as individual and competing. Women's and children's rights may well be in need of separation, given social pressures for women to subordinate their interests to those of their children, as where the sensitive mother is enjoined by the child-centred pedagogy to disguise her household labour as play (e.g. Walkerdine and Lucy, 1989). Similarly, increasingly health education campaigns are inviting pregnant women to subordinate their rights (e.g. to drink and smoke) to those of their 'unborn children'. Where this is extended to 'pre-pregnant' women we begin to see how the categories of woman, mother and child are in danger of imploding. But nevertheless, this does not mean that these categories *are* absolutely separable. This would be to accept the discourse of the Western patriarchal legal system as truth.

Perhaps there is something more uneasy at work here in the separation between women and children marked by the adoption of a liberal rights discourse, something that goes beyond even warding off the infantilization of women and the feminization of children (Burman, 1995a). Perhaps if we treat women and children as separate categories, we do not then have to attend to the ways feminists have been, and are, divided over discussions about children and childcare (see for example, Attar, 1988, 1992; as opposed to Wallsgrove, 1985). Mary Daly's (1981) description of mothers who initiate girls into oppressive practices of femininity as 'token torturers' is scarcely mother-friendly. Even within first-wave British feminism, disputes emerged over the roles of mothers, and of the relative responsibilities of mothers and the state for childcare – between empowering women through giving them the vote and improving public facilities for mothers and children (Riley, 1987). Twenty-four-hour creche provision may have been a longstanding demand of second-wave feminism, but the current revival of celebratory motherhood (in an era of economic and social decline) restates more positively the old refrain: why have children if you don't want to look after or be with them?

Here we encounter the full force of critiques of feminism as played out through differences in women's relationships to children and families. Black feminists have argued against the representation of the family as only functioning as a site of oppression for women, since it is also a source of support against a racist society (Amos and Parmar, 1984; Glenn et al., 1995). Heterosexual privilege has long been equated with motherhood – although the increasing numbers of lesbian mothers by donor insemination (DI) perhaps shows this as the partial fiction it always has been. Nevertheless 'fitness to mother' in the sense of bearing, caring for, and, crucially, access to services for assisted mothering and child custody, are all heavily influenced by norms about what makes an appropriate family environment in which children can grow up (Alldred, 1995). These (examples of) structural divisions between women replay themselves anew (across divisions of class and able-bodiedness) in the mutual suspicions, jealousies and antagonisms between feminist mothers and non-mothers.

Without subscribing to romantic notions of relatedness or 'different voices' (e.g. Fulani, 1998; Gilligan, 1982), we can still recognize the limits of a 'rights' model – be it reproductive rights, children's rights or women's rights – for the useful but flawed legal instrument it is, and try to move on beyond the unhelpful polarities it reinscribes; on this, in their attention to diversity, undecidability and structural ambivalence, feminist poststructuralisms may be helpful.

But even the apparatus of deconstruction, including deconstructing developmental psychology, presumes the structure it sets out to dismantle. It is thus covertly dependent on, or even maintaining of, it. Further, the idea of deconstructing developmental psychology may provoke specific and contradictory reactions, particularly for women: of horror or sadism. That this is so is intimated by the images of dismemberment associated with deconstruction. Treating deconstruction as equivalent to ejection or explosion of the child subject constitutes a perniciously individualist and reductionist reading of what should be the rejection or reformulation of an entire body of *theory*: talk of throwing the baby out with the bathwater suffers from similar limitations. While children, like women, are considered both appealing and appalling (Burman, 1994b, in press a), their status as quintessential humanist subjects does not necessarily favour either. Similarly, it is probably both unhelpful and impossible simply to replace an exclusive focus on the child with one on the woman as subject. This is where developmental psychology in its lifespan varieties meets the psychology of women (e.g. Josselson, 1987). The problem is not simply the gendered character of the implicit subject and trajectory of developmental psychology (though this *is* also a problem). Feminizing the child, or taking the woman as central to the developmental account is useful, but not enough, since the unitary subject still remains.

Sixth dilemma: the child as postmodern subject?

If poststructuralism and postmodernism have deconstructed the liberal humanist subject, reproduced in the rational, unitary subject of modern psychology (Henriques et al., 1984), what kind of subjects inhabit postmodernity? Notwithstanding the proclamations of the death of the subject, a new model of subjectivity has been engendered that emphasizes sponteneity, play, plurality and fragmentation. Such subjectivities explicitly challenge dominant conceptualizations of political organization deemed inappropriate to these 'new times' of rapid political change, of epistemological, ecological and economic uncertainty, and new social movements. But far from dispensing with the Enlightenment subject, residues of the old remain to haunt us within the new. As a reversal of the serious, integrated, single-minded adult, the romantic subject of postmodernism is the child. While Frederick Jameson's (1984) influential account of postmodernity celebrates play, bricolage, timelessness and schizophrenia (or internal disintegration) as tokens of postmodern subjectivities, I will focus here on Jean-François Lyotard's portrayal (but see also Burman, 1992b). As the author of one of the key works heralding postmodernity (Lyotard, 1984), Lyotard's writings on childhood are particularly worthy of attention.

Lyotard's *The Postmodern Explained to Children* (1992) is undoubtedly a playful and polyvalent text, not only in its title, which beguilingly appears to promise clarity and simplicity, nor in the pedagogical position of master/teacher he covertly assumes to complement that of the child–reader. The book is introduced by its editor/translators as exemplifying Lyotard's conception of the postmodern in its fragmentary, non-linear, incomplete form. In some senses it does indeed convey some of the central preoccupations of Lyotard's ideas; and in that respect the trope of the child works in the typical modern manner of indicating an inner core of truth, stripped of trappings and defences.

Where Lyotard writes explicitly about childhood, he is treating this not as a lifestage of immaturity or inferiority, but as the moment of creative chaos that precedes thought. (Here he alludes both to Nietzsche and Benjamin.) In his discussion of the teaching and practice of philosophy, he designates childhood as a state of mind, as 'the possibility of risk of being adrift' (1992: 116). Thus:

> Philosophical writing is ahead of where it is supposed to be. Like a child, it is premature and insubstantial. We recommence, but cannot rely on it getting to thought itself, there, at the end. For the thought is here, muddled up in the unthought, trying to sort out the impertinent babble of childhood. (Lyotard, 1992: 119)

The openness and unbounded state of the exploring philosopher cannot be entered into 'without renewing ties with the season of childhood, the season of the mind's possibilities' (1992: 116). Childhood is like postmodernism: that which is ineffable, intangible, unarticulable, unrepresentable (see Lyotard, 1983) – but what a modern-style mystery of childhood this is:

> The postmodern would be that which in the modern invokes the unpresentable in presentation itself, which refuses the consolation of correct forms, refuses the consensus of taste permitting a common experience for the impossible, and inquires into new presentations – not to take pleasure in them but to better produce the feeling that there is something unpresentable . . . (Lyotard, 1992: 24)

Although cast as a mode of writing, as intimating the inchoate character of innovation and creativity, this romance of the child ultimately appeals to an embodied form, and presumed collective memory, with all its attendant normalizations and cultural assumptions. There is no equivocation about the child as subject, as an interpellated, putatively general, historical memory:

> . . . we must extend the line of the body in the line of writing. . . . Following this line . . . means that we use these forms in an attempt to bear witness to what really matters: the childhood of an encounter, the welcome extended to the marvel that (something) is happening, the respect for the event. Don't forget, you were and are this yourself: the welcomed marvel, the respected event, the childhood shared by your parents. (Lyotard, 1992: 112)

Once again the minds and bodies of children have become homogenized into the child, every child, that dimly remembered part of ourselves 'we' were and are: the postmodern has mutated into the worst excesses of the modern by reinstalling the familiar subject of Western everyman in a post-Enlightenment form.

Seventh dilemma: the child, the woman or the cyborg?

If the child irretrievably harks back to modernism, then perhaps there are other metaphors for less oppressive psychological and political subjectivities. Developmental psychology is complicit with the problems of modernity, and anti-developmental theories – though vital – stop at critique rather than creative formulation of new models. Yet if, ultimately, even non-foundationalist postmodernism retains a commitment to a humanist subject, is it possible, or desirable, to try to dispense with a model of the subject? Given the political ambiguities of postmodernism, feminists are debating forms of available conceptions of subjectivity and (individual and collective) change (Bondi, 1993; Nicholson and Seidman, 1995). In this chapter I have discussed the limits of child-centred models of development, and how women or even women-centred varieties fall prey to some of the same difficulties of essentialism and reification. Perhaps Donna Haraway's (1991) cyborg manifesto, with its speculative political possibilities, offers an alternative set of metaphors on which to base a (feminist) developmental psychology.

The cyborg is ostensibly antithetical to any conventional developmental narrative: it is an entity without history, or a history of embodiment; it is neither human nor machine; it transgresses categories of gender; it is of uncertain or unallocated sexual orientation; and of no known 'race' or culture. As such, the cyborg usefully highlights the typical investments and applications of developmental psychology, and in particular resists the resort to 'nature', since by definition it is an artefactual construction, a hybrid without precedent and origins. As such the metaphor of the cyborg has gained an enthusiastic reception in feminist and postmodernist circles (Lykke and Braidotti, 1996). Still, once again, we find the monster cyborg suffers from the legacies of monstrous women and children, as indicated by the bad press it has received in popular culture (Creed, 1987).

There are other reservations or limits to its radical potential. Just as the dominant cultural representation of the cyborg as invulnerable superman threatens to eclipse the figurative possibilities of this new life form, so too it reminds us of how developmental psychology has been powerfully informed by, as well as contributing to, the project of 'artificial intelligence' (see Rutkowska, 1993). Haraway is very clear that she invokes the cyborg as *mythical possibility*, as a reminder of possibilities that technophilic and anti-scientific feminists might fail to notice. But, as she acknowledges, this vision is one that we will have to struggle hard to recast in feminist-friendly ways, given the cyborg's origins in advanced war technology and (productive and reproductive) labour replacement (Macaulay and Gordo Lopez, 1995).

While the cyborg may lack its own history, it functions within historical circumstances. Haraway's challenge is for us to recognize that it can be (re)formulated to promote feminist ends. (We might note how the original subtitle of her piece: 'science, technology and socialist feminism in the 1980s' is often forgotten.) If theories of subjectivity are inevitable and indispensible tools to envisage changed social arrangements, then perhaps the cyborg offers a different set of models and images that are less caught up in the trappings of tradition and modernity. While no image is innocent, or without history (cyborgs abound in all mythologies – ancient and new), what the cyborg offers the critic of developmental psychology is an alternative vantage point on its terms of reference – as neither parent nor child, and with neither absolute standpoint nor immutable difference.

At the risk of reiterating the modern story of the child as intimating more general lessons and strategies, I want to end by asserting the relevance of debates about development, change and political subjectivities for feminist politics (modern or postmodern). In this chapter I have commented on some current models in circulation, and in particular highlighted the varied and enduring character of the resort to the child – exemplified by, but not confined to, the child of developmental psychology. If turning from the child to the woman or even the cyborg fails to resolve some of the difficulties, then there are two possible conclusions we might draw: first, that no metaphor can guarantee a progressive outcome: rather, what matters is what we do with it; and secondly, that common to all three tropes – the child, the woman and the cyborg – is that they remain singular, isolated, and thus recuperable into the individualist narrative of liberal bourgeois development.

Perhaps rather than (only) leaping into new figurative utopias, there is still much mundane work of feminist (psychological) critique to be done. Along with elaborating new inspirational images, one very material and grounding critical practice of developmental psychology is to challenge the elision of the general into the singular, with all its attendant homogenization of the diversity of gendered, cultural and historical practices. This is more modest than the grand project of reconstructing a developmental psychology that can prefigure better days, but that always runs the risk of reproducing the same oppressive structures it set out to counter. Yet it can draw on imaginary alternatives and deconstructionist destabilizations to engage in a more informed way with the complexities and poignancies of the intersections between women and children, and between women, as well as between women and men, that are brought to the fore by the feminist critique of developmental psychology. At the very least we can start to document the diversities of what we, as children, women or cyborgs, are and do: we might even find that there is already more resistance for, and will to, change than we thought.

Acknowledgement

Thanks to the editors for their enthusiasm, commitment and hard work, and to Angel Gordo-Lopez for his intellectual and translation support.

Note

1 The terms North and South are used to refer to the richer and poorer countries of the world, as historically produced through the colonial and imperialist de-development, and which map historically on to the positions of people of European and non-European origins. This is not to underestimate the major difference in advantage and disadvantage experienced within peoples and countries of the North and South.

References

Alldred, P. (1995) '"Fit to parent"? Developmental psychology and non-traditional families', in E. Burman, P. Alldred, C. Bewley, B. Goldberg, C. Heenan, D. Marks, J. Marshall, K. Taylor, R. Ullah and S. Warner (1995) *Challenging Women: Psychology's Exclusions, Feminist Possibilities.* Buckingham: Open University Press.

Alldred, P. (1996) 'Whose expertise? Conceptualising mothers' resistance to advice about childcare', in E. Burman, G. Aitken, P. Alldred, R. Allwood, T. Billington, B. Goldberg, A. Gordo Lopez, C. Heenan, D. Marks, S. Warner, *Psychology Discourse Practice: From Regulation to Resistance.* London: Taylor & Francis.

Amos, V. and Parmar, P. (1984) 'Challenging imperial feminism', *Feminist Review* 17: 3–20.

Attar, D. (1988) 'Who's holding the bottle? The politics of breastfeeding', *Trouble and Strife* 13: 33–9.

Attar, D. (1992) 'The demand that time forgot', *Trouble and Strife* 23: 24–9.

Bondi, L. (1993) 'Locating identity politics', in M. Keith and J. Pale (eds), *Place and the Politics of Identity.* London: Routledge.

Boyden, J. (1993) 'The development of indicators for the monitoring of the Convention on the Rights of the Child', Report for Redda Barnan.

Black, M. (1992) *A Cause for Our Times: Oxfam – the First Fifty Years.* Oxfam: Oxford.

Burman, E. (1992a) 'Feminism and discourse in developmental psychology: power, subjectivity and interpretation', *Feminism and Psychology* 2 (1): 45–60.

Burman, E. (1992b) 'Developmental psychology and the postmodern child', in J. Doherty, E. Graham and M. Malek (eds), *Postmodernism and the Social Sciences.* London: Macmillan.

Burman, E. (1994a) *Deconstructing Developmental Psychology.* London: Routledge.

Burman, E. (1994b) 'Innocents abroad: projecting Western fantasies of childhood onto the iconography of emergencies', *Disasters: Journal of Disaster Studies and Management* 18 (3): 238–53.

Burman, E. (1995a) 'What is it? Masculinity and femininity in the cultural representation of childhood', in S. Wilkinson and C. Kitzinger (eds), *Feminism and Discourse: Psychological Perspectives.* London: Sage.

Burman, E. (1995b) 'The abnormal distribution of development: child development and policies for Southern women', *Gender, Place and Culture* 2 (1): 21–36.

Burman, E. (1996a) 'Local, global or globalized: child development and international child rights legislation', *Childhood: A Global Journal of Child Research* 3 (1): 45–66.

Burman, E. (1996b) 'Continuities and discontinuities in interpretative and textual approaches to developmental psychology', *Human Development* 39: 330–49.

Burman, E. (1996c) 'Telling stories: psychologists, children and the production of "false memories"', *Theory & Psychology* 7 (3): 291–309.

Burman, E. (1996d) 'False memories, true hopes and the angelic: revenge of the postmodern on therapy', *New Formations* 30: 122–34.

Burman, E. (in press a) 'Appealing and appalling children', *Free Associations* 43.

Burman, E. (in press b) 'Minding the gap: positivism, psychology and the politics of qualitative methods', *Journal of Social Issues.*

Burman, E. (in press c) 'Disciplinary apprentices: "qualitative methods" in student psychological research', *International Journal of Social Research Methodology, Theory and Practice*.

Coulson, M. and Bhavnani, K. (1990) 'Making a difference: questioning women's studies', in E. Burman (ed.), *Feminists and Psychological Practice*. London: Sage.

Cowen, M. and Shenton, R. (1996) *Doctrines of Development*. London: Routledge.

Creed, B. (1987) 'Horror and the monstrous feminine: an imaginary abjection', *Screen* 28 (1): 44–70.

Crush, J. (ed.) (1995) *Power of Development*. London: Routledge.

Daly, M. (1981) *Gyn/Ecology*. London: The Women's Press.

Downick, S. and Grundberg, S. (eds) (1980) *Why Children?* London: The Women's Press.

Evans, M. (1990) 'The problem of gender for women's studies', *Women's Studies International Forum* 13 (5): 457–63.

Foucault, M. (1981) *The History of Sexuality. Vol. 1: An Introduction*. Harmondsworth: Penguin.

Freeman, M. and Veerman, P. (eds) (1992) *The Ideologies of Children's Rights*. Dordrecht: Martinus Nijhoff.

Fulani, L. (1998) 'Beyond the ethic of care: the Kohlberg–Gilligan controversy revamped', in E. Burman (ed.), *Deconstructing Feminist Psychology*. London: Sage.

Gilligan, C. (1992) *In a Different Voice*. Cambridge, MA: Harvard University Press.

Glenn, E., Chang, G. and Forcey, L. (eds) (1995) *Mothering: Ideology, Experience, and Agency*. New York: Routledge.

Gordon, T. (1990) *Feminist Mothers*. London: Macmillan.

Haraway, D. (1989) *Primate Visions: Gender, Race and Nature in the World of Modern Science*. London: Verso.

Haraway, D. (1991) *Simians, Cyborgs and Women*. London: Verso.

Henriques, J., Hollway, W., Urwin, C., Venn, C. and Walkerdine, V. (1984) *Changing the Subject: Psychology, Social Regulation and Subjectivity*. London: Methuen.

Hollway, W. (1989) *Subjectivity and Method in Psychology*. London: Sage.

Jameson, F. (1984) 'Postmodernism, or the cultural logic of late capitalism', *New Left Review* 146: 53–93.

Johnson, D. (1992) 'Cultural and regional pluralism in the drafting of the UN Convention on the Right of the Child', in M. Freeman and P. Veerman (eds), *The Ideologies of Children's Rights*. Dordrecht: Martinus Nijhoff Publishers.

Josselson, J. (1987) *Finding Herself: Pathways to Identity Development in Women*. San Francisco and London: Jossey-Bass.

Kessen, W. (1979) 'The American child and other cultural inventions', *American Psychologist* 34 (10): 815–20.

Lieven, E. (1980) '"If it's natural, we can't change it"', in Cambridge Women's Studies Group, *Women in Society: Interdisciplinary Studies*. London: Virago.

Lykke, N. and Braidotti, R. (eds) (1996) *Between Monsters, Goddesses and Cyborgs: Feminist Confrontations with Science, Medicine and Cyberspace*. London: Zed.

Lyotard, J.F. (1983) 'Presentations', in A. Montifiore (ed.), *Philosophy in France Today*. Cambridge: Cambridge University Press.

Lyotard, J.F. (1984) *The Postmodern Condition: A Report on Knowledge*. Manchester: Manchester University Press.

Lyotard, J.F. (1992) *The Postmodern Explained to Children: Correspondence 1982–1985*. London: Turnaround.

McNeil, M. (1992) 'Pedagogical practice and problems: reflections on teaching about gender relations', in H. Hinds, A. Phoenix and J. Stacey (eds), *Working Out: New Directions for Women's Studies.* London: Falmer Press.

Macaulay, R. and Gordo Lopez, A.J. (1995) 'From cognitive psychologies to mythologies: advancing cyborg textualities for a narrative of resistance', in C.H. Gray, H. Figueroa-Sarriera and S. Mentor (eds), *The Cyborg Handbook.* New York and London: Routledge.

Mayall, B. (1996) 'Politics and practice in research with children', *Changes: An International Journal of Psychology and Psychotherapy* (Special Issue on 'Qualitative Research') 14 (3): 199–203.

Maynard, M. and Purvis, J. (eds) (1994) *Researching Women's Lives from a Feminist Perspective.* London: Taylor & Francis.

Mehta, O. (1995) *Westernizing the Third World.* London and New York: Zed.

Middleton, N. (1971) *When Family Failed: The Treatment of the Child in the Care of the Community in the First Half of the Twentieth Century.* London: Victor Gollancz.

Miller, L., Rustin, M., and Shuttleworth, J. (eds) (1989) *Closely Observed Infants.* London: Duckworth.

Mitchell, S. (1988) *Relational Concepts in Psychoanalysis.* Cambridge, MA: Harvard University Press.

Morss, J. (1990) *The Biologizing of Childhood.* New York: Lawrence Erlbaum.

Morss, J. (1995) *Growing Critical: Alternatives to Developmental Psychology.* London: Routledge.

New, C. and David, M. (1985) *For the Children's Sake: Making Childcare More than Women's Business.* Harmondsworth: Penguin.

Nicholson, L. and Seidman, S. (eds) (1995) *Social Postmodernism: Beyond Identity Politics.* Cambridge: Cambridge University Press.

O'Hagan, K. and Dillenberger, K. (1995) *The Abuse of Women within Childcare Work.* Buckingham: Open University Press.

Oakley, A. (1981) *From Here to Maternity: Becoming a Mother.* Harmondsworth: Penguin.

Pateman, C. (1989) *The Disorder of Women.* Cambridge: Polity Press.

Peace, G. and Hulme, D. (1993) *Children and Income Generating Programmes: A Report for Save the Children UK.* Institute of Development Planning and Management: University of Manchester.

Peters, J. and Wolper, A. (eds) (1995) *Women's Rights, Human Rights: International Feminist Perspectives.* London: Routledge.

Phoenix, A. (1987) 'Theories of gender and black families', in G. Weiner and M. Arnot (eds), *Gender Under Scrutiny.* London: Hutchinson.

Rao, A. (1995) 'The politics of gender and culture in international human rights discourse', in J. Peters and A. Wolper (eds), *Women's Rights, Human Rights: International Feminist Perspectives.* London: Routledge.

Ribbens, J. (1994) *Mothers and their Children: A Feminist Sociology of Childbearing.* London: Sage.

Riley, D. (1987) 'The serious burdens of love', in A. Phillips (ed.), *Feminism and Equality.* Oxford: Blackwell.

Rose, N. (1985) *The Psychological Complex.* London: Routledge and Kegan Paul.

Rutkowska, J. (1993) *The Computational Infant: Looking for Developmental Cognitive Science.* London: Harvester Wheatsheaf.

Scott, S. (1997) 'Feminists and false memories: a case of postmodern amnesia', in L.

Brown and E. Burman (eds), *Feminist Responses to the False Memory Debate*, Special Feature of *Feminism and Psychology* 7 (1).

Steedman, C. (1995) *Strange Dislocations: Childhood and Sense of Human Interiority, 1790–1930*. London: Virago.

Thorne, B. (1987) 'Re-visioning women and social change: where are the children?', *Gender & Society* 1 (1): 85–109.

Urwin, C. (1985) 'Constructing motherhood: the persuasion of normal development', in C. Steedman, C. Urwin and V. Walkerdine (eds), *Language, Gender and Childhood*. London: Routledge and Kegan Paul.

Vittachi, A. (1989) *Stolen Childhood: In Search of the Rights of the Child*. Cambridge: Polity Press.

Walkerdine, V. (1985) 'On the regulation of speaking and silence: subjectivity, class and gender in contemporary schooling', in C. Steedman, C. Urwin and V. Walkerdine (eds), *Language, Gender and Childhood*. London: Routledge and Kegan Paul.

Walkerdine, V. (1988) *The Mastery of Reason*. London: Routledge.

Walkerdine, V. and Lucy, H. (1989) *Democracy in the Kitchen: Regulating Mothers and Socialising Daughters*. London: Virago.

Wallsgrove, R. (1985) 'Thicker than water?', *Trouble and Strife* 7: 26–8.

Wilkinson, S. (1988) 'The role of reflexivity in feminist psychology', *Women's Studies International Forum* 11 (5): 493–502.

Wilkinson, S. and Kitzinger, C. (eds) (1996) *Representing the Other: A Feminism & Psychology Reader*. London: Sage.

Wingfield, R. and Saddiqui, H. (1995/6) 'Fundamental questions: from Southall to Beijing', *Trouble and Strife* 32: 53–62.

Woodhead, M. (1990) 'Psychology and the cultural construction of children's needs', in A. James and A. Prout (eds), *Constructing and Reconstructing Childhood*. Basingstoke: Falmer Press.

Woodhead, M. (1996) *In Search of the Rainbow: Pathways to Quality in Large-Scale Programmes for Young Disadvantaged Children*. The Hague: Bernard van Leer Foundation.

Index

academy
  crises in, 18
  reflexivity in, 38
accountability, in NLFs, 36–7
accountable reflexivity, Gill's concept of, 36–7, 186
age
  concept in developmental psychology, 213
  and power in research relationship, 181
agency
  and structure in feminist standpoint theory, 60
  of subject in feminist standpoint theory, 83, 84
  see also practice
aggression, Squire's study of, 65–6
  content of interviews, 66–74, 80
  narrative language and subjectivity, 75–83, 86
  research procedures, 67, 83
Alcoff, L., 32
Aldridge, Judith, 25
Anthony, E.J., 141–2
anthropology, postmodern, 22–3, 37
Armistead, Cathleen, 26
Ashmore, Malcolm, 35, 36
Asian experiences of parenting, analysis of, 121–6
authority
  of author in NLFs, 35–6
  of researcher, 22
autobiography
  awareness of structural constraints in, 52–3
  as narrative construction of self, 53–7
  see also memory work
autonomy, as ideal in FMHC, 194–5
avoidance
  as defence to shame, 139–40
  as means of resistance, 143–6

Bakhtin, Mikhail, 94–5, 111
Bar On, Bat-Ami, 30
Bartky, S.L., 139
Belenky, M.F., 203
Bhavnani, Kum-Kum, 32, 175
Billig, Michael, 23, 168
Brownmiller, Susan, 49
Butler, Judith, 111

Changing the Subject, 4
child
  in modernity, 213
  as postmodern subject, 224–6
  see also developmental psychology
childcare *see* motherhood and childcare
class
  and listening to girls' voices, 96–8
  ventriloquation of conventional femininity, 98–102
  ventriloquation of renegade femininity, 103–9
  and power in research relationship, 181–2
  and research on aggression, 71–2
client centred approach of FMHC, 193–4
Clifford, James, 22–3, 37
collective memory work, 50–2, 54, 56
conflict talk, gender differences in, 91
connected mode of procedural knowledge, 203, 204
connection, concept in FMHC of, 194–5, 197
Connell, R.W.
  notion of subjectivity, 166
  theory of gender relations, 157–60, 162, 163
consciousness-raising groups, 50, 198–9, 203